GHOSTLY HERTFORDSHIRE

A Haunted History

Damien O'Dell

Pen Press Publishers Ltd

First published in Great Britain by
Pen Press Publishers Ltd
39-41, North Road
Islington
London N7 9DP

ISBN 1-905203-73-X

Printed and bound in the UK

A catalogue record of this book is available from
the British Library

Cover Design and Map Illustrations
by Paul Watts

Dedication

This book is dedicated to everyone who has been involved with Anglia Paranormal Investigation Society since its inception in October 2002.

My particular thanks go to my good friends Paul Keech, Vice Chairman, and Carol Greenall, Secretary, for their enthusiastic, unwavering and wholehearted support in making APIS the effective organisation it has become and a society of which I am proud to be a part.

As always, my wife Vicki deserves a special mention for her unfailing assistance and guidance in every aspect of my paranormal endeavours.

About the Author

Damien O'Dell has enjoyed a lifelong interest in the paranormal and is an Accredited Investigator with the Association for the Scientific Study of Anomalous Phenomena (ASSAP). He has been Team Leader of his own paranormal investigation group, APIS (Anglia Paranormal Investigation Society), on numerous highly successful vigils, including one which was conducted live 'on air', at night in BBC Radio Three Counties' haunted radio station at Luton! On Halloween of 2002 he founded APIS with just four original members. He is Chairman of a society which now boasts over 50 members and is continuing to grow; it is already one of the largest and most highly respected paranormal investigation groups in the country. Members meet regularly in Bedfordshire and carry out vigils all over the UK. Damien has trained every member of APIS in the science of paranormal investigation and is also involved, with Keith Paull, a fourth generation dowser, in training APIS investigators in the art of dowsing. Damien is the organiser of the Anglia Paranormal Investigators' Seminar, held annually at The Weatherley Centre in Biggleswade, Bedfordshire. This event draws together the many various paranormal investigation societies throughout East Anglia as well as those members of the public who have a deep and abiding interest in the subject of the supernatural and each year the attendance increases substantially.

Born and brought up in West London, 55 year-old Damien resides in Baldock, Hertfordshire, where he has lived since 1986, with his wife Vicki, daughter Sarah and their cat, Kym. He divides his time between writing, running APIS, giving talks and teaching people about the paranormal. He says that his 'scariest moment', so far, was while witnessing poltergeist activity in Wilden, Bedfordshire, but something much more scary could be just around the corner and that is what makes ghost hunting exciting!

About the Book

Damien O'Dell's second book about the paranormal is quite literally close to home, his 'adopted' home of Hertfordshire, where he has lived for nearly twenty years, and as you might expect he has uncovered a rich new seam of spooky stories in his 'own backyard'. They may seem strange but are, nonetheless, true. There is a mixture of the 'classic' true ghost stories of the county but with a fresh perspective, and many brand new stories, which are recounted here for the very first time.

The author doesn't rely on reading reports and compiling lists of supposedly haunted sites, instead he researches every story personally, sometimes in the company of friends from Anglia Paranormal Investigation Society, in order to provide first-hand experience wherever possible of the people, places and events that he writes about. He has stayed with the winning formula that he employed in his first book – a careful blend of hauntings and history aided by a strong dash of illustrations, allied to personal observations gained through his own experience.

Not all the ghosts he encounters are pleasant, such as 'George Armatage', a seventeenth-century misogynist who was also a smuggler, murderer and leader of a gang of cut-throats that ended up committing suicide to evade the hangman's noose. What follows is a sometimes hair-raising, in-depth investigation into Hertfordshire's numerous hauntings… welcome to *Ghostly Hertfordshire* – a haunted history.

Ghostly Hertfordshire
BEDFORDSHIRE
Lilley
Markyate
HARPENDEN
Wheathampstead
TRING
BERKHAMSTED
HEMEL HEMPSTEAD
Bovingdon
BUCKINGHAMSHIRE
Leavesden
Abbots Langley
Sarratt
WATFORD
Aldenham
Croxley Green
BUSHEY
RICKMANSWORTH
South Oxhey

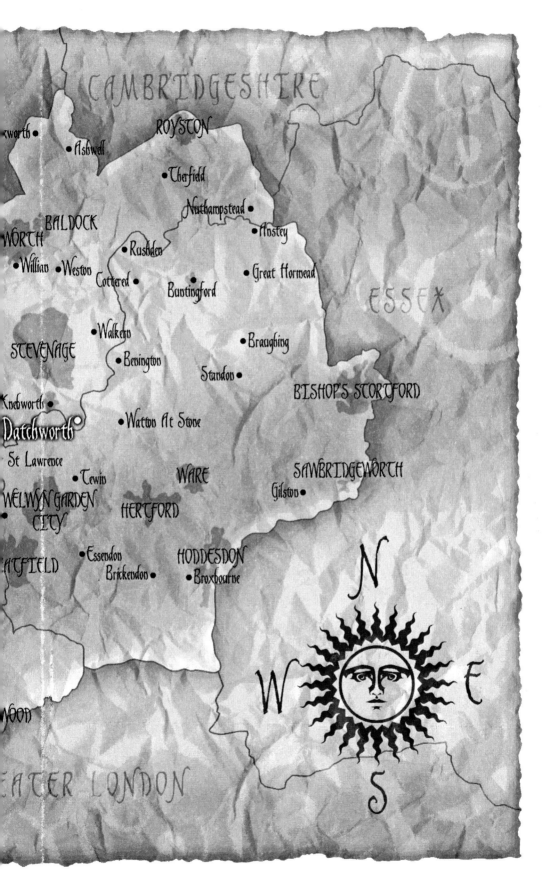

Contents

Illustrations

Acknowledgements

As always, no book of mine was ever written without the kind co-operation of a number of friends, both new and old. Thank you to the many people who helped in the making of this book. My thanks are especially due for the contributions from the following good people:

'Fan' Anderson

Duncan Campbell

Carol Greenall

Val Hume

Gordon Metcalfe

Maureen Maddren

Martin Small

Stevenage Museum

Andrew Thompson

Peter Underwood

Paul Watts (for his superb covers)

Steve Webster

And, as always, my life partner and constant support, a very special wife and mother: Vicki.

Foreword

As a native of Hertfordshire, where I lived for the first twenty-eight years of my life, it gives me great pleasure to contribute this brief note to the first comprehensive volume devoted to the ghostly population of the county.

These Hertfordshire ghosts really are a varied and fascinating crowd and Damien O'Dell has presented the vast and impressive evidence in a lucid and most interesting way. We are gently led from one ghostly episode to another, never knowing what will be round the corner and we are never disappointed. This is an original collection of intriguing stories that must puzzle even the most ardent of sceptics.

This is a book that is to be thoroughly recommended as it will assuredly play a prominent part in presenting for posterity some of the really interesting stories of our national heritage.

Peter Underwood
Life President of the Ghost Club Society

Introduction

'Hertfordshire is not really a county for ghosts...' so wrote an author for whom I hold a high regard, in her enjoyable work, *Victoria Glendinning's Hertfordshire*. Victoria's Hertfordshire history is impeccably researched but she doesn't know her Hertfordshire hauntings! This writer went on to say 'There are not many ghosts, and they are all banal...' I beg to differ Mrs Glendinning, and *Ghostly Hertfordshire* is an attempt to set the record straight – Hertfordshire is awash with apparitions, replete with restless revenants, and as for being banal, well... bah humbug! I don't think that readers will be the least bit bothered by banality in *Ghostly Hertfordshire*...

It was always my intention to write a series of 'Ghostly' titles, about East Anglia. After *Ghostly Bedfordshire*, the first book in the series was successfully launched (now in its second edition, with additional new material and retitled *Ghostly Bedfordshire... Reinvestigated*), the next project was to set about researching *Ghostly Hertfordshire*. This is the county I have called home for these past twenty years and I spent almost two years working in Hertford (in a reputedly haunted building – of course – but more of that later on). This was useful from a research point of view and an eye-opener in terms of the sheer volume of reported hauntings that originate in our county town.

It is odd though, how my writing follows me around. During the writing of my first book I took the family off for a break in Whitby, a seaside town that we all love. Whitby is a town big on character and atmosphere, for me it is easy to see how it could inspire a writer like Bram Stoker as a setting for the opening of *Dracula*. We were sitting at the breakfast table on the first morning at our guest house (or should that be ghost house?) in Normanby Terrace, when our 'neighbours' enquired of our landlord as to whether the property was haunted. Of course my ears pricked up while at the same time my mind was thinking 'even on holiday I can't escape the paranormal'. It turned out that the guest house we had chosen was indeed haunted. The landlord had sounded rather circumspect when he replied, and for good reason – it was our room that was haunted not our 'neighbours' room downstairs! These good people complained that their strange nocturnal experiences included their kettle being regularly switched on by some invisible agency (it strikes me as strange, the fascination that kettles have for ghosts), and their bathroom door being gradually forced shut despite their attempts to firmly wedge it open...

I decided to tackle our genial host, John Harrison, and tell him that I was currently writing a book about hauntings. He then admitted that he hadn't said much to the people who had the paranormal experiences because it was the attic room, number nine, where I was staying with my wife and daughter that was the most haunted part of the house and where hauntings were usually reported! It seemed that the ghost had moved its locale – maybe it sensed a ghost-hunter in the place and decided to move on... When I questioned him further an interesting story began to emerge. The ghost of number 13 was that of a Victorian serving-girl who tragically died young at the villa when it was used as the weekend retreat of a Yorkshire mill-owner. She regularly lets herself into the sitting room, John told me, and lights the gas fire 'for the cats' on cold winter nights despite the fact that the owner locks the room and makes sure the gas is off last thing at night...

So – here we are at last – the second book in the series and I hope it has the same success as its predecessor! I would like to say a big thank you to all the people who helped to make it possible, especially those of you who preferred to remain anonymous after contributing some fascinating stories. For those folk who have enjoyed my work so far I can assure you that there will be several more books in the series to come, *Ghostly Cambridgeshire* is, even now, in its infancy...

Hertfordshire is still a great place to live despite the many changes brought about as a result of modern living conditions. The old, slower-paced way of life in our villages has changed dramatically in the last hundred years or so, with far fewer natives both living and working in their locality. The loss of scores of country pubs and other places of employment like saddleries, forges, wheelwrights and bakehouses mean that more and more village residents are commuters now, endlessly shuttling between our county and London or Cambridge where high salaries can be expected. Natives of Hertfordshire were once known as Hertfordshire 'Hedgehogs' in reference to their slow-moving countryman ways. Now we are just as caught up in the frenetic modern tempo as anyone else and the hedgehogs aren't so plentiful any more, mainly due to the 'road kill' so symptomatic of the age of the motor car. New housing developments and the inevitable increase in tarmac due to bypasses, new roads and other 'improvements' erode the green acres of the countryside yet there are still peaceful pockets to be found in places like the 'golden triangle' between the A1 and the A10 main roads, where some villages exist that retain their restful charms. New employers have made Hertfordshire less dependent on her traditional role as supplier of foodstuffs to our populous neighbour, London. Now

Hertfordshire is home to the likes of the British film industry and the powerful pharmaceutical industry, two fields of endeavour of which we can be justifiably proud. It is not surprising that so many footballers, pop singers ('Beckingham Palace' is within our county boundary), actors and best-selling authors have chosen to make their home in Hertfordshire. The women's fiction writer Sarah Harrison lives in Ashwell, thriller-writer Frederick Forsythe resides near Hertford and popular novelist Ken Follett has a second home in Old Stevenage, to name but a few examples of successful writers resident in our neck of the woods.

More books are published about ghosts in Great Britain than in any other country in the world. We probably have more ghosts than any other country in the world! Recent research by scientists revealed that the most popular ghost that a person is likely to encounter is a monk or a highwayman. The Hampshire Ghost Club carried out their own research and reached very different conclusions. You are more likely to encounter a male ghost or a female ghost – about ten times more likely than you are to see a monk or a highwayman. My money is on the Hampshire Ghost Club – I never did trust scientists anyway!

Another snippet that I came across recently concerned ghost story-telling, with the most popular time for recounting ghost stories being All Hallows' Eve, (commonly known as Halloween), the spookiest night of the year by far, followed by Christmas Eve, the holiest night. For some strange reason, in Hertfordshire, it was traditional to tell ghost stories on February 13th, the eve of St Valentine's Day, for what reason I know not... answers on a postcard please.

'Do you believe in ghosts?' After all this time at the sharp end of research into the subject I would say that it is not that simple a question any more. What I do believe in, passionately, is the paranormal. I believe that there are things beyond our present understanding. I believe that when we understand more about the human mind we will reach more of an understanding about 'ghosts'. Part of my 'spiritual quest' is to attempt to clear some of the myth and mystery surrounding 'hauntings'. I am of the opinion that in many cases people haunt houses rather than ghosts. The answer to anomalous phenomena may often lie in the living human spirit rather than in the return of spirits of the deceased, although there is some rather convincing evidence that the dead can and do interact with the living from time to time.

Mankind has 'blamed the dead' from the earliest times for matters outside his control or understanding, from failed crops to mysterious sudden deaths or even persistent 'bad luck'. The power of the mind is easily underrated, I am certain that its full capabilities would fill us with awe were they to be unleashed. For instance I suspect that one day poltergeist activity will be proven to be attributable to mind-power rather than spirit-power. We may then uncover some amazing revelations. Poltergeist phenomena has been responsible for strange effects such as moving extremely heavy furniture with ease (which would prove difficult to budge even for a strong man), for starting spontaneous fires, for throwing showers of stones, for making small objects appear or disappear, for causing loud rapping in walls and a whole host of other 'party tricks'. What if it were the human mind, alone and unaided, that was responsible for causing all these effects?

Everyone must reach their own conclusions on the nature of ghosts and hauntings. I hope that this book, with its wide variety of true ghostly occurrences, will help you to begin to draw your own conclusions. As for me, detective Joe Friday summed it up well with his words in the TV series *Dragnet*... 'Just give me the facts ma'am' ... and that's what I have tried to do in *Ghostly Hertfordshire*, just give you the facts...

Damien O'Dell
Baldock, Hertfordshire
May 2005

BOOK ONE

North Hertfordshire Nightmares

Chapter One

BALDOCK

I moved to Baldock twenty years ago after spending almost half a lifetime in London. During that time I have seen it grow from a sleepy little North Hertfordshire market town to another bustling, 'dormitory', one more stop on the ever-extending London commuter belt, always threatened with absorption by its sprawling neighbour to the south, Stevenage. It is an ancient town, which gets its name, allegedly, from a corruption of Baghdad, due to the influence of the Knights Templar, an eminent Order of soldier-monks, who fought in the Holy Land and were rewarded with various gifts of lands and properties, including a large parcel of acreage in Hertfordshire. Baldock was just one of their properties and the Templars had a strong presence in the town and its surrounding areas.

The group known as the Knights Templars was founded around 1118 to protect pilgrims to Jerusalem and the Holy Land. At first they called themselves 'The poor fellow soldiers of Jesus Christ' but in recognition of their service they were given a former mosque over the site of the Temple of Solomon and henceforward were known as the Knights of the Temple of Solomon, or Knights Templar. They rapidly rose to eminence in the Crusades and played an important role in the freeing of Palestine. The Templars enjoyed spectacular wealth and influence; with royal patronage they became a prominent order right across Europe, within fifty years they owned some 7,000 manors across the Continent, together with vast treasures. Prominent in farming, they also created the forerunner of the banking system because they accepted valuables for safe deposit or transit. In addition they maintained a fleet of ships which they used for trading and for provisioning their forces in Palestine. Their headquarters in England was situated at The Temple in London and any place name containing the word 'Temple' had Templar associations.

There were at least five classes of brothers within the Order from the highest noble knights to labourers and artisans. Everyone served the Grand Master but they were attached locally to a province in the charge of a Grand Preceptor or Grand Prior. By the end of the 13th century the Templars had fallen into disrepute and were accused of heresy leading to their persecution. In France members of the order were imprisoned in 1307 and some were subsequently executed by burning. The persecution quickly spread throughout Europe but delays by Edward II in England allowed many Templars to escape to Scotland or even to go underground. The order was finally extinguished by Pope Clement in 1312. Their persecution marked a shameful chapter in the history of Roman Catholicism. It is probable that both the Church and many European Kings throughout Europe wanted to lay claim to the great Templar lands and treasures.

BALDOCK'S 'LOCAL' HAUNTS…

As a ghost-hunter, what intrigued me was the lack of mention of, or interest in, Baldock's spirit population. In all the multitude of reference works in my extensive library of the paranormal, I could find no mention of my adopted home town. Did this mean that Baldock rated a minus in the manifestations measurement map? Far from it, but then if you believe in some kind of Fate, perhaps I was 'Fated' to put the record straight concerning Baldock's ghostly population…

In times past neighbouring Letchworth Garden City used to be a Quaker Town, where pubs were not just frowned upon, they were non-existent. In these more enlightened times Letchworth has its fair share of pubs, but it was not always so and local people took their pleasure in nearby Baldock. For a small town it was chock full of hostelries, at one time there were as many as a dozen inns in what was, in those times a rural backwater. Baldock also boasted its own brewery. Sadly, with the introduction of the breathalyser, cheap booze junkets to France and the Chancellor's fondness for raising revenue at the expense of the inn's imbibers many of those lovely old places have been turned into desirable residences for the upwardly mobile. They are good places to start, however, in our search for 'the darker side' of Baldock Town, as paranormal reports are numerous.

A pub that I know well is The Cock, as it is conveniently situated at the end of the High Street closest to where I live. I have talked with John and Lone (who is Danish) on several occasions about the hauntings at their pub and found them to be extremely credible witnesses. They have been at The Cock for about four years now but the pub had probably been haunted for quite a time before their arrival. John and Lone's suspicions were first aroused by their dogs, normally quiet and well behaved, they would bark rather loudly and excitedly at an upstairs cupboard, in a room that remains cold, whatever the weather outside. Downstairs, in the bar, bottles left at the front of the shelves will, overnight, wind up right at the back. At the end of the bar a picture was seen to fly off the wall at right angles and smash on the floor. John has experimented with dowsing rods and discovered that they reacted violently within the pub, crossing over as he held them. An amateur psychic researcher theorised that the place may be haunted by three ghosts, two are a couple (possibly a former landlord and landlady) and the outside of the building is haunted too.

One pub that I remember as certainly having the reputation for being haunted was The Eagle, which stood in Icknield Way, but it was demolished some years back to make way for a new housing development. The Eagle was reputedly haunted by the 'pot boy', not really a boy but usually an older man given the duties of collecting beer glasses and doing odd jobs like sweeping up and emptying the ash trays. Some thirty to forty years ago the old man who was The Eagle's pot boy was barred from the landlady's sitting room because she was both house-proud and snobbish; she thought he was beneath her. In an ironic twist of Fate the pot boy collapsed while working at the pub and was taken into the off-limits sitting room and laid on the settee, where he chanced to expire. Not long after his death, banging was heard from the cellar and the racket was attributed to an indignant pot boy, exhibiting his annoyance at having been allowed into the sitting room just the one time.

Across the road The Orange Tree continues to make a living, despite many rumours as to its 'imminent demise' it has managed to cling on to survival. I particularly enjoy The Orange Tree in summer, when the attractions of its garden are most apparent. I have seen many landlords and landladies come and go over the years and it must be one of Green King's least profitable establishments, but long may it flourish as part of my town. It too, had a mischievous ghost, one that delighted in turning the ice-making machine off. The ice-maker's overhead switch was never turned off normally, so it couldn't be switched off accidentally. On the shelf behind the bar it's a tight fit to get twelve glasses together yet on occasion one had been known to jump off, with a loud smash, onto the floor.

I think I only ever visited The Bull's Head, in Church Street the once, so maybe it's partly my fault that it didn't survive as a business! I remember it as a cosy, characterful, little olde worlde boozer with a roaring log fire, so it must have been during the winter, that solitary visit. There was a persistent rumour in circulation, concerning the attic; a room up there, directly under the pitch of the roof, was persistently cold and it has allegedly remained untouched by human visitation for over forty years, but you can never find anyone who wants to talk about it…

This same Church Street is where the 'old, bent man' has been sighted by residents, walking past their windows dressed in clothes 'not of this century'. Church Street has been home to at least one, if not two, other pubs to my knowledge, long since converted to private houses. So you'll see what I mean by 'chock full of pubs'.

The first house in the street, next to the churchyard takes its name from the church, St Mary's House. It is said that the ghost of a boy haunts the kitchen (reputedly a boy who was killed when scaffolding fell on him). Another curiosity concerning Church Street is 'the bodies in the wall' tale. Many years ago, during renovations to houses in this street, some skeletons were discovered in the walls. At one time it was the custom, if you were too poor to afford a proper church burial, to dispose of the remains of your nearest and dearest at home, by walling up their remains in your cottage! Perhaps not unsurprisingly, St Mary's itself has a resident ghost – John Smith, former rector from 1832–1870. He was famous for deciphering and transcribing (while studying at St John's, Cambridge) the cryptic shorthand of Samuel Pepys' diary. It ran to six volumes and languished in the diarist's library for almost a hundred years before John Smith's translation. You can still see the former rector's grave in the churchyard, his shade, however, has often been seen sitting at the back of St Mary's.

The George and Dragon is one of Baldock's abiding landmarks, at the crossroads between Church Street, Hitchin Street, Whitehorse Street and High Street. Many an old postcard of the town features a view that includes this famous historic coaching inn. It must be about ten years or more ago, that I first came across reports of ghostly occurrences there. It was during the time that The George was closed, and it was put up for sale by the brewery, Green King. I was in another pub in Baldock, The Rose and Crown Hotel, when I met one of Green King's travelling managers. It was his job to stay at the brewery's properties while they were empty, to keep an eye on them as a sort of temporary caretaker. We got talking and I happened to mention that The Rose and Crown Hotel was haunted. He then proceeded to tell me that The George and Dragon was also haunted, as he had discovered for himself. While alone there at night he regularly heard noises from the rooms upstairs but he knew that the building was secure and that he was the only person inside it. He was quick to check out the source of the noises, but discovered no trace of any human visitors. When I asked him if he was scared he shook his head and said that it never bothered him, he was used to all manner of strange happenings in his line of work... I returned to The Rose and Crown in August '04 and met the current landlord, Roger Nicholls, and he was able to confirm that the place is still very much haunted. Roger had heard his name being called when he was alone in the building and ghostly footsteps and noises, as of things being moved about, were heard too. The ghost haunts room 10 and goes by the name of Elizabeth, as children who have stayed at the inn have confirmed – they have even played with her!

There is a much older story associated with this old coaching inn and it concerns a notorious highwayman known as 'Shock Oliver'. In the seventeenth century he was the terror of the neighbourhood, known to have held up two men returning from Baldock's October Fair (still held annually, but without the highwaymen). Eventually this criminal's luck ran out, he was caught and hanged at St Albans around 1790. He had lived in St Neots, so his body was returned there via Baldock, where his wife worked. She was a cook at 'The George and Dragon' so that was where 'Shock Oliver' lay in his coffin overnight. Disturbances in the kitchen and the cellar have been attributed to 'Shock Oliver's haunting. The ghost of a man has been reported in the bar too, and it is interesting that staff referred to it as 'Ollie'…

I mentioned The Rose and Crown earlier, I was told many years ago, by the landlord and landlady at that time, that one of the bedrooms was definitely haunted. It may be the troubled spirit of a housemaid who committed suicide, about a hundred years ago, at the inn, after discovering that she was pregnant, by the butcher's boy. Clocks often stop in that room. A young couple claimed to have seen another ghost, this time it was an old lady with white hair and a long cardigan who was at the end of a corridor one moment and then disappeared the next. It is small wonder that a landlord felt 'eerie' in the cellar; some thirty years ago a regular's request for his ashes to be scattered down there was agreed to and was duly carried out…

Another pub that has disappeared from Baldock's landscape is The Chequers, in Whitehorse Street; it was a very small, intimate sort of establishment which is now converted into offices. It only closed a few years ago and when the landlord and landlady were preparing to go, prior to the closure, the Area Manager from Greene King called to say goodbye and to say how sorry he was that The Chequers had to close. He was taken aback by the landlord's comment, 'I'll not be sorry to leave it though, at least I'll be rid of her.' The Area Manager looked quizzically at the wife as he had always believed that the couple had got on well together. The landlord quickly corrected him, 'No not my wife, we've got a ghost.' It transpired that the landlord had woken up one night to see the figure of a woman, seemingly bundled up in clothes, leaning over him, but on turning over he saw that his wife was sleeping peacefully beside him. He turned back, but the mysterious figure had vanished. With that he felt a searing pain in his arm, he clutched it, the pain gradually subsided and he managed to get back to sleep. On waking in the morning his arm still felt tender, so he checked it and found teeth marks on the sore spot, which he showed to the Area Manager, who subsequently repeated the weird tale to some of

Baldock's residents. Is it the same spirit that was seen just across the road in the former Howard's Watch and Clock Shop? People have, in the past, claimed to have seen through the window an old lady sitting in a chair there.

From haunted pubs we move on to a haunted restaurant. Like so many county towns, Baldock has seen, with the coming of supermarket giants Tescos, the disappearance of a whole variety of small shops, so that nowadays Baldock is a great place to have a drink or to dine out (we have no less than three Indian restaurants and a world-class fish and chip shop)! One of these places has a haunted history and it is Il Fiorno, an Italian restaurant, once regularly patronised by the late, fine actor, Nigel Hawthorne, (of TV's *Yes Minister* and the movie, *The Madness of King George* fame) when he lived at the nearby village of Radwell. The building is originally 17th century, behind an 18th century façade, so reports of a ghostly 'Cavalier type', dressed in a large black hat, black cloak and black boots would certainly fit in with the period of origin. These accounts date back to when the site was run as Hanscombes, the bakers shop. There have been many businesses at what is now Il Fiorno's restaurant; a few years ago I recall it being a French restaurant, the 'Montmartre', the home of 'The Healing Chair', said to cure whomever sat in it of their ailment. It was put to the test by a diner, celebrating a wedding anniversary, who also happened to be feeling rather groggy as he was suffering with an extremely heavy cold. He sat in the corner, in 'The Chair', and the next day the cold had gone. A psychosomatic cure, coincidence, or could the ghostly man in black have been a physician – hence 'The Healing Chair'?

Moving down the High Street was The Mayflower, a shop where I was accustomed to buy my Sunday newspapers, Dennis used to run it and my daughter's beloved 'Brown Owl' at Brownies worked there, it was a friendly little shop. Alas, it too, is no more, another victim of the changing times, it closed about a year ago. Currently it's a combined sweetshop and gift shop called Truly Scrumptious, selling sweets, crystals, paintings, ornaments and other gifts. Numerous phenomena have been witnessed here over the years, including the following incidents from the recent past, when it was still The Mayflower. Various items frequently rearranged themselves, the contents of boxes on high shelves would often be disturbed, for instance little toy pistol cap boxes were found opened and all the reels left in a heap on the floor. One day the owner of The Mayflower was talking to a female sales representative. The shop's sales assistant was tidying up in the back of the shop, but when the representative came in the assistant took over at the counter so that the owner and the rep could talk at the back of the shop while checking the stock. After a few minutes the young lady went on her way and the assistant returned to her tidying up and called out to the owner in surprise to ask what he had been up to. For there in the middle of the floor, on the spot where he had stood with the salesperson, were two golden wedding glasses, which had been taken out of their box and placed on the ground. Sounds like the ghost had a sense of humour, and thought that the two of them would have made a lovely couple! On another occasion, Dennis was behind the counter when he heard the door open. The counter was directly opposite the cold drinks cabinet in the tiny shop, affording the person behind the counter a reflection of anyone coming in, only there was no one reflected there on this occasion. Shortly after this the door opened again and a woman came in, a box of chocolates flew off the shelf, nearly hitting her... The flat above the shop is not immune to the attentions of the ghostly presence. Things have often been moved around up here as well. On one notable occasion a couple living in the flat watched, fascinated, as two coasters moved down a perfectly level table from one end to the other.

Next door to the old Mayflower is The Gates, home to the 'electrical' ghost, which seemed to have a fascination for all things electrical – there was probably no electricity in this spirit's time! A young mother living here opened a can of spaghetti for her child when she remembered an important phone call she had to make. She placed the pan of spaghetti on the hob with the intention of first making her call, then returning to begin heating the meal. Imagine her surprise when she came back to find her food merrily bubbling away. She did a double take and rechecked the hob, only to find it as she had left it – switched off. The microwave used to switch itself on and off with some regularity and the young mum was wont to refer to her ghost as 'the man in the cupboard'. An elderly gentleman living in one of the other flats claimed to have seen the ghost; he described him as wearing clothes similar to those that would have been worn by a Cavalier. In this same house there was an incident in which someone reported watching in amazement as an electric hairdryer switched itself on and off.

Across Baldock's famously wide High Street can be found Costcutters, reputedly haunted by the ghosts of a young boy and girl dressed in Victorian clothes, one witness described the pair so vividly that it made her mother's flesh creep. There is also reputed to be a violent ghost that has been known to throw people against the wall!

Just behind the High Street is Baldock's most haunted road – Pembroke Road. There are a number of haunted houses documented here, and probably a few others that are not. Jean and Tom moved into Pembroke Road some fifteen years ago, having moved from another part of the town and wishing to live in a more central location. Before finding their present house they viewed one nearby, in The Orchard, nicely tucked away off Pinnock's Lane. I had some friends who used to own 'Granny Smith's', a lovely little chalet bungalow in this private road, which is one of my favourite areas of Baldock. After Jean and Tom had been shown around the property the owner asked if they minded that the place was haunted. As they are a level-headed couple they replied that it didn't bother them, and they were told that every so often a Roman soldier appeared at the top of the stairs.

Roman soldiers figure in other Baldock sightings, one has startled motorists when he has been seen crossing nearby Clothall Road. When the huge Barratts housing estate was first built, some twenty odd years ago, on Clothall Common, numerous Roman artefacts were unearthed. A Roman burial ground containing hundreds of bodies in tightly packed rows was also found, and, rather sinisterly, a lot of the graves contained corpses which were buried face down. There were to be many additions to this estate, which continued to grow right up till final completion a few years ago – now there are several thousand houses here. I had a first-hand report from a woman who lived in Rye Gardens on the sprawling estate; she was shaken to look up from her ironing to see a Roman soldier staring at her. Not surprisingly she left Rye Gardens after spending just a few years in her brand new four bedroom detached home.

To return to Pembroke Road – Jean and Tom didn't buy the house with its Roman soldier in The Orchard, they moved to Pembroke Road – but they didn't escape Baldock's ghosts, because the house they bought had its own invisible occupants. A friend of their son was staying over for a few weeks and one evening the couple were sitting in their living room when they heard footfalls bounding up the stairs. They hadn't heard anyone come in, but assumed it was the young man. They then heard doors closing upstairs and thought it a little strange that he hadn't popped his head around the door to say hello as he usually did. After a little while they thought they would have a look upstairs to see if he was all right and to offer him a cup of coffee. There was no one there. They checked every room, but whoever or whatever went upstairs, it was no living soul. The footsteps and closing doors have subsequently been heard on several occasions. There is also a smell of tobacco smoke in the house, although none of the family smokes and the house is detached, set in its own grounds. Jean and Tom must have got used to their ghost, for they still live in the same house.

A young couple, also living in Pembroke Road, reported seeing a Roman soldier several years ago. He was seen to walk across the bedroom, but the floor was at the height of his knees. During his time that particular level, whether it was a building or a mound was obviously at a lower level than the present floor. He seemed unaware of the couple's presence and just continued walking, straight on through the wall.

Another home in Pembroke Road that has mysterious occurrences is a Victorian terraced cottage. The couple that live here, George and Wendy, are both keen horse riders and one day George had thrown his jodhpurs on the settee as he wanted to watch TV. He was watching a boxing match when he saw, out of the corner of his eye, some movement. He was then astonished to witness his jodhpurs rising up of their own accord, then moving a foot or two along the settee before settling down again.

On another occasion a teddy bear that used to sit propped up by a cushion was seen to lurch sideways at the same time as a dent appeared in the supporting cushion. Wendy has heard what she assumed to be George's footsteps behind her in the kitchen and has moved aside to let him pass only to discover nobody there. At night both George and Wendy have felt 'someone' sit on the end of the bed. Wendy isn't keen to be left on her own in the house at night but George is quite philosophical. He has the distinct impression that their ghost is a benevolent one, possibly someone who previously lived in the house a long time and was happy there, too happy to leave in fact...

Raban Court is a well known landmark, an ancient, timbered building, standing at the crossroads of Royston Road, Station Road, Clothall Road and Whitehorse Street. It's one of those places that you expect to be haunted and it is, by a friendly spirit. About ten years ago a lady who lived there shared her story with some other Baldock residents. She had a problem with her arms so she visited her doctor, who gave her treatment but nothing seemed to ease the aches and pains. She would lie awake, night after night, unable to sleep. On one such night she laid with her arms outside the blankets, hoping that the pain would go away so that she could get some sleep. Then she sensed a presence, which walked around the bed before stopping and standing by her side, while pulling some invisible covers over her arms. Soon she fell asleep to enjoy the most restful night that she had enjoyed for a long time. Many people say that they sleep very soundly in Raban Court, despite the heavy traffic that thunders past day and night (roll on the bypass, due to be completed in Spring 2006). There is also a phantom smell which is often remarked on – that of tobacco, and a jester has been spotted, at gallery level, in Raban Court.

A stone's throw away is Bell Row, where the tiny Baldock Library was sited before we got our improved, larger, 'proper' town library in the High Street, some years ago. Now the old library premises are occupied by a Balti restaurant, one which the wife and I often frequent. A little further along Bell Row is a house with an interesting history... I am grateful to Doug Elgood for this snippet... 'My wife and I moved into 4 Bell Row, Baldock, in July of 1973. It was company property, owned by Sketchleys at that time; the house has a bay window overlooking the High Street right by the zebra crossing. After we had been there for a couple of months we used to experience the most awful smells suddenly appearing in the flat that would disappear after a short while. This went on for some time until we called the environmental health people, who could find no source or explanation for the occurrence. We also had a cupboard door at the top of the stairs which could not be opened properly as it scraped along the floorboards. Many a time we would discover it wide open when no one had either been in it or even near it. After a while we began to spend quite a bit of time at my parents' home in Letchworth, because we couldn't bear to be in the flat for too long a period as everything would just start happening over again.

As we felt so uneasy in the flat, I decided to 'borrow' my mother's dog for a while to keep us company, especially when one of us was home alone. On the first visit the dog wet herself all the way upstairs and subsequently cried all night, on many occasions, for no apparent reason. When you were alone there you would often feel someone in the same room, or behind your shoulder. While passing the old flat we have often looked up, to see if anyone was living there, and over the years we have come to the conclusion that while it may be occupied for a short time, it soon looks empty again. It leads us to believe that we may not have been the only ones to have had one visitor too many...'

The most gruesome spectre to ever haunt Baldock's environs has to be 'the headless peddler'; fortunately you are unlikely to encounter him now, for he was last seen back in the 1870s. Some time in the early 1800s a peddler left Baldock Fair carrying a goodly amount of money on him as he had successfully sold most of his wares. He didn't make it home and his horse was found wandering on the road between Bygrave and Ashwell, of the peddler himself there was no trace. It was a few years later that the hauntings started, the figure of a headless peddler was repeatedly seen, wandering the Bygrave Road and the sightings were reported for a number of years. Daniel Fossey was implicated in the peddler's robbery and Fossey was also one of the men who had earlier claimed that highwayman Shock Oliver had tried to rob them on the Clothall Road, which charge had led directly to Oliver's arrest and subsequent hanging.

Suspicion had surrounded Fossey concerning the peddler, because shortly after the latter's disappearance Daniel Fossey seemed to come into money, since he moved from his farm in

Bygrave to a bigger one in Wallington. Many years later, after his death, work was being carried out at Fossey's old farm in Bygrave, when the skeleton of a headless man, as well as the remains of a woman and child, was discovered there. Later still, a skull was found at another of Daniel Fossey's former homes, Wallington farm. It was given a Christian burial soon after its discovery around 1870 and the hauntings on the Bygrave Road promptly ceased. It was assumed by the locals that the unfortunate peddler had been waylaid by Fossey as he made his way to Ashwell, the poor man was then murdered and his head cut off. That would account for his ghost wandering the road in search of its missing head...

HINXWORTH

Situated about three miles north of Baldock, Hinxworth is the most northerly village in Hertfordshire, not well known, an out of the way place, yet situated just over a mile from the roaring traffic on the teeming A1 there is a church, St Nicholas's, which has stood here since the 12th century, with its avenue of ten lime trees, a living memorial to the Clutterbuck family, the parents and eight children who resided here long, long ago. There is a pub, The Three Horseshoes, a village hall and some scattered old houses with a cluster of new homes built in more recent times and that's it. It was the out of the way nature of the place that attracted the writer Monica Dickens, who bought a thatched cottage here in 1947 and she spent four happy years in her country retreat.

Hinxworth Place is also tucked away, as I can attest, having cycled across the fields on my mountain bike in the summer to look over the old place, a small manor house with its cobbled courtyard and statuary in the garden. It seems a perfect location for a haunted house, a lonely place somehow, with open fields as far as the eye can see on one side. It is a much altered manor house that dates from around 1470 with a noisily haunted history; over a period of many years, particularly on autumn nights, screams and thuds were heard from the direction of the stairs, also a baby's crying and the sound of water gushing from a squeaking pump in the yard, which was all witnessed as recently as 1968. This was thought to be a replay of events from the distant past, from the 1800s in fact, when the couple who lived here left their children, including a little baby, in the charge of a nursemaid one evening while they walked across the fields to the church. The young son of the household thought it would be fun to dress up in a sheet and to make weird noises in order to scare his sister, which he succeeded in doing only too well, with tragic consequences. The girl (or her maid) attacked 'the ghost' with a poker, causing the brother to fall downstairs, screaming. The cook found him and tried to help the lad by putting his head under the pump to revive him with the water, but he died.

This was not the only haunting. A procession of monks has been reported on several occasions, walking through the walls of the house and a single monk was seen in the porchway leading to the courtyard during the 19th century. Heavy footsteps were heard in an upper corridor by the houseowner in the 1960s and they seemed to continue moving outside the existing house. It was later confirmed from old plans of the property that there used to be a wing with a staircase at the point where the footsteps were heard descending the non-existent stairs.

ASHWELL

Ashwell lies about half way between Baldock and Royston, and there are six approach roads into it. At one time this picturesque community was surrounded by windmills on almost every surrounding hill, but now the only remnant is the well-restored example at Cromer village, which is worth a visit. Ashwell, although it is a village was once a town, when the Normans invaded England it was the sixth largest town in Hertfordshire. It is hard to believe when you see the scale of the place now. Land here is extremely fertile and house prices reflect the added value that is put on living in such a chic yet ancient village. Many residents commute to lucrative London jobs and are quite happy to pay the premium that is asked for Ashwell properties. It has to be said that the place does have charm a-plenty and my wife Vicki and I looked at a property here when we first moved out of London. My present link with the village is that I am a member of the local writer's circle, the Morden and District writers (MAD Writers, rather appropriately, for short). We are proud to number successful novelist Sarah Harrison, who lives in the village, as our President. Unlike many other Hertfordshire villages Ashwell has managed to retain its post office, its butchers' shop and its excellent bakery, Day's.

Dominating the village skyline is the impressive bulk of St Mary the Virgin's Church with its traditional Hertfordshire 'spike' steeple. A church has stood on this site since the 14th century. The high tower had only reached 12ft in height when the Black Death swept the village after decimating Europe and all work on the tower ceased for a number of years. Ashwell became known as Hertfordshire's Plague village, such was the heavy toll taken of villagers' lives. Some remarkable Latin graffiti can be seen on the north wall of St Mary the Virgin, which translates as: '1350 – miserable wild distracted the dregs of the people alone survive to witness and tell the tale and in the end with a tempest Maurus this year thunders mightily in all the world 1361'. This is a reference to the storm on St

Maur's day 15th January 1361 which may have cleared the air of any lingering infection of the Black Death. On the first pillar near the south door there is another medieval message which translates as: 'the corners are not pointed correctly – I spit on them', which is a rebuke from the original architect. Several people have reported strange happenings at the church, the best documented of these being the sighting, in1850, of a headless black figure, which was seen in Ashwell Churchyard, gliding silently along from the rectory to the church door, by chorister Georgianna Covington, who managed to get through the chancel door after her terrifying encounter before promptly fainting and falling to the ground right in front of the assembled choir. Perhaps this frightening vision was connected with the fact that part of the churchyard, opposite the Bushel and Strike pub, is occupied by a massive medieval plague pit.

The High Street is one of the most attractive of its kind in the whole of the county; with its traditional pubs and, in a hollow beside High Street, the little river Rhee rises clean and pure to form a pool in the chalk that is shaded by ash trees, hence the place-name:

'Some Ashen trees and water bubbling, springing
Just where the chalky hillside meets the plain,
And gathered all about them clustering clinging
The village homesteads have for ages lain.'

Once, watercress grown at Ashwell Springs was taken to London regularly, to be sold to the street cries of 'Ashwell Hed Watercrease'.

There is also the site of a Merchant Taylors' School here, which has recently been redeveloped to provide 'executive homes' and a lovely little museum is perfectly located in a 15th century house, but then where else would one house a museum?

As for hauntings Ashwell has its share, Bear House, a well known old local landmark, opposite the VG stores, is the place where the ghost of an old man has regularly been seen, sitting quietly (and no doubt contentedly) drinking his beer. The most sinister haunting, however, is at Tower Cottage, Swan Street, which is so called because there was a tunnel (since bricked up) which connected the cottage to the tower of St Mary the Virgin. I recently interviewed the daughter of my friend Sarah Harrison, 'Fan' Anderson, who had moved out of Tower Cottage after only three months' occupancy. It was ten years ago, in the summer of 1995, that the twenty-one-year-old single mother moved, with her baby Ollie, into the Grade Two Listed 16th century cottage by the church. 'Fan' joined a long list of tenants who have rented Tower Cottage over the years, from absentee owners, who live in Australia.

Although it looked 'cute', from the day that the young mum moved in she had a bad feeling about her new home, which was small on the outside but surprisingly spacious inside. It had an attic and a big cellar, outside there was a toilet and various other outbuildings. Her best friend helped with the removals and neither one wanted to be alone, as they unpacked in different rooms they called out to each other for reassurance. That night the real fear began. As Fan explained, she 'felt the fear of a child', she was 'terrified without knowing why' as she lay in her bed, sharing the room with her one-year-old son, who slept soundly. It was so bad that she was too scared to go downstairs, too frightened even to go out to the toilet and she just lay in bed wishing it was morning.

It didn't get any better at Tower Cottage and on numerous occasions Fan went to sleep at her mum's house in Steeple Morden. Even during the hot July days it was 'never welcoming' at the cottage, she felt anxious on her own and there was often a bad smell in the main bedroom. She wondered if a mouse had died under the floorboards, but each time she thought about doing something about the nasty smell it would go away again. The young mum wondered about her unexplained feelings, the unpleasant feel of the place, the fact that she never seemed able to relax here. For her little boy, Ollie, it was a different story; he seemed content and able to sleep particularly well in his new home.

Things soon reached a climax, on the night of the 31st July of that very hot summer Fan suddenly awoke, at 3.55am. She was sure of the time because her bedroom window overlooked the church clock. It was that time between night and dawn when 'the sky had gone from black to navy blue'. The girl's heart was thumping as, in the corner of her large bedroom there appeared some 'fuzzy dots of light' which began to join up to form an image of a tall man, who was looking intently at Fan. She wanted to call out but felt unable to, the atmosphere in the room was heavily charged with distress and unhappiness, 'time seemed to stand still' and no sounds could be heard. The tall, thin man appeared to be unwell, he was distressed, in need, and his skull looked badly deformed. Fan continued that 'As he held my gaze he seemed as real as you are. When he turned slightly the floorboards creaked.' She admitted that she had never been so frightened in her life, yet her little boy lay sound asleep. Somehow she managed to reach down and grabbed the phone that lay beside her bed, she was about to dial her father, and as she looked up again her 'intruder' had disappeared. Within ten minutes her father was at her front door and he searched the place thoroughly for any signs of the unwanted 'visitor' but there was no trace of him. Unable to remain in her bedroom, his terrified daughter spent the remainder of the night on the sofa and was never to sleep in the cottage again for the next six weeks, preferring to stay with her mother at night time.

Next morning Sarah, Fran's mum, rang with some sad news. One of Fran's distant uncles, John, had died the previous evening. He had suffered with cancer of the head and neck. Some time later Fran was shown a photograph of her uncle John, whom she hadn't seen since she was a child. She rushed out to the toilet and was violently sick from the shock that she felt – he was the 'intruder' that she had seen in her bedroom… Fran was unable to work out why an uncle that she hardly knew, and who lived a long way off, in the West Country, should choose to return to haunt her of all people. Her days of fear were, however, far from over…

The rector, the Reverend Patrick Bright, came in answer to Fran's appeal, and he blessed Tower Cottage. Still Fran refused to spend her nights at her rented home. Even during the day, when she had been with her friend Emma in the sitting room they had heard movements on the bedroom floorboards, directly overhead. Fran described balls of light that she had seen, which sounded very like orbs to me ('round lights, with streaks attached'). She had also taken a photograph of the upstairs from the garden and there seemed to be the head and shoulders of a woman at one of the windows.

One morning, as she returned with another friend, they discovered every single door in the place, even the fridge door, thrown open, so they went around shutting them again. They also had to close all the drawers in every room, since they, too, had been yanked open.

Fran decided to do some research on her cottage and spent some time in the library. It was here that she learned about the tunnel from her cellar which ran below the road and came out underneath the church tower. She checked the cellar and could see where the tunnel had been bricked up. There was also reputedly a monks' hiding place beneath her cottage and garden. She continued to delve into the history and made contact with other villagers as well as former occupants – a strange story began to emerge. Tower Cottage looked like something of a 'ghost magnet', with different occupants reporting a variety of ghostly sightings and there had been a fairly rapid turnover of tenants. It sounded to me as though the site itself may have been a focus for paranormal energy and Fran confirmed my thoughts by telling me that several ley lines were known to intersect at this point. Some previous tenants, about twenty years previously, had reported ghosts of what could have been ancient market traders, but they were only seen from the knees upwards. In order to reach Tower Cottage you have to go up several steps. It turned out that before the cottage was built a street market existed on this site, and it would, therefore, have been on a lower level.

Marge Kite is a well-known local medium who lives in Ashwell and it was no surprise when I learned that she had paid a visit to ghostly Tower Cottage. Marge was soon picking up horrible impressions; she didn't want to stay long in the place, the atmosphere was 'highly charged' and she didn't like being there. There was the ghost of a woman, Ivy, who had lost a child and Ivy didn't like Fran. Ivy's story was revealed; she had been made pregnant by a priest and had had the child at the cottage. Ivy had been thought to be a witch by her neighbours and the fact that she was a single parent hadn't helped back in the sixteenth century. Her child had died in what was now Fran's bedroom. The medium asked if Ollie, Fran's son, had been disturbed in his sleep and the young mum had answered no, he wasn't always a good sleeper yet when he was at the cottage he had particularly peaceful slumbers. Marge relayed that this was because Ivy was 'looking after him'. She also asked Fran if she had done anything wrong and commented, somewhat darkly I thought, that 'What goes around comes around.' I reassured Fran that this may have applied to a former life, if you believe in reincarnation that is…

The weirdness continued, one night Christine Schofield, who lived opposite Tower Cottage, at Swan Cottage, heard a baby crying at her neighbour's home all night. It was so persistent that she got up and knocked on the door but got no reply, which wasn't surprising since Fran and Ollie were staying at Sarah Harrison's home and Tower Cottage was quite empty.

As previously mentioned Tower Cottage is situated in Swan Street and at nearby Church Path the end house is called Dove Cottage, where the windows overlook the graveyard and next door there was a fire in the past in which a woman and two children died. Footsteps have often been heard, running or walking briskly past Dove Cottage, when there has been nobody seen to account for them. Fran wondered if it was Ivy's ghostly footsteps, as she made her way to the church for secret assignations with her priestly lover.

A week before she finally moved out Fran returned to her cottage to discover every single tap in the place turned on, which necessitated a tour of the whole house to turn them off again. Her dad was with her and where he had displayed scepticism before she now noticed that he seemed anxious. As Fran crossed the low-ceilinged corridor that separated the bedroom from the bathroom a fresh shock awaited her. There in the bedroom doorway stood a woman. She was attractive, very tall, in her late 30s or early 40s and wearing a long dress with her hair piled up. Somehow the room seemed darker than usual but the woman was real enough, down to the rustle of her dress and the creak of the floorboards as she moved. Fran called for her dad but this new apparition vanished before he reached the bedroom.

I was struck by the intensity of Fran's experiences, fascinated by her story and felt strongly sympathetic for this attractive, personable and intelligent young woman, who undoubtedly had suffered a terrifying and traumatic few months in a badly haunted property ten years before I met her.

Chapter Two

HITCHIN

Hitchin has been at the centre of any number of true ghostly experiences, the vast majority of them, not unexpectedly, are centred in and around the streets of the Old Town. There is an excellent ghost walk, organised by Hitchin Museum, which is a sure indication of the town's sizeable phantom population. The walk winds its way around the narrow streets and picturesque courtyards which radiate outwards from the central, cobbled market square, where timber-framed houses, shops, restaurants and pubs lend a medieval atmosphere.

The river Hiz meanders through, dividing the town into east and west, with parks and attractive open spaces along the riverbanks. The Icknield Way, an ancient trading route which runs from east to west across Hertfordshire, passes through the town and affords some lovely views across the county. It forms part of the route between the Wash, east along Peddars Way and south towards the Dorset coast via the Ridgeway Path.

For centuries Hitchin has been a market town, it once enjoyed a thriving wool trade when sheep grazed on the hillsides and there was wheat, barley and lavender grown too, which added to the general prosperity of the area. Commerce and industry have continued to make Hitchin one of the business centres of North Hertfordshire. The town has grown steadily but the real increase in population happened with the coming of the railway line between London and the North of England and now the population is in excess of 30,000.

The Old Town is dominated by the venerable, ancient church of St Mary and several nearby shops in St Mary's Square are haunted including the bridal gown suppliers, Jayne Boulton, which used to be a bookshop. During alterations to a wall a shoe was found and after that manifestations began. Just over the road, at Charisma, some staff have been pelted with beads by an unseen presence and the electric lights have come on at night when nobody has been in the place.

Not far away is Queen Street, which was once called Dead Street because not a single soul living there during the great plague of 1665 survived...

The market square is a busy place at night, popular with 'thirty-somethings' who are spoilt for choice when it comes to 'eateries', the immediate surroundings are packed with a vast spectrum of different places to dine out. What many diners may be unaware of is that they may be in close proximity to spirits not found in bottles. Bar Amigo is haunted by the spirits of an old man and a little girl who, with arms linked, have been seen to walk straight through a wall.

Just across the way from the square, in the High Street, is Woolworth's, haunted by the 'lavender lady', whose scent has been smelt by staff and whose form has been seen by them. The most interesting story surrounding the ghost is that one of the manageresses of Woolworth's who was at a meeting in the Sun Hotel when her mobile was called, but nobody spoke when she answered the call. The manageress then dialled 1471 and was astonished to find that she had been called from the Woolworth's building, at night, when she knew that it was empty! Had the 'lavender lady' contacted her?

Between the High Street and Churchyard Walk is Arams Alley, a narrow thoroughfare where regular sightings of a former notorious resident of Hitchin have been recorded. He was Eugene Aram, scholar, friend of the writer Lord Lytton of Knebworth House, usher at a local boys' school in Hitchin... and a murderer. Aram created a new life for himself in Hitchin, where he hid out for at least eight years after murdering a tramp in Yorkshire, but by a strange coincidence he was recognised by someone passing through Hitchin who had known him in his former life and eventually he was brought to justice in King's Lynn, Norfolk, where he was hanged in 1758.

Sun Street's Sun Hotel is one of the most notorious and interesting of Hitchin's many haunted historical buildings, as it has multiple ghostly reports surrounding it. The dumb waiter inside the place has been known to go up and down by itself and after functions in the ballroom an invisible presence often moves things around. Guests have heard voices in the night from the archway outside, where the horse-drawn coaches used to pass underneath, calling out 'mind your head', it is believed that a long-ago coach passenger suffered decapitation here.

At the other end of the building, near the car park, some ladies reported being struck on the shins by ghostly wood and the distinctive sounds of clacking woods have also been reported in the vicinity. This used to be the site of an ancient bowling green used by local clergymen and, as far as I know, is the only example of anyone experiencing phantom bowling balls!

On a more sinister note there is one particular guest bedroom in the hotel (I cannot divulge which one) where no guest has stayed for more than one night as it is haunted (to a scary degree) by the most famous person to ever haunt the hotel, Lord Havisham. This former aristocrat has also been seen, oddly enough, carrying a fish under one arm as he passes through the building. He was a 19th century contemporary of the Duke of Bedford, who used to pay off his friend's gambling debts until one day, when he decided that enough was enough. Faced with debts that he could not repay Havisham committed suicide and his ghost is still active in the 21st century. He has plenty of company, for people have also been frightened by a woman's ghost as well as that of a monk, who has been observed crossing the bar room and also behind the bar (presumably he prefers Abbott ale).

One room that I can mention is room 10, as it well known to be haunted by the ghost of a woman whose body is felt by guests, lying across their faces in the night and almost suffocating them, but the more psychically aware refuse to sleep in the room upon entering it.

Further along Sun Street, at number 10 and 11 is a Queen Anne building, the premises of Philpotts, the house furnishers. It has a history of frightening anyone foolish enough to want to spend a night upstairs, which area has for many years been used only as a storeroom. There are rumours of some gruesome event taking place up there, some say that a person was locked in and died behind a trapdoor. A family living here heard knocking sounds and when they opened the hatch they were told to leave and allegedly were injured by the spirits that inhabit the top floor. Investigations into the hauntings are also reported to have gone drastically wrong and nowadays nobody is offering to try and record any paranormal activity here. It is small wonder then that the windows remain boarded up to this day.

In a house at the corner of Sun Street and Bridge Street a lady has reported seeing a soldier wearing the clothes and trappings of the Civil War, standing by the old fireplace, it is thought to be the spirit of a soldier who disappeared while billeted here.

Running parallel with Sun Street, the other side of Market Place, runs Bucklersbury which also has its share of haunted buildings. At number 8a, which is the flat two floors above Hawkins the clothiers, footsteps are regularly heard walking on the landing, cold spots are experienced and the spirit of a woman wearing a blue dress has been seen as well as that of a tall thin man with straggly hair and a 'vampiric' appearance. Parliamentarian officers were quartered in these buildings, while their troops remained out of doors or at the local inns, if they were lucky, during the Civil War.

My friend Andy Thompson lived in this flat for a time and he too heard the footsteps, he also heard scratching noises in his bedroom, coming from the door leading to the next bedroom, but when he fully woke up they stopped. One night he thought that someone had broken in, as he went to investigate he was confronted by a Civil War soldier standing on the landing, Andy looked in the mirror but the figure was not reflected in it. He described it as follows, 'He was wearing a red tunic, a very big man, bearded and with a scar on his face, I was only about three or four steps below him on the stairs and saw him quite plainly.'

Another strange occurrence that Andy recalled took place during a party at the flat, everyone had been sitting and talking in a big circle in the middle of the room when someone got up and left. The others thought that this individual had gone to the toilet, but the 'person' didn't return and everyone began to wonder who it was, only to realise that every guest was accounted for, on checking outside the room nobody else was found, so who was it? Everyone in that circle was certain that 'someone else' had joined them...

Andy used a tape recorder in an attempt to capture some of the many inexplicable noises heard in the place and one evening, with a small group of friends, he was startled to hear fearsomely loud snarling, growling animal-like sounds on the landing, which were recorded on tape.

Duncan Campbell, another friend of mine, was under no illusions about the flat, he had also lived there for a while and he confirmed the story about the frightening tape recording as he had been present at the time and recalled that everyone had felt quite shaken by the experience. One sultry July night he had another even more alarming experience as he tried to find sleep. He heard scratching noises in the woodwork by the door, then footsteps approaching his bed before the mattress dipped under an invisible weight, all the time the room was freezing cold despite the heat of a summer's evening outside, and finally 'something' scratched his face. He dived under the covers, unwilling to face his invisible assailant and next day there was a red weal on his face as a memento of the paranormal attack.

In the same street The George pub has a certain reputation, with heavy footsteps similarly reported at night time, when animals and even landlords, have refused to venture down into the cellar. Further along is the Red Hart pub, probably the oldest pub in Hitchin, dating back to Elizabethan times and notorious as the site of the town's last public hanging. Gas taps have been turned off by an invisible entity and at least one manifestation has been recorded in a bedroom, where the ghost of an old man was seen at night, sitting in an armchair.

Bucklersbury leads down to Tilehouse Street and another haunted pub, the Coopers Arms, where a ghostly, one-legged monk (also a phantom cat) has been sighted, and the cellar is reputedly an uncomfortable place to be. A regular's tankard was reported, back in 1971, to have moved of its own accord.

There are thought to be monastic origins associated with this area. The most famous resident of Tilehouse Street was George Chapman (1560–1634) poet, translator and playwright, best known for his translations of Homer's *Iliad* and *Odyssey*. His former home, 'the Chapmans', is reputedly haunted by his ghost, which has been seen, quill pen in hand, at the window. Number 84, an elegant town house, is also notoriously haunted and it is frequently up for sale. Its ghost is a 19th century midshipman, in a blue Naval uniform and when a legal firm had the premises in the 1980s and 90s there were a number of reported sightings of a figure which walked through the walls here.

Not far away in the shadowy Halls Yard, the partial apparition of a lady has been seen, but only as far down as her knees…

There is a flat above Ladbrokes betting shop in Bancroft which the local estate agents admit is hard to let. This is haunted by a ghostly cat; tenants have claimed that they have been scratched on the legs by this spirit animal. What is known is that a former tenant in the 1970s owned a cat, which was run over and shortly afterwards the grieving owner committed suicide.

My personal favourite 'haunt' would be Hitchin Priory, an attractive place set in its own parkland, which extends to 29 acres and which was owned by the same family, the Delmay-Radcliffes, for four hundred years. Presently it is a conference and training centre, but it dates back to the 14th century, when it was a Carmelite (also known as White Friars) monastery. It is probably the most haunted building in the town and night porters have witnessed a phantom coach and horses in the grounds at the back of the priory on several occasions. Other visitors include a troop of Roman soldiers also seen and heard, marching through the grounds.

Security guards have heard people talking in one of the rooms where no people should have been. An astonished guard opened the door to find a group of card players in old-fashioned dress, he went to get another witness, but on their return the room not only looked completely different but it was also devoid of any people. The security man realised afterwards that no one in the room had acknowledged his presence; they hadn't even looked up from their game. It was as if they were in a different time zone – had the man suffered some kind of 'time slip'? After the event he confessed that he hadn't been frightened at the time, but then he hadn't been expecting to see what he saw, some oddly-dressed people playing cards…

Other apparitions are associated with the Priory including a mysterious 'grey lady', last reported in 1980 by the caretaker when the place was used as an education centre. Nothing is known about her, but she has also been seen outside the Priory, sometimes on cold nights, wearing no coat, just a long grey dress. I wonder if she has anything to do with the report from 1816, when butcher Richard Atkins claimed a sighting of a woman in a handsome red cloak and black hat who had been walking towards him in Priory Park but she disappeared as he looked away, he walked towards the spot where he last saw her only to discover that there was nowhere that she could have hidden. Unsurprisingly, given the early history of the site, phantom monks are also regularly seen by the staff here. The most frequently mentioned out of Hitchin Piriory's plethora of phantoms is an anniversary ghost, reputed to appear on June 15th and it is a ghostly Cavalier, called Goring.

North-west of Hitchin lies the village of Pirton, where there is a Tudor mansion, dating from about 1510, called High Down House, which was built by the Dowcras family of Lilley. Every year, on the 15th June, a headless Cavalier is said to ride his white horse, at midnight, from High Down House to Hitchin Priory, where he might have found sanctuary, it is the ghost of Goring. This unfortunate Cavalier soldier took shelter in a small roof chamber. (This chamber is also haunted by the appearance of a beautiful young woman, who was reported by a startled guest during the 1980s, sitting on the edge of the bed and she is probably the spirit of Goring's former girlfriend).

During the summer of 1648 Goring had been visiting a lady friend (a dangerous assignation as the area was crawling with Parliamentarian troopers) at High Down House when he was surprised by the Roundheads, but he managed to escape via a secret underground passage and hid in a hollow wych-elm. The Parliamentarian troops were occupying Hitchin and the surrounding areas, under the command of Colonel Scoop, and they discovered Goring's hiding place, dragged him to the foot of the tree and ruthlessly cut him down. His murder was witnessed from afar by his girlfriend, who soon after collapsed and died of shock.

MYSTERIOUS MINSDEN

South of Hitchin, on the B651, is an inn called the Royal Oak, near here you can park in Hitchwood Lane car park and then about a hundred yards up a dirt track on the left can be found the ruins of Minsden Chapel. It dates from the fourteenth century, when it was a chapel-of-ease for the use of pilgrims, and it has long been associated with a ghostly monk. Sightings have usually been preceded by the tolling of ghostly bells, when the sounds died away the monk was seen, under the ivy-covered arch on the south side, walking with his head bowed, he mounted invisible steps before he disappeared. Soon after 'sweet and plaintive music' would briefly fill the air before quiet descended once more. A remarkable photograph was thought to have captured an image of this ghostly monk. It was taken by W.T. Latchmore in 1907 and was reproduced on page 92, volume II of *The History of Hitchin* by Reginald Hine. The 'Latchmore photograph' caused great excitement at the time but, sadly for the cause of genuine paranormal investigation, this photograph was later admitted to be a fake.

It is said that Minsden Chapel was once the property of the Knights of St John of Jerusalem, what is known is that the Knights Templars were located at nearby Temple Dinsley, now the site occupied by the Princess Helena College, in Preston, where they are rumoured to have kept a great treasure. The Knights Templars were also associated with the church at St Ippolitts dedicated to the patron saint of horses, St Hippolytus. Legend has it that before riding off to the Crusades the knights had their horses blessed at this church.

By 1690 Minsden was already little more than a ruin, but as it was such a romantic spot it was used for al fresco marriages, right up to 1738 when it was deemed unsafe to conduct any more weddings. The chapel is most strongly linked with the Hitchin attorney, writer and historian, Reginald Hine, who became quite obsessed with the place. He leased the ruins for his lifetime, completed one of his books there, called *Confessions of a an Uncommon Attorney*, in 1943, he even had his ashes scattered in the grounds, after his death in 1949, and his memorial stone can be found here in the undergrowth. After Hine's death his wife made the ruins his memorial, keeping the walls and arches safe from the invading creeper, ivy and brambles. Reginald Hine was passionate about protecting 'his' Minsden and he laid down a promise, 'Trespassers and sacrilegious persons take warning, for I will proceed against them with the utmost rigour of the law and after my death and burial, I will endeavour, in all ghostly ways, to protect and haunt its hallowed walls.' Some people believe that he carried out his promise after his tragic death. He had retired from the legal profession and was talking with friends at Hitchin railway station when the train approached, he casually said, 'Wait a minute,' with that he walked into the path of the train and died instantly. A note was left, addressed to the local coroner...

All Hallows Eve is the night when Minsden's ghosts have traditionally been most active, with a host of stories concerning horses and dogs behaving as though they have seen or sensed some invisible presence as they climb towards Minsden Chapel on that particular night. Dame Margerie, a local resident and benefactress of the chapel, who lived in the 14th century, is another spirit reputed to haunt the ruins, along with the reported haunting in the 1980s, of a small, flute-playing boy.

The 19th century ghost-hunter Elliott O'Donnell was a visitor here at Halloween on several occasions and he reported feeling 'extraordinarily uncanny', conscious of something scrutinising him although nothing was seen or heard. On another occasion, when discussing the case with modern-day ghost-hunter Peter Underwood, O'Donnell claimed to have heard 'sweet music' and thought that he had glimpsed 'a white-robed figure standing in one of the archways'. Peter Underwood met Reginald Hine and obtained his permission to investigate the site, which Peter, together with his brother and a friend, duly did. During their preliminary visit both Peter and his friend heard a brief, unaccounted snatch of music, while the ghost-hunter's brother heard nothing.

My friend Sarah Hopkins, who lives in Hitchin, visited the ruins in recent years and found it a peaceful spot. There is not much to see now, just lots of undergrowth and a few stone columns, but she took a series of photographs most of which were unremarkable except for one which has been preserved in APIS's archives. In this remarkable photograph a curious orange glow appears, hovering a few feet off the ground, which some people think looks like the head and shoulders of a monk kneeling at prayer. There was certainly no odd light effect visible at the time that the photograph was taken, only the camera itself recorded the weird orange glow. This is typical of a 'stage one' manifestation, that is the genesis of an energy mass, often referred to as an orb because it is usually round in shape. 'Stage ones' are not visible to the naked eye and require a digital camera or video recorder to 'see' them for us. They vary in colour, with white, red, pink, orange, blue, grey and black orbs having been reported. They appear as flashes of light as well as the more widely known orb effects. A 'full manifestation', that is recognisably a human figure, which may interact with the viewer, requires a lot more energy to make an appearance. Certainly no fault could be found with Sarah's camera and this photograph would seem to fall into that 1% of such photographs which simply defy explanation.

LILLEY – VILLAGE OF THE UNEXPLAINED

Situated four miles west of Hitchin on the A505 is the 'village of mysteries' – Lilley, where the famed alchemist Johann Kellerman lived in the 19th century. Accounts of him vary, on the one hand we have the secretive recluse, rarely seen outside his own home, who spoke with a strong foreign accent and who guarded the privacy of his large house with man-traps and barricades while he toiled away at the furnace in his cellar on his ceaseless quest to turn base metals into gold. On the other hand we hear of his kinder side, his willingness to help villagers in distress. On one occasion he heard of a party of gypsies who missed their way in the snow and ended up stranded in a dell near the turning to Lilley Hoo, Kellerman had them dug out. Strangest of all was the alchemist's sudden vanishing trick, one day he just disappeared without a trace.

One of the best things about Lilley is the nearby Icknield Way, this ancient lane is best seen at the part that runs out of the Hexton Road above Lilley Hoo, across the top of Telegraph Hill, it makes for country walking at its finest. Nearly everyone who knows Hertfordshire well knows the lines from the poem by Rupert Brook:

'The Roman road to Wendover
By Tring and Lilley Hoo.'

When he was an undergraduate at Cambridge University Rupert Brook became well acquainted with Hertfordshire through his walks along the country lanes. The above-mentioned lines of verse are not strictly accurate however; as the Icknield Way, which he would have followed, is actually pre-Roman. The oddities of the county boundary mean that almost everything between Tring and Lilley Hoo is, in fact, in Bedfordshire.

Lilley's mysterious reputation was further enhanced some 70 years after Johann Kellerman vanished, in about 1895, with the haunting at the village sweet shop. Fanny Ebbs ran her shop near the Silver Lion pub and one night she saw the ghost of a man appear through her bedroom wall then turn and walk down the stairs. Fanny followed the apparition through the shop and into her kitchen and watched dumbfounded as he went to the brick fireplace, knelt down and took up the hearth bricks to reveal a hidden large black kettle.

From the kettle the ghost counted out scores of gold sovereigns and then counted them all back again before revealing a second pot which was similarly checked before both pots were replaced. After the spirit had disappeared again, back through the bedroom wall, the sweetshop owner searched the hearth and found the miser's hoard, which she took, but put everything else back as it had been. The ghost returned the next night and, finding all its treasure missing, it never came back. Fanny Ebbs continued to run her sweetshop but when she died the remains of her fortune were left to the people of the parish.

By far the biggest mystery of Lilley is its haunted pub, the Lilley Arms, formerly known as the Sugar Loaf, which has an extremely well catalogued collection of ghosts. My group, Anglia Paranormal Investigation Society, held its 2004 Christmas Dinner here in the atmospheric old Crooked Barn, which we had to ourselves. I had the ideal opportunity to talk with Sylvia Brown, who has been the licensee together with her husband Peter, for over twenty years. She had numerous stories of hauntings to tell and so did most of her staff, enough to convince the most hardened sceptic that there was something mysterious about the place. One of Sylvia's stories was about her attic, while she was cleaning up there one day she knocked over a bowl of walnuts, so she picked them up, put them back on the shelf and carried on cleaning. While her back was to the shelf she heard some taps and clicks behind her and when she turned around, a matter of seconds later, the walnuts had been carefully positioned in a straight line on the attic floor! I told her that this was typical of poltergeist behaviour.

In 2001 a film crew arrived and ended up staying for three nights at the Lilley Arms, after deciding that here was something well worth investigating. The six psychic investigators, who included two mediums, were not disappointed. A cold draught constantly played around the saloon bar and the upstairs living room and the continual activity meant that Sylvia found difficulty sleeping for the duration of the investigation.

Several orbs of light, thought to be first stages in a ghost manifestation, were seen in the bar and upstairs. Christmas decorations have always been difficult to put up in the saloon bar, which is now the dining room and dowsers have located two energy lines which cross right in the middle of the room. The Browns showed the mediums the decoration which spanned the bar and about an hour later this same decoration began to twist before falling down as if invisible hands had pulled it. A photograph was taken which showed an orb near to some more Christmas decorations and everyone in the room was aware of a chill in the air that was so strong that their breath could be seen. Directly after the photograph was shot, three people witnessed the decorations snapping in the exact place where the orb had been seen!

The most frightening events of the whole long drawn out vigil occurred in the Crooked Barn at the back of the pub. One of the mediums asked if anyone had committed suicide in there and at that the video cameraman felt his whole face being stretched back. He later described the experience as if 'something' was all over him making him taller. It was so scary that he had to stop filming as the temperature plummeted and the mediums saw a tall gaunt figure lying on the floor.

So who are the ghosts that haunt the Lilley Arms? They are many and they are varied. When the pub was called the Sugar Loaf about two hundred years ago there was a terrible fire which may have killed a number of people. One of the ghosts is reckoned to be that of Frances Mitchell who ran a millinery business at Stotfold in 1786, and she often arrived in a coach from Hitchin, supposedly to see Tom Connisbee, landlord of the inn from 1780 onwards. There is a chair in the corner of the restaurant known as Tom's Chair where a ghost has been seen and where candles have been found to be inexplicably alight. Connisbee is also thought to be the ghost that sometimes playfully pokes people in the back. A medium, during the three day vigil, asked Sylvia to tell him he was in the wrong century and the landlady, in a semi-trance, retorted in a masculine voice, 'No, you are in the wrong century!'

At least one ghost is what a paranormal investigator has categorised 'a lander', i.e. it doesn't haunt a building so much as a piece of ground. This spirit is said to be that of a shepherd who wasn't welcome at the inn and who haunts the yard outside. A multitude of other 'haunters' have been identified including John, who was a former handyman, a small deaf and dumb girl, a Pirton postman of the 18th century, another 'lander', a small girl called Rose Anne who is attached to the orchard, where she likes to play, and there is also the ghost of a former kitchen hand as well. One summer a few years back a six-year-old boy visiting the pub saw the shepherd's shade and in his own words, 'a see-through dog' as well.

Sylvia wonders if the ghost of the alchemist of Lilley, Johann Kellerman, is amongst the motley crew of ghosts. What is known is that his laboratory was just across the road, and it has been surmised that there may have been an escape tunnel from his house to the cellars of the pub. It is strongly rumoured that he was murdered, hence his sudden disappearance.

Chapter Three
KNEBWORTH

Knebworth derives from Chenepeworde, meaning 'the house on the hill', as mentioned in the Domesday Book of 1086, when it was a small manor house built like a fortress and surrounded by hundreds of acres of land. It was given to one of William the Conqueror's stewards, a knight called Eudo Dapifer. Over the following four hundred years the house changed ownership a number of times until, in 1492, the first Lytton arrived at Knebworth and it has remained in the same family ever since, over five hundred years, quite unusual when so many ancient family 'seats' have passed into other hands.

Many people over the years have earned a living and have been accommodated on the great estate. Sir Robert Lytton came first, and he was known as Sir Robert of the Peak. He was Keeper of the Wardrobe to Henry VII. He came down from Derbyshire and set about pulling down the Manor House, which he replaced with a huge mansion of red Tudor brick. The four sides were built around a central courtyard with a gate-house and so it was to remain for some four hundred years, when, due to long-term neglect three sides were demolished and stucco was added to the remaining wing in the nineteenth century.

Knebworth's 'family ghost' was known as 'the Yellow Boy' or 'the Radiant Boy' and only if a member of the Lyttons was due to die a violent death would this phantom child appear, and by his gestures he would indicate the manner of their passing. Not surprisingly the room he was said to haunt was carefully avoided by the family but they had no qualms about offering it to their guests. One such guest was politician Lord Castlereagh, who stayed in this room when he was Foreign Secretary. He complained in the morning about a night-time visitation by the apparently solid figure of a young boy with yellow hair who looked directly at Castlereagh while drawing his fingers slowly across his own throat several times before he disappeared. In 1822 Lord Castlereagh did indeed die a violent death, by cutting his throat with a penknife...

'Radiant Boys' are a world-wide phenomenon and there are several well documented cases recorded around the UK. Knebworth's 'Yellow Boy' is one such typical manifestation. These ghosts appear as beautiful male children, tightly surrounded by an unearthly bright light of different colours, but most often white or blue. Nobody knows the identity of these other-worldly visitors or the purpose of their visitations. There is, however, a commonly held opinion that they are the spirits of children who were murdered by their parents. More often than not the sighting of such a spectre is an omen of ill fortune for the spectator...

In 1843, when he succeeded to the Knebworth estate, Sir Edward Bulwer Lytton (1803–73), by then an established, famous novelist, changed the character of the Tudor mansion completely. He modernised it, commissioned copper domes, gargoyles and more castellations to be added, as was the fashion in Victorian times, to create his own Gothic fantasy and the great house now had the status of a palace.

In terms of books sold this eminent Victorian was, perhaps, the male equivalent of J.K. Rowling in his day. It was said of him, 'Everything he wrote, sold as though it were bread displayed to a hungry crowd.' What was equally impressive was his versatility, he wrote immensely successful novels in a variety of genres popular at the time – over a career that spanned 45 years he wrote 24 novels alone, that included historical romances, tales of magic, spiritualism and science, novels of high society, light novels of middle-class domestic life and philosophical novels. He also found the time to pen 10 plays, 11 volumes of poetry, two collections of essays, numerous short stories, a pioneering sociological study, a history of Athens and translations of Horace and Schiller. Sir Edward somehow managed to combine both a writing career and a political career; he was an MP for over 16 years. He was a lifelong friend of Charles Dickens, whom he greatly influenced, and Dickens was a frequent visitor to Knebworth House. Sir Edward Bulwer Lytton was a man of many interests, among them was an enthusiasm for the occult and two of his most chilling ghost stories are *The House and the Brain* and the *The Haunted and the Haunters*. During the mid 19th century he was widely regarded as England's leading man of letters. He will forever be remembered as the author who first penned those immortal opening lines, '*It was a dark and stormy night...*' These will always be the ideal conditions for a good haunting because the static electricity in the air during a thunderstorm provides the energy that spirits require to produce their manifestations.

Sir Edward delighted in presiding over his palace at Knebworth and would often greet his many guests clad in his rich velvet suits. His friends were an eclectic bunch, drawn from politicians, writers, artists and fellow students of the occult. He was responsible for making the idea of occultism fashionable in England and visitors included many famous mediums. The most eminent of these was Daniel Dunglas Home, the remarkably gifted Scottish medium and spiritualist for whom the word 'psychic' was coined. It is difficult to comprehend the world-wide celebrity achieved by this rather effeminate-looking man whose fame in the Victorian world would totally eclipse that of someone like Derek Acorah, for instance, in the current Elizabethan era. Acorah is the beneficiary of twenty-first century advantages such as the ability to reach a vast public via regular television broadcasts. Home's international standing was attained mainly by personal demonstrations of his powers, made during meetings with members of European high society.

Home was said to be able to move objects by the power of his thoughts alone. He was also credited with the ability to change the dimensions of his body as well as being impervious to fire and intense heat when in a trance. He could, allegedly, materialise ghostly forms and the most dramatic of all effects – he was able to levitate at will! Hundreds of witnesses, in various parts of the world, over a forty year period, attested to his unique powers. It is regrettable that this all took place before the era of the Society for Psychical Research, which wasn't founded till the late nineteenth century and also before the invention of the snapshot camera.

Daniel Dunglas Home moved with his family from Edinburgh to Connecticut when he was nine years old, he was a sickly child who grew up to an adulthood where his health was never robust. By the time he was nineteen he experienced his first spontaneous levitation and eventually learned to control it to such an extent that observers later claimed that he seemed able to fly. He left America and came to England in the summer of 1855 and he was welcomed into society by Sir Edward Bulwer-Lytton, who invited him to visit his Park Lane residence. Later he was a guest at Knebworth, where a number of séances were held which provided thought-provoking material for Sir Edward's novel *The Haunted and the Haunters.*

In 1868, at Lord Adare's house in London, Home while in a trance, produced his most famous phenomenon. He was seen by several prominent witnesses to float out of a third floor window and then to float back in again via a different window. That same year witnesses at another trance medium session attested to a most shocking demonstration when Home stuck his head in a fire and handled red-hot coals without any injury whatsoever!

Home did not know how or why he was chosen to be the recipient of such awe-inspiring psychic gifts and explained that he was just the medium for the spirits, over which he had no control and his main spirit guide was called Bryan. Tragically this fascinating individual, the 'original psychic' died at the early age of forty-four in 1886 and is largely forgotten today.

Sir Edward Bulwer-Lytton was raised to the peerage in 1866, he was known thereafter as Lord Lytton and his son Robert, was first Earl of Lytton (1831–91) who succeeded to the title in 1873. Robert became the first Viceroy of India in 1876 and lived at Knebworth with his son, Victor, and his son-in-law, Sir Edward Lutyens, who altered the property and designed the formal garden to the west of the house.

In modern times Knebworth House is recognised as a striking stately home and may seem familiar to many people as the backdrop for numerous films (it has appeared, for example, as Wayne Manor, home to Bruce Wayne, alias Batman, in that entertaining series of movies). It has also played host to quite a few spectacular outdoor vintage-car rallies, fairs, pageants, 'events' and of course, pop concerts in its 260 acres of parkland and the cream of the music business have played here, Robbie Williams, the Rolling Stones, Led Zeppelin and Pink Floyd among them.

The village grew up around the great house and villagers continue to attend the 12th century church of St Mary's, which stands in Knebworth Park. One inn remains in the village, the lovely old Lytton Arms and some attractive old cottages add to the character but the village has lost much of its own identity and is in serious danger of amalgamation, as it becomes swallowed up by the ever encroaching urban sprawl of the Stevenage shopping corridor to the north and Welwyn Garden City's overspill to the south.

Knebworth House still has its ghosts, in fairly recent times an American guest, staying in the Queen Elizabeth room, was startled one morning when she awoke to find the unexplained presence of a stranger, a young girl with long blonde hair, who was leaning over the four-poster bed. A female spirit reportedly haunts the picture gallery too. The strongest presence of all, however, perhaps quite naturally, remains the most interesting man who ever lived in Knebworth House. This multi-talented man felt passionate about his ancestral home and altered it so much during his lifetime, he entertained so many exciting personalities of his era, and he was a politician, an occultist and a best-selling author, Edward Bulwer-Lytton. His spirit is felt by family, staff members and visitors alike, particularly strongly in the old study and adjoining drawing room that he used to frequent and this is a good example of a peaceful earth-bound spirit bound to a location by his love and affection for this very special place.

Nup End

A few years ago Nup End farmhouse, a property which reputedly dates back to Cromwellian times and is situated on the outskirts of Knebworth, was converted into apartments by Mr Tony Bly. Close by are the offices of A.D. Bly, a groundworks and civil engineering company owned by Tony, and both the farmhouse and the contractors' offices are haunted. There is a separate, small outbuilding in the farmhouse grounds, which is similarly affected. Terry Goddard is a computer engineer who leased the outbuilding as a tenant to A.D. Bly for over five years until late summer/early autumn in 2004. He was working at 2am in his office one morning when he looked up to see a farm worker standing in front of the desk who smiled at Terry before abruptly vanishing. Terry saw this same apparition in the corridor on another occasion. Then there were the other phenomena, like the taps being turned on and off in the kitchen, the handle on the front door going down on its own and the door opening and closing by itself as well as the doorbell being rung but nobody being found outside. There was also one of the hallmarks of a genuine haunting – abnormally high electricity bills. Ghosts seem to 'tap into' the available electricity supply in order to gain the energy necessary to produce their repertoire of anomalous phenomena.

Anglia Paranormal Investigation Society has mounted several night-time vigils, beginning in March 2004, which have recorded paranormal activity at Nup End. These have included the movement of trigger objects i.e. pebbles left on a tray containing sand were moved. Trigger objects are an essential part of any self-respecting ghost hunter's kit. They are used to attract the attention of ghosts and the idea is to leave them in a place where they will not be disturbed by members of the investigating team. APIS has found the use of trigger objects to be a particularly effective ghost research technique.

Those members of our Society who are 'sensitive' have picked up a number of strong psychic impressions of both male and female spirits, the names Vivien, Kevin, Ron, Helen and Tom were received, along with David Isaacs, a man with dark, curly hair, a longish beard and an injured hand. The presence of a seven or eight-year-old girl with mousy brown hair in ringlets, wearing an old-fashioned knee-length dress was detected; she was accompanied by a small black and white terrier. There was an impression that this child had died suddenly, on a road. More than one team member has experienced unexplained breezes or draughts on the stairs, the sound of something metallic being put down has been heard and the feeling of being watched has been reported.

All of our investigations have been organised by Carol Greenall (APIS's Secretary) who works for A.D. Bly. In March 2005, as part of a small group of four investigators, Andy Garrett (an APIS Team Leader); saw his very first complete manifestation. This is an exciting, 'landmark occasion' in any ghost hunter's life! As Andy stood near the window a man walked along the side of the building over what are now flower beds. The passer-by seemed to be marching briskly along and Andy caught sight of a white shirt with

34

big cuffs and large buttons. The investigating team wondered who it could be, but on going outside there was no sign of anyone other than themselves!

While undertaking another vigil in the farmhouse Andy and Carol have sensed a bad atmosphere in the garden, as though something nasty was lying in wait, and inside the building they have heard knocking sounds upstairs when they have been downstairs and the only (human) occupants in the farmhouse.

About three years ago Carol was working alone in the reception area of A.D Bly's main offices at Nup End when she suddenly felt the atmosphere turn freezing cold and she saw a hazy shape take form by the fax machine, the misty outline then crossed the floor and went through the wall. She compared notes with the receptionist who confirmed that she had also seen this misty shape and the two sightings were about twelve months apart. A number of staff, both male and female, have told Carol that the place has 'a funny feel at night' and that they do not like being there on their own…

GHOSTLY DATCHWORTH

Datchworth is a most impressive place, turn left opposite the Chequers pub coming out of Knebworth into Woolmer Green and you enter a completely different world to the hubbub that is Knebworth town centre. Winding country lanes, acres and acres of open farmland, bluebell woods, beautiful houses tucked away down sweeping drives, hidden thatched cottages, a large open pond, an ancient Green… this little exclusive enclave has everything going for it. Small wonder that people like boxing promoter Frank Warren and film critic Barry Norman live here. It seems impossible that you are in fact a mere mile south of Knebworth.

Long regarded as Hertfordshire's 'most haunted village' (as it is reputedly inhabited by at least 12 ghosts), Datchworth is an ancient village, originally known as Decewrthe as far back as 969. By the time of the Domesday Book in 1086 it was called Daceuuorde, 'Enclosure of a man called Daecca'. Datchworth is a scattered community which is made up of a number of 'Greens' – Datchworth Green, Bulls Green and Burnham Green, (as well as Mardleybury) indicating the clearance and cultivation of woodland after the Domesday records were made.

At the highest point, with panoramic views across the Hertfordshire countryside, stands All Saints Church, a small, plain edifice that is visible from several miles around. Its churchyard is reputed to be haunted by a strange chattering sound and shadowy figures have been seen amongst the gravestones. The church is sited at the top of narrow, unlit Rectory Lane; this byway has the spookiest reputation with reports of phantom footsteps and appearances of a ghostly cart with dead bodies inside, a grisly hangover from the 1760s. A family named Eaves starved to death in the ruined poorhouse at Datchworth Green during the famine of 1762 and their final journey was made in a cart up Rectory Lane, where their remains were buried in a mass grave in the churchyard. In 1998 Carlton Television visited Rectory Lane to make a feature film for its *London Tonight* programme and the presenter confessed that he felt the atmosphere there 'unsettling'.

Rectory Lane was also investigated one autumn night in the 1970s by journalist Evelyn Hall-King and psychic Eileen Ison, when they visited Datchworth in search of material for a magazine article about Britain's most haunted places. At the end of their findings Evelyn and Eileen concluded that Datchworth was the second most haunted location in the UK – I would like to know which location came out top! They were walking along Rectory Lane in the dark and the rain when the psychic suddenly started moaning and bending over, as if receiving invisible blows, which indeed she actually felt was the case. She was receiving a paranormal impression of being viciously beaten about the head and shoulders. 'The horses,' she said, 'They're coming, can't you hear them?' The journalist surmised that her friend might have been receiving the 'psychic echoes' of a killing carried out some two hundred years previously, when highway robber Walter Clibbon met his end in the neighbourhood. His grave is half way along the Datchworth to Bramfield road, a couple of miles from where they were presently standing, and it is marked by a plain wooden post. Clibbon had terrorised the neighbourhood for many years and his death brought forth celebrations from the local people when his body was brought to The Horns public house, where it stayed overnight.

Walter Clibbon, sometimes dubbed 'the murderous pie-man of Hertford' was a vicious criminal of the late 18th century, whose gang preyed on traders returning from the four annual fairs and regular Saturday markets held at Hertford County Town. What nobody could understand at the time was how the robbers were always able to select their victims from the most successful farmers and peddlers, who were carrying the most money on the day. The answer was simple, the gang's ringleader, Walter Clibbon, led a double life. By day he blended in with the crowds, he came from Babbs Green, Wareside, so he was a local and he attended the fairs and markets as he was a pie-man by trade. This gave him the perfect opportunity to mix with the crowds and to see and to hear about who was making the most money while he sold his pies. Clibbon's real business however, was robbery, which he carried out at night with the help of his two sons. As darkness fell these footpads dressed themselves up in anonymous smock-frocks, home-made linen garments worn by Hertfordshire farm labourers right up to the end of the 19th century, and blacked up their faces with soot. With their expert local knowledge they were able to carefully choose the best ambush spots. One of their many victims was a comfortably off farmer from Bennington called Kent and he put up a fierce resistance when attacked by the Clibbon gang, so they murdered him. His badly battered body was unceremoniously dumped in his own cart and his horses found their way home alone.

Trade began to decline at Hertford and traders took to leaving before dark and travelling in groups but the robberies continued... until the night of December the 28th, 1782. That evening the footpads ambushed a young man named Whittenbury in some woods to the west of Hertford and he prudently offered no resistance. When they had taken their ill-gotten gains Whittenbury drove his cart hell for leather to nearby Queen Hoo Hall, to seek help from his uncle Benjamin Whittenbury, who was at home. Young Whittenbury's father however, had been visiting but had just left with another uncle, so Benjamin and his nephew set off after them. They decided to take Ben's servant, George North, as well as a dog, and armed themselves with a stout stick and a gun. They were themselves then ambushed by the Clibbon crew before they could meet up with the rest of the family, in dense woodland at Oakenvalley Bottom. The younger Whittenbury was knocked down, his uncle was a powerful man and put up more of a fight but he was outnumbered and overpowered so he called for his servant to shoot. George North fired the gun at almost point blank range, felling one of the gang and scattering the other two. The badly injured Walter Clibbon was then tied to a horse and dragged to Bull's Green where the angry locals bludgeoned him to death. One of the accomplices escaped but the other was caught and hanged at the next Lent Assizes.

As a murderer Walter Clibbon, like suicides and the insane, was denied a burial in consecrated ground. Such was the anger and hatred aroused by the deceased that he was accorded the very worst of burials. His body was interred at the side of the road where he had been shot in Oakenvalley Bottom. In accordance with the superstitions of the day his body was staked, 'to keep it down' and to stop his unquiet spirit from roaming the area. 'Clibbon's Post', a simple, stout piece of wood with the felon's name carved on it, can be seen to this present day, the original has long since rotted away but it has always been replaced when necessary, usually at the expense of the resident of Queen Hoo Hall. Was it successful in 'laying his ghost'? There are those who say they have seen the dim shape of a horse pulling a writhing body along the lanes and others have heard the sound of hooves or ghostly moaning. As in the case of highwayman 'Black Tom' who was hanged in Bedford in 1607 (see *Ghostly Bedfordshire…Revisited*) the traditional stake through the heart only works in vampire movies…

One local lady psychic seems to have encountered 'time slips' as she has driven along Datchworth's lanes at twilight. She has claimed to have seen, on more than one occasion, people in old-fashioned country clothing labouring in the fields, as they would have done a hundred or more years ago.

There are at least three well-known haunted lanes around Datchworth. One is Hollybush Lane, where a red-headed woman wearing bright clothing is said to haunt a family home and her appearance is accompanied by the sound of tinkling bells. Another haunted lane is Hawkins Hall Lane, which is frequented by the ghost of a little old lady – who happens to be headless! She has often been spotted in the evenings, shuffling along in what has been described as a purposeful way. She appears to be stooped with age if seen from behind but met head on (sorry I couldn't resist it) it is plain that she has no head. Legend has it that, back in the 19th century an old woman hanged herself with a piece of wire in her Knebworth cottage after the sudden death of her husband. What is not forthcoming is what her connection to Hollybush Lane was. The third haunted lane is close by, Bury Lane, and at one of the houses there a family has reported a dark shape seen flitting past the back window. The man of the house once had a clear sighting of an old man peering through the same window, so he hurried out to confront him but found no trace of anyone there.

The White Horse pub at Burnham Green is only one of two in the county to be named after a ghost (the other is the Wicked Lady at Wheathampstead). The story is that during the Civil War Cromwell's troops caught and beheaded one of the King's men at his farm in the area. They then tried to take away his fine white horse as a prize but the magnificent animal put up such a struggle that they beheaded the horse as well. Afterwards there were sightings of a headless white horse galloping down the lane from Burnham Green. Local people say that animals are wary of Whitehorse Lane to this day.

Is the title 'most haunted village' really deserved? Maybe once upon a time but in modern times there seemed to have been some doubt, so I decided to investigate for myself. The answers surprised me when my initial enquiries turned out positive from the start. A good friend of mine was able to confirm one of the stories surrounding Datchworth as he knew a witness to the haunting personally. It would have been around 1990 and Graham Young, a Hertfordshire lad in his early twenties, was driving through Burnham Green, a couple of miles from Datchworth, late one night. He was not far from the White Horse pub when a horse and rider came galloping up behind him, so he pulled over into the bank as it was a narrow lane, to let the horseman pass. Horse and rider continued on their way, galloping past the stationary car. It was only when Graham looked at the car's clock that he thought that there was something odd, it was 11.45pm, rather late for someone to be out riding in these dark and narrow lanes. He looked up again to see that both horse and rider had completely disappeared and it was only then that he realised that what he'd actually seen was a ghost. Sightings of this ghostly horseman are extremely rare, over a twenty year period there have been only three or four recorded.

One of the strangest encounters in Datchworth that I investigated occurred in the 1980s on the Bramfield Road, between Bramfield and Bulls Green. Mr Archer, a local young man who was in his late 20s at the time, was driving along when a woman in white, wearing Victorian clothes, suddenly stepped out onto the road. The young man braked hard but couldn't avoid hitting her, he stopped a little further on, near the site of a Roman villa and turned to see a man emerge from the woods, who picked up the fallen woman and carried her back off the road. Archer hurried to the spot, which was about a hundred yards from Clibbon's Post, opposite some woodland known as 'The Block', but there was no trace whatsoever of either the woman or the man. I discussed the mysterious sighting with Barry Davies, a gamekeeper whose mother still lives at Burnham Green. He confirmed that Archer hadn't been drinking when he saw the apparitions, was certainly not the type to invent such a story and that he had never been able to account for his unwanted unearthly experience.

Datchworth Green, popular for cricket games and the June fete, is associated with a number of hauntings, one is said to be an old lady seen pushing a barrow and gathering in firewood. A woman who was walking along the road beside the Green one evening heard what sounded like a coach and horses racing along behind her. She turned around but could see nothing yet the noise became much louder and instinctively she backed into the hedge just in time to experience a rushing wind, furious galloping hoofbeats, rattling coachwork and jingling harnesses – but no visible physical presence of a coach…

Another spectral presence encountered on Datchworth Green is of a lady in old-fashioned dress who appears to float above ground level and is always seen standing by the swings. A house on the Green is haunted by sounds rather than sights; Pettits has a restless ghost and footsteps are frequently heard on the stairs and pacing from room to room when there is nobody about to account for them. The Plough public house beside the Green had a strange story in fairly recent times. The landlady was plagued by the vision of a man when she looked into her mirror. Mirrors are often the focus for paranormal activity, particularly where two mirrors face each other. Mirrors reflect electromagnetic energy, which is what spirits use to materialise, and if two mirrors face each other they may magnify that energy and create some kind of 'energy portal' that ghosts can use, both to travel and to manifest. The landlady went to a spiritualist for advice (I would have recommended simply moving the mirrors) and was told that she had a ghostly admirer by the name of 'Jacques', who had lived in the 1700s and presumably the clairvoyant helped this 'lost soul' to move on…

A Roman road, edged with ash and oak trees, skirts the south side of the Green and at the far corner it comes to a quaint thatched cottage, 'Hopkyns Hoo', which was built as a farmhouse in 1570. It is situated where three old green lanes meet and in the garden there is a small duck pond, the remnant of a large moat which surrounded the farmhouse and its main outbuildings on what would have been an extensive farm in its day. This charming period dwelling has survived possible demolition, which was considered after the First World War, as it had been left empty and fallen into disrepair, but the main internal timbers were found to be in passable condition, so the place was, happily, reprieved. The residents at 'Hopkyns Hoo' have had some strange incidents and fairly recent reports suggest poltergeist activity. This includes a house alarm going off quite regularly for no obvious reason even when it has been turned off, and household items that seem to completely disappear.

At the east end of Datchworth Green is the whipping post, a grim reminder of harsher times when vagrants who didn't want to work in the parish received a whipping. It was last used in 1665 for the public flogging of two vagabonds. Stocks and a cage stood close by but no trace of them remains now.

MARDLEYBURY

That part of the haunted area of Datchworth known as Mardleybury and Mardley Heath deserve a mention of their own; they have roads with such romantic names, redolent of the highwayman, like Turpin's Ride, Hangman's Lane and the high viewpoint, Robbery Bottom Lane and not far away is Hanging Hill Wood. There is another wood in this area, Bramfield Woods, where lived a legendary witch with the colourful name of Sally Rainbow, but her intentions were decidedly dark. She made herself a comfortable living by taking money from local farmers in return for not putting the 'evil eye' on their cattle!

Ancient Mardleybury Manor House, overlooking Mardleybury Pond is the scene of ghostly sights, sounds and smells with clothes thrown around and objects moved and the smell of incense has been detected when nobody has lit any and an assortment of noises have been heard, variously described as crunching sounds, bangs and heavy breathing, also pictures have dropped off walls. On one occasion some very heavy flooring was moved about by whatever unseen force is present in the old house, but the owners don't seem to have been perturbed by these incidents and seem to be convinced that 'it' is a friendly presence!

Mardleybury Pond is reputedly haunted by the apparition of a long-haired young woman wearing a flowing gown or cloak that is usually seen by lone travellers. There was a much-publicised all-night vigil organised by the British Psychic and Occult Society in 1984 when a misty white figure was observed at 4.15am, it hovered briefly above the water at the far end of the pond before disappearing. A photograph was taken but there was no figure in the developed print.

Motorists have been forced to brake hard on the sharp bend just before the pond on seeing a totally unexpected vision of the 'pond lady'. A Welwyn man encountered the spook as he approached the Woolmer Green turning, anxious to avoid hitting what he perceived to be a woman in his path he veered off the road and collided with a tree... I would dearly have loved to see the insurance report form wouldn't you?

Chapter Four

LETCHWORTH

Letchworth's most distinguished resident must surely have been the internationally-acclaimed actor, the late Lord Laurence Olivier. Many people who currently live in the Garden City are unaware of the town's connection with one of the greatest actors who has ever lived. Laurence Kerr Olivier moved here with his parents in December1919, when he was just 12 years old. It must have seemed a promising fresh start for his father, the Reverend Gerard Kerr Olivier, who took up the ministry at the church of St Michael's and All Saints and moved his wife Agnes and their three children into the handsome Queen Anne house that was provided with his new position. Tragedy was soon to mar the situation, however, with Agnes's premature death at 48 from a brain tumour, in March 1920. This shattering event led Laurence Olivier to remark, nearly fifty years later, 'I often think, and say, that perhaps I've never got over it'.

By 1924 the seventeen-year-old Olivier was studying acting at the Central School of Speech Training and Drama at London's Royal Albert Hall. During the vacations he travelled up from his attic bedsitter in Paddington to St Christopher's School in Letchworth, where he started work as second assistant stage manager and general understudy in the school's theatre, for payment of £4 per week. Letchworth was, the following year, privileged to witness Olivier's professional stage debut at St Christopher's theatre, where he played Lennox in their production of *Macbeth*.

Letchworth is justifiably proud of its heritage as the first 'Garden City'. Garden Cities were designed to ease London's overcrowding, as were the 'New Towns'. Ebenezer Howard's vision of a rural Utopia was outlined in his book *Tomorrow* (1898) and a few years later the Garden City Pioneer Company was formed. In 1901 the parishes of Letchworth, Norton and Willian had a combined population of 566, yet by 1919, when the Oliviers came to stay, the population of Letchworth Garden City had soared to 10,000 inhabitants. Since then it has steadily risen to about 35,000.

For 60 years Letchworth was a temperance town but in recent times, with the relaxation of opening hours, it has made up for that with the opening of two new large pubs, the Hog's Head and the Three Magnets. The opening of the vast Morrisons supermarket was welcomed by many and the transformation of Kennedy Gardens into the renamed and beautifully maintained Broadway Gardens, complete with impressive new fountains, has been a definite improvement to the environment. Letchworth Town is not noted for ghost stories, but its environs have some intriguing tales – particularly the surrounding villages of Willian and Weston…

WILLIAN'S WRAITHS,
INCLUDING THE NOTORIOUS 'PHANTOM JOGGER'.

Willian is a village just off Letchworth Gate, so close to Letchworth that it is usually considered part of the town. It has some intriguing hauntings as I discovered when I went investigating… The post office is an extremely old building. Sheila and Bob Leverett moved in about fourteen years ago, and the place underwent considerable alterations and a major clearout. Late one evening, after a hard day's work, as they sat relaxing in their lounge, they saw the figure of a little boy, smartly dressed, wearing a bow tie, who disappeared as suddenly as he had appeared. Then other things started disappearing around the house, various items would vanish only to reappear in different locations. Other odd occurrences were experienced, like the night the Leveretts were walking through the village, around one in the morning, when they clearly heard the sounds of children playing, from what was once the schoolhouse and is now a private residence. In the former school playground, behind a hedge, a little girl could be seen standing there.

Back at the post office both Georgina and Jessica, two of the Leverett's daughters witnessed strange goings-on. Doors that had been left open would be suddenly closed behind them and ghostly talking and giggling was heard, which frightened both girls. Everything was moved off a shelf one time and on another notable occasion a picture flew off the wall with such violence that shards of glass landed on a nearby mattress, yet the picture's hook was still in place on the wall.

I was not surprised to learn that the pub next door was also haunted; The Fox and Duck is certainly old, and believed to date from the sixteenth century. At one time it had been a private residence. I spoke with Lorraine Russell, the manager, who had worked here for over three years and had first experienced her ghostly visitor about eighteen months after moving in. She told me about a lady's ghost, which was seen by at least three people in different locations; in the kitchen, in the passageway and coming down the stairs. It seemed to be a 'calm presence' rather than a frightening one, a tidy one that moved ashtrays which had been left on the bar into neat stacks, and the ghost was sometimes experienced a 'cold feeling'. Andy Thompson, who once worked at the pub, had spotted the ghostly lady walking downstairs and Steve

Banks, who managed with Lorraine, caught the spirit's reflection, mimicking him in the mirror as he was combing his hair. Light bulbs have been known to fly out of the chandelier for no apparent reason. Strangest of all was Lorraine's close encounter, as she was cleaning some pictures in the hallway, when the ghost actually walked through her! Unusually Lorraine experienced a 'warm feeling' rather than the cold chill usually reported in such circumstances. Andy Thompson confirmed other manifestations, like beer mats being found piled up by 'something' and bad feelings experienced as well as impressions that 'someone' haunted the cellars. The ghost was seen just a year or so ago and was described as 'misty and small, only around five feet tall...'

Undoubtedly the scariest spook to pass through Willian is the notorious 'phantom jogger'. Most witnesses to the 'phantom jogger' don't wish to discuss the experience, but I was lucky enough to track down one soul who was a bit braver than the rest. Gail Peacock is a well-known Bedfordshire medium, who recounted her spine-chilling brush with the paranormal in some detail. It was back in June 1998, around twilight, as Gail drove through Willian, that she had a 'feeling of apprehension'. The hedgerow along this stretch of road is quite dense and the medium had 'an overwhelming sense of dread, that something bad was going to happen...' the car would break down, or worse still, she would run someone over. So cautious did this make her that she slowed right down to crawling pace, about twenty miles an hour, as she approached a left-hand bend. She checked her mirrors and felt a 'surreal, daydream-like impression' of 'something' at the edge of her peripheral vision. Next moment in her right-hand wing-mirror there suddenly appeared the image of a jogger. No other cars or pedestrians were about. As the runner drew alongside, he was so close that Gail could see his fair, slightly curly, mid-length hair, his white running vest with red piping and matching white shorts with red stripe down the sides. The man had a malevolent, sneering expression, which somehow made the medium feel threatened. He exuded an almost palpable sense of menace, of evil. Without warning he cut right in front of the moving car, causing Gail to brake sharply, yet there was no impact as expected. The car stopped, its engine idling, while the shaking driver wondered how such a solid figure could manage to run through an extremely dense hedgerow. The woman got out of her car and her close inspection revealed no dent on its bodywork, she raised her gaze to a clear, uninterrupted view over open, empty fields.

The unsettling experience left Gail wondering who or what she had encountered, so she made her way to nearby Letchworth Hall Hotel where she poured out her strange story to the receptionist, who registered no surprise whatsoever. Instead she showed a notebook which she had been keeping, listing other visitors' description of their encounter with the apparition. There was a startling similarity to all the accounts. I was particularly struck by the earnestness of the medium's report and the intensity of the experience for her. Seldom have I come across an interviewee who recalled such detail that I almost felt that I was there with her, experiencing this lady's shock and horror, as it dawned on her that what she had come across could only have been a ghost and an evil-intentioned one at that. Some idea of the depth of her impression may be gained by the realisation that she recalled these nightmarish details for me seven years after the event. It is something that will live with her forever and even after all this time she still drives through this part of Willian with great trepidation...

I made enquiries at nearby Letchworth Hall Hotel, where, reputedly, other frightened victims of the malign jogger's apparition have reported their encounters, only to find that the hotel has its own ghost, the former owner of Letchworth Hall, the Reverend William Alington, whose ghost has been encountered in both the ballroom and on the landing, by a number of witnesses. The Reverend died in the 1860s and was allegedly suspended from his office for drinking and inappropriate behaviour with his parishioners.

THE WESTON POLTERGEIST

Another village not far from Letchworth with a story to tell is Weston. It is a highly desirable rural location to live in – except for one house... It was a simple farm worker's cottage, built in the 17th century; it had once variously served as the village post office and as the police station. One long-term resident was to famously describe its being 'as haunted as Hell'! When our story began however, it could have been the dream cottage for Jill Brown, but instead it became a nightmare...

'When I mention the goings-on to people they always say to me "How could you stay there?" In reality there were long periods of calm and when freaky things occurred we just had to live with them. All in all we stayed in the house for seven years. We bought it in 1995 but didn't live in it straight away. I didn't ever really like the house but it was where we wanted to be and the right price. I'm not sure when things started to happen but I'm sure it was after a couple of years living there. I do remember that the cat would sit on a cupboard just staring at the wall in the lounge which seemed very odd. One morning I came downstairs and the lounge furniture was about a foot away from the wall, it was very heavy to move it back again. The taps would be turned on at night – it became a regular occurrence, and once, when there was a lot of unrest in the house there was a loud bang as my son's wardrobe door flew open and my son's clothes emptied themselves out onto the floor. His wastepaper basket also flew across the room, emptying rubbish everywhere. He was in bed at the time but strangely was not particularly upset by the events. I remember it was a Sunday night, as I had spent the evening ironing and was cross that the clothes I had spent time ironing were strewn across the floor. I tried to keep calm as I cleared up the mess and my son went back to sleep in his bedroom, inside I felt anything but calm.

After this event I thought the house needed some help, although no one had seen any ghosts there was definitely some unrest. I always felt that whatever it was went with the house and not necessarily with the occupants. I enquired about getting the house blessed by the local vicar, but didn't get a good reaction there. I phoned the previous owner and asked about her experiences in the place. She told me that she had always liked living there, but that there was a benevolent, mischievous presence about, whenever anything went missing she would just have to ask for it back... I felt much better about things after this conversation, but when I thought about all the things that had gone missing I would have a large pile! Around this time a colleague offered to visit, to use her dowsing rods. I was interested in this theory of energy channels causing unrest, it seemed to make sense. When she came over she was very uneasy – didn't want to stay long or even to sit down. She said she could instantly feel cold spots in the lounge, close to where the cat would sit looking at the wall. She found two energy channels running from a corner of the lounge to the back door. I thought it all very interesting but didn't know what to do with this information. A while later, I also dowsed the lounge using a basic ring and thread, It freaked me when the thread would spin almost horizontally at a certain spot!

Little did I know that something entirely different from my previous weird experiences in the house was due to happen to me. I was almost asleep in bed when I felt the most tender, loving kiss on my cheek. When I think about it now it still makes me feel emotional. After a while I turned the light on and was shocked to find... only an empty room, yet I could still feel that kiss on my cheek... It was soon after this that that I went on holiday to France with the kids, but I think I took something extra in the car with us, because the same thing happened in France; I was kissed on the cheek again, just as I was falling asleep. It worried me greatly this time, because my theory about "it" belonging to the house seemed to have gone out of the window. The kissing never happened again and the house was fairly quiet when we returned – now I wondered if I had left "it" behind in France!

The next big event in my story was meeting my partner, David, who instantly disliked the house, which was rather upsetting as it was, after all, our home and supposedly in a most desirable location. For the first few nights that he stayed there he felt a great pressure on his chest, as if someone was bearing down on him. He would often sleepwalk and seemed almost 'possessed', often we would have to 'rescue' him in the night and point him in the right direction, back to bed. His personal things would go missing so often that he didn't like to leave anything in the house. I thought that when we moved they would turn up, but sadly they never have been found. Taps were frequently turned on at night; thankfully the noise from the water tank in the loft would wake me. Although we were really anxious to move by this time it took a good year to sell the place. During this waiting time we spoke with a man who had spent his whole life in Weston and he said that he wouldn't like to live in our house because it was as haunted as Hell. He explained that even the builders had refused to be in the place alone when it was being renovated.

It was a great relief when we eventually found a buyer and a new house to move to. I worried that "it" would misbehave before we went, what with the disruption, boxes lying everywhere etc. We were treated to one more "tap episode" the night before we left and mercifully that was all. Since moving to the new home we can't help noticing that the cat never sits staring at the wall any more…'

I also talked with Dave, Jill's partner, and he confirmed everything that she had said, the house was always cold, always hard to get warm. There had been loads of viewings in the year that they had tried to sell the cottage. A local had told Dave that when Sally, the previous owner, had an extension put on no builders would stay on the job and their tools were always going missing. He had regularly found video tapes, books and keys that would just disappear, only to turn up in exactly the same spot a couple of months later, but sometimes things vanished entirely, never to be seen again. He witnessed the taps that came on unaided; they would often nearly flood the house. There was one weird effect when he was in the bathroom one day and couldn't locate the door to get out again – 'It was as if the room had changed altogether, the door had disappeared!'

The new female vicar that was asked to help them just laughed, admitting that she wouldn't know what to do… Jill's husband, Tom Brown, it transpired, had got sick in the house, suffering with rheumatoid arthritis, diabetes, a thyroid defect and other auto-immune problems. One of Jill's children, Jack, suffered with depression, and he had regularly heard scratching and banging noises in his bedroom, one time all four walls were banged at once, which really spooked him. The more I talked with them the more obvious it became that their former home had left a deep impression on the whole family, an impression that they were, unfortunately, unlikely to ever forget.

Chapter Five

ROYSTON

Royston is as far north as you can go in Hertfordshire and it has the feel of being out of place, as though it belongs in neighbouring Cambridgeshire, maybe because it is so close to the border of that county. Hertfordshire has a population of over one million and Royston's share is currently 13,600 people and growing rapidly, with new housing developments springing up on all sides of the town. Royston gets its name from the lady Roisia (meaning Rose), who was married to William the Conqueror's steward, Eudo Dapifer, owner of Newsells, the local Manor House. A cross was erected by her (or restored by her) at the junction of two prehistoric (later Romanised) roads, improved by the Romans to provide easier access for the military to Britain's hinterlands. These roads were Ermine Street and the Icknield Way. The base of Roisia's cross (or foot stone) is all that remains of the cross and it may be found at the bottom of the High Street. Crossroads, in ancient times, were considered sacred and early in the Christian era the practice of erecting crosses at crossroads was developed. Ermine Street was the Romans' Great North Road; it runs all the way from London to York and the Icknield Way runs from Salisbury Plain to East Anglia. The area around the crossroads became known as Roisia's Cross, then later, when the town grew up around it the name was Roisia's Town, eventually abbreviated to Royston.

In 1603 King James VI of Scotland stopped at Royston en route to London, to be crowned King James I of England. He obviously liked what he saw for even before his coronation the King decided to establish a residence in the town and soon established a series of buildings for members of his court, his horses and his hunting dogs. He created strict rules against anyone taking game within 14 miles of Royston and he indulged in the royal sport locally on a regular basis. Royston offered the advantage of being conveniently close to London yet far enough away to deter intrusion.

HAIR-RAISING HAUNTINGS… AT HENRICK'S

The most interesting true ghost story in Royston concerns a building in Fish Hill that is believed to date back to the time of King James I; it is presently home to a busy hairdressing salon called Henrick's. I heard, through some friends who live in the town, that the shop was haunted, so I contacted the owner, Mark Henrick. We had an initial meeting in July 2004, during which time I had the opportunity to talk with Mark and various members of his staff at the salon. Mark had by this time been running his business for about a year from the Grade Two Listed building at Fish Hill, which has had many changes of use, just prior to Mark's tenancy it was a pine furniture shop for many years, but originally the building had comprised two cottages and a barn.

Ever since Mark Henrick first started up his business paranormal activity has occurred in the hairdressers at Fish Hill. Electrical problems have plagued the place with fuses constantly blowing, there have been as many as sixteen electrical problems experienced in one day and lights have gone on and off by themselves. He told me that sometimes 'something' will not let you flip the trip switch. Other unaccountable incidents have included a mirror 'shooting off the wall and smashing', yet leaving a nearby member of staff unscathed. Weird noises have been reported and Mark said 'There is always a feeling of someone else being present' when he is alone in his salon. Radio stations have been retuned, heaters have turned off and on by themselves and Emma, a young member of staff, has had various small items thrown at her, such as bottle tops which have not come from the salon, but have come out of nowhere. This was particularly interesting for me because 'apports' (mostly small objects which materialise from thin air or transport through solid matter) are a classic sign of poltergeist activity, as is interference with electrical equipment, so I now knew what we were dealing with.

I had been preceded at Henrick's by a number of investigators. Peter Foreman is a highly experienced dowser from Hatfield and on his visit to the shop he received some extremely strong impressions. In the cellar he became most agitated, got very red in the face and started shaking as he sensed that a fire had originated here and he also sensed the presence of a man in the far corner. On the first floor, in the shower room/toilet area Peter picked up the spirit of another man 'with a troubled past'. He also encountered a female spirit by the sun cubicle area and as he stood by a small cupboard on the landing its door inexplicably flew open. In the upstairs waiting room Peter discovered 'a large energy mass' and his dowsing rods rotated at a great rate, away from it they stopped moving altogether and the dowser was left feeling dizzy.

The medium from Ashwell, previously mentioned in the haunting of Tower Cottage, called Marge Kite, was another former visitor and she had detected the presence of a man and a dog in spirit form in the toning table room, while a female entity has been associated with the beauty room and her name may have been Rosemary, a 'cold spot' has been felt in a corner of this room, by the couch.

My friends from Cambridge Paranormal Research Society carried out a vigil in February, four months prior to my first visit. They identified 'a six foot mass of electrical energy' and in the treatment room they felt 'someone was wandering about and getting on and off the treatment table'. According to CPRS twelve separate spirits were haunting the premises.

It was a warm day on the 10th July when I carried out my initial observations at Henrick's yet I noticed it was distinctly colder as I made my way upstairs, to where most of the paranormal activity seemed to be focussed. My inbuilt 'haunted building detector' was confirming that I was in a genuinely haunted place – my back felt distinctly cold. Normally you would expect a building to be warmer upstairs. I noticed a space on one wall and was told that a clock had been hung here, but every morning it would be found on the floor face up, working perfectly. This carried on for two weeks and so the clock was removed. Mark and I agreed that my group, Anglia Paranormal Investigation Society (APIS) would hold a vigil on the night of Tuesday 28th September. This night was chosen because the nightclub over the road would be closed and it was also the night of the full moon, usually a good time for paranormal activity.

I called back in August to confirm the details of the APIS vigil with Mark and in the intervening weeks yet more activity had taken place. Marta, the nail technician, felt someone squeeze her back, but turned around to find nobody there. A flickering and fusing light was also reported along with the radio volume control, which had gone up and down on its own and lastly a picture was seen to 'jump off the wall', it bounced downstairs and smashed.

On the day before the planned vigil I returned to collect the keys to the shop and there was some extremely interesting news to learn about. Some mediums, led by Gail Peacock, a Bedfordshire medium (mentioned earlier in the Willian phantom jogger case) had recently held their own investigation at the hairdressers, along with some of Mark's staff one evening, from 7.30pm to 10.30pm. The results were rather exciting; a tape recorder left on in the salon had captured a child's voice repeating 'help me, help me...' (I listened to this tape and, although I had to strain to hear the words at first, a little like a bad phone connection from a foreign country, it eventually became clear that it was exactly as described).

Gail was also seen, by several witnesses to 'transfigure' (that is her features completely changed – to those of a man in this case). She seemed to be temporarily possessed by another entity, as she went up the stairs she 'froze' on the second step from the top. She started swearing, her face changed, I was told that her chin was different, her eyes became dark and she even had a moustache, while there were distinctive red marks around her throat. The entity was a man who clearly hated women, he was holding on to a little girl, somebody had stopped him from making money and he had committed suicide. Gail later told me that she had been levitated up the stairs, without her feet actually touching them. The two young members of staff I spoke to were certain that they had witnessed the medium's face become dramatically altered. Transfiguration is a rarity among psychic mediums so I was particularly pleased to come across this example.

Another fascinating insight into the Henrick's hauntings was provided by Louise Morton, a psychic artist from Blunham, Bedfordshire, who is able to turn her impressions into sketches. I found her input particularly valuable because she provided us with the details of the 'main protagonist', responsible for the more hair-raising happenings at the hairdressers. Not only was she able to show us what he looked like, but she received his name and identified the period he lived in. He sounds like an extremely insalubrious character indeed, not only a suicide but also a misogynist, possibly a smuggler and probably a murderer too. 'Get my name right you bitch', was his greeting to Louise, 'Lord George Armatage'. Louise's drawings were decidedly creepy; they showed a man with hypnotic, staring eyes, strong arched eyebrows, a rather thin face with shoulder-length hair and a droopy moustache. Overall my impression seemed to be that it was an intense, cruel face, this man would show no mercy, take no pity. Her description of his dress was also fairly detailed. He wore a shirt with a ruffled front, he had long black boots, he carried a cane with a brass top and bottom and he stood at the top of the stairs. He was alive at the time of Charles I, in the 1600s. On another visit to Henrick's Armatage showed himself as he was when he died, aged 40 – 'my own demise' he explained to Louise, his eyes were closed and his tongue was hanging out. 'I felt no pain; I was intoxicated when the knife cut my throat.'

Louise got visions and communications from some of the other restless spirits in the salon who told the psychic that 'George was a swanky yob who was going to stand trial at Newgate, that's why he took his life and many were glad of it. He was head of a large gang of cut-throats, aiding and abetting stealing. Where some got hung for a loaf of bread he got away with murder and more for years.' Louise received a name and a date – Betty – 1672. She also picked up impressions of the building as it was in times past, of a side building for horses and staff, a pub opposite this site, a horse tethered on the back wall, the kitchen lined with riding boots, it had been used as a tack room. In the salon the floor had been lower at the partition and a young boy appeared, his image superimposed itself on a poster in the window, he would have been about fourteen years old, his name was James, he was very sad and he wanted to move on. A middle aged lady was here too, aged about fifty. Louise had a feeling that there had been a well on the grounds. Another man came through, this time a happy-go-lucky personality, from a later age. His name was Tom Skinner and he was 'A justice of the law, with rouge a'plenty, I used to come a'courting and used to check this abode and its clientele.'

Upstairs Louise encountered the spirit of a young girl, called Millie or Molly in the attic room, who had worn callipers on her legs because she had polio. Millie's presence was felt by several other mediums who were with Louise at the time; they all felt an extreme heaviness in their legs as they walked up the stairs. An elderly lady, called Betty inhabited the attic once, she too had suffered problems with her legs, which had been ulcerated and eventually turned gangrenous. She lived here when the house was 'used for letting to rough people, I stayed here and used to lock myself in at times.' Betty had wanted to die, she had been fed up with the cold, with penniless hunger and she 'used to see, like you (psychically) and I left before my body gave up. The room used to fill up with smoke from the lower chimney downstairs. I had a pauper's grave, I'm only the dogsbody and when ill no one to attend me. Years of toil and sweat and graft for nowt, 'tis a trial this life o' mine, glad to break its bones and go...'

The APIS team of twelve investigators assembled at 10pm on the night of the 28th September and we familiarised ourselves with the layout of the building, checked our log books and discussed our plans. Next we set up our equipment, which includes night vision video cameras, temperature and humidity gauges, vibration detectors, electro-magnetic frequency meters, walkie-talkies and analogue and digital tape recorders. At 11pm we began our watches, in teams of two, for an hour at a time, followed by a break of 30 minutes. Then we began the second watch, at 11.30pm with a different combination of team members and a change of location (so that everybody gets to work with everybody else and in every different location). We carried right on through till 4.30am on the Wednesday morning.

In our team we had a guest, newspaper reporter Louise Sassoon, from *The Royston Crow*. There were also eleven members of APIS; each one had a part to play in the investigation, including our two principal psychic mediums, Joan Dancer and Ian Eddolls. We don't just rely on our electronic measuring and recording equipment but factor in our mediums' psychic impressions as well. Nigel Brockwell, an electronics engineer, is also APIS's Technical Consultant, who builds the investigative equipment that we use. The other members of the team that night were Carol Greenall (Secretary), Andy Garrett (one of our Team Leaders), Moira Gray, Mark Head, Ryan Chambers, Paul O'Dell and Andy Thompson (Investigators).

We didn't have long to wait for unexplained activity and psychic impressions to happen. On the first watch (11pm – 12 midnight) on the ground floor shadows were seen in the salon and Andy Garrett could smell the scent of roses. Meanwhile, upstairs, in the sun-bed room area Joan, Paul and Louise all distinctly heard a loud exhalation of air. Joan also received an impression of heat and believed that there was a fire in that room in the past. In the nail room and beauty room Nigel and Ian were witness to the electric heater coming on then going off again as soon as a flash photograph was taken outside the room.

Ian picked up many impressions; the name Penny, the years 1832 and 1879, also Leonora James, aged 10 and the year 1772. He asked Leonora if anyone 'bad' was there, but she left, saying 'Don't let him find me.' About half an hour later there came the sound of something falling/bouncing from the room above and shortly afterwards the heater came on again and went off again two minutes later. I was up on the top floor on this first watch with Andy Thompson and I am certain that nothing dropped on the floor while we were up there. We did, however, see a flash of light around the edge of the closed door, Andy felt cold and he heard a definite shuffling sound from the stairs. The battery unaccountably drained right down on our night vision camcorder and at that point we both felt cold. Andy, who was nearer to the door, then heard what sounded like voices just outside the room.

During the first coffee break the strangeness continued. As my brother Paul waited to use the toilet in the salon a large bottle of hair conditioner fell to the floor with a bang right in front of him. He later explained to me that there was no reason for it to suddenly fall off the shelf, one second it was there and the next it was on the floor. He was both mystified and adamant that nobody had been near enough to knock or push the bottle off the shelf; it hadn't been teetering on the end but had been neatly stacked. I experimented, jumped up and down quite hard right by the shelf to see if I could dislodge any of the bottles, perhaps there was a springy floorboard? Try as I might I couldn't make any of those bottles move, they were secure on that shelf. Nigel quietly informed me that he too had witnessed exactly the same thing as Paul, he had been standing nearby and he had been equally mystified by it. I have noticed at other vigils which APIS has conducted, that unexplained incidents quite regularly seem to occur when the investigators are off-guard, often on a break, so this was a typical example.

The second watch was quieter, with Ryan and Ian stationed downstairs. Shortly after 1am Ryan felt cold and Ian got a psychic impression, this time it was of a middle-aged woman clutching her chest in distress. She was standing in the corner then fell to the floor before disappearing; the year 1873 was associated with this event. Later on Ian felt as though he was outside in wind, rain and cold, together with a horse and cart. On the top floor attic room Joan and Nigel were teamed together. At 12.45am Nigel noted in the log a four inch vertical line of light on the wall opposite the door, which moved about a foot to the left and then back before disappearing. Joan felt that the current premises had originally been three dwellings converted into one. She had the impression of a double bed in the room and two children playing with a train set.

On the third watch the unexplained occurrences continued, Nigel and I saw that the remote thermometers, which had been placed upstairs, had stopped working. Joan and Ian were in the first floor reception area and they felt cold, particularly around their legs. Joan used her crystal to do some dowsing, with interesting impressions. A man had committed suicide by the fireplace and a middle-aged lady had died of a heart attack. Ian then dowsed to determine the cause of the suicide's death and got a tight feeling in his throat which, he felt, might have been the result of poisoning. Joan also had a strong sensation in her throat but it was as if it had been cut... Joan and Ian also recorded a high electro-magnetic frequency (EMF) reading by the fireplace, which is often an indication that a spirit is present.

After the third watch we had our customary debriefing, while Ian returned upstairs, as he was anxious to collect some final impressions from the spirits in the attic room. Joan mentioned that 'something' had touched her hand after she had heard a 'clinking sound' upstairs, also at one point it felt like something was tugging at her hair. She heard music, like a military band at some point in the evening, at the front of the building. After his final visit to the top floor Ian reported that he had received a psychic impression of three people; a woman who had died of old age and two young brothers who had been hiding and who had died of smoke inhalation. These two incidents were a year apart and Ian received further impressions of two names and two associated years – David Lawrence 1743 and Mrs Bessie Edwards 1833.

The most remarkable event of an incident-packed night was at 3.30am when Mark took some photographs of the exterior of the building with his digital camera. I had locked up and turned off all the lights and it was only when the photographs were printed that we saw that on one of the prints there was a glow from the upstairs window. The photograph reproduced in this book shows an eerie glow from the upstairs window. It is not the kind of light given off by an electric light, but seems more like the glow that might emanate from a fire inside the place! It is also possible to make out an orb, floating at roof height; it definitely wasn't the moon because that was positioned behind Mark's right shoulder as he took the shot. Not only was I a witness to the circumstances surrounding this unexplained photograph but so were Ian, Nigel, Joan and Andy Thompson. I compared notes with psychic artist Louise Morton and she had a communication from 'Lord George Armatage'. 'I was responsible for the light in the photograph. Nobody knows the truth of my atrocities, yes or it wouldn't be the perfect crime. Harbouring and abetting, I would have got away with it if it wasn't for that blackguard…' Chilling stuff indeed, we don't know who 'that blackguard' was, but somebody seems to have spoilt our misogynist criminal Armatage's plans – if indeed that was his real name…

We were naturally quite excited to see, just a fortnight after our investigation, the Friday night programme, *Ghostly Tales of the Unexpected*. The medium Lizzie Falconer gave her views, during her visit to Royston when she investigated Henrick's. What was particularly interesting was that Lizzie's main impressions tallied closely with those of the mediums that I had worked with; she seemed to make some kind of sense of the strange happenings. She homed in on the man who had slit his own throat and it was because he was so resentful that his former home had been turned into a hairdressing salon that the manifestations had begun.

This case seemed to revolve around 'Lord George Armatage' (as the spirit identified himself) plus a number of 'supporting characters' from various eras. The change of use from a furniture shop to a women's hairdressing salon appears to have triggered the manifestations of this principal, evil character whose anger and malign influence has, for so long, been directed at womankind in general. That would account for all the paranormal activity suddenly taking off since Mark Henrick's arrival, prior to the last year or so there does not appear to have been this level of hauntings experienced anywhere in Fish Hill, Royston. There often appears to be a trigger for paranormal phenomena, a factor which precipitates a manifestation of some sort, often the catalyst is building work, and these alterations to the fabric of a property seem to stir up spirits that may have lain dormant for a long time, maybe even centuries. It is as though the former inhabitants are resentful of modern day intrusions to 'their' homes. What was noteworthy here was the fact that a number of mediums, working independently and without prior knowledge of either the case or of each other's involvement, had received the same basic impressions of the principal angry spirit, a suicide who had slashed his throat, in his own home, during the seventeenth century.

I would have to agree with my friends from Cambridge Paranormal Research Society, that there are, indeed, probably twelve spirits that have been haunting the site at Fish Hill, many of them children or young people and they belong in different centuries. As well as the evil Armatage there were the children from 1743, one of whom identified himself as David Lawrence, who supposedly perished from smoke inhalation in a fire while in hiding with his brother. Several mediums and a dowser felt strongly that there had been a fire in the house. Then there was ten-year-old Leonora James, from 1772, Millie or Molly with the callipered legs and sad, fourteen year old James. There was a spirit lady simply identified as Penny connected with 1832 and 1879 – her birthday and dying day perhaps? Then there was another lady, possibly called Rosemary and poor Bessie Edwards with her gangrenous legs, from 1833 and the happy-go-lucky Tom Skinner.

One of APIS's founding members, our trusted dowser Keith Paull, has dowsed the premises at Fish Hill and he discovered an extremely strong haunting energy line (which spirits use to draw energy in order to manifest themselves). This is invariably a strong indicator that a place is haunted. It may be that because the spirit of the suicide (Armatage) began his activities that other entities were also attracted to the place they had known in their lifetime. They may have used the energies of the many visiting psychic mediums and paranormal investigators, as well as the existing energy lines which cross the building, to make their presence known. What we do know for sure is that Henrick's Hairdressing, in Fish Hill Royston, is currently Royston's most haunted site.

BANYERS HOTEL

I visited the Banyers Hotel in Melbourn Street, Royston, on several occasions, and spoke with the friendly and helpful staff there, who are in no doubt that they have some non-paying guests, for this is a haunted hotel. My first meeting, in July '03 was with the manager, John Guisberg, and he told me that he had stayed overnight about 30–40 times. On one occasion, when John was sleeping at the hotel on his own, he heard a baby crying. This was between midnight and 1am on a Wednesday or Thursday night. Puzzled, he turned off the television and noticed that the sound seemed to be coming from near the window, so he opened it, but finding nothing outside he wondered if the noise might be coming through the vents in the windowsill. The crying was persistent, and he decided to get dressed and to search all the rooms. Nothing was found, but the sounds of distress, which John described as high-pitched and definitely female, continued. Since he was thoroughly awakened he thought that he might as well search the rest of the premises, both inside and out. By now it was about 3 or 4am, there were no cars outside and no lights on. The security light, which is triggered if anyone comes within five yards, remained off. He was investigating outside when there was a final, even louder burst of crying which then abruptly stopped altogether. John was completely candid, 'It was so frightening that I nearly went home.' This had only happened about six months before our discussion.

John has been roused before, by other noises during his overnight stays prior to the 'crying baby' incident. He has heard heavy hand raps on the front door in the middle of the night, yet when he has gone to answer them there is nobody there. He told me that the knocking may be repeated then stopped when he gets downstairs, to find no sign of any earthly visitor. He sometimes hears conversation in the bar when he is alone in the hotel, but once again, upon investigation the place is found to be empty. John also showed me the notorious room number 1, the haunted room (not room 4 as erroneously reported in some accounts of the hotel's history), where the ghost of a Cavalier has been seen in the past. Room 1 is a solid, oak-panelled place which is listed; it has been kept in original condition, despite refurbishments to other parts of the hotel. The ghostly Cavalier is affectionately known by the locals as 'Henry', obviously a gentleman amongst ghosts, for he takes off his cape and politely bows before any startled hotel guest that he may meet.

A year later, on the 27th July '04, I met manager Dawn Adams, who gave me a second tour of the hotel, this time to parts of it that I hadn't seen before. We naturally discussed room 1 and she told me that guests have often reported it being 'very cold' – when checked the radiators have been found to be hot. We tried to look into the tunnel in the cellar which once linked the church to the vicarage (as the Banyers used to be). 'He' wouldn't let us explore any further than the cellar, all four lights in the cellar simply refused to work, despite being on different circuits – we checked the mains switch – it was in the 'on' position. 'He' was the Reverend Banyer (vicar of Royston from 1739 till his death in 1751), after whom the hotel was named and it appeared that he did not like me. As a seasoned paranormal investigator I am quite used to this sort of thing. My psychically-developed friends tell me that often the ghosts know when I am coming, or when a vigil is going to take place, and act accordingly. Dawn believes the 'presence' of the Reverend Banyer can be felt down in the cellars.

Back upstairs in the bar Dawn recounted how four weeks ago she had been in this bar at the corner nearest to the TV, having a quiet drink with Delia (the owner) when they had both spotted, out of the corners of their eyes, a figure behind the bar, right by the Pepsi dispenser. 'It was a man, he was all in white, white hair, trousers and jacket, and he appeared to be about 45 years of age.' His image was only briefly glimpsed, and then it was gone... This is fairly common in my experience, where ghosts are concerned; they are often viewed in a witness's peripheral vision, and for the briefest of moments, so Dawn's account had the ring of truth to it.

Bernard Lee had been the chef at the Banyers for many years and he clearly recalled for me a night seven years ago, when he was enjoying a pint with a couple of friends in the same bar and suddenly 'The clock just flew off the wall, about eight feet across the room', it scared the trio, who finished their drinks rather rapidly and left the bar in a hurry. Was this an example of the Reverend Banyer making his displeasure of late night drinking clearly known? I also wondered if Stacey, the barmaid, had a story to tell, she did – just three weeks ago a drip tray 'Just flipped out and landed on the floor', and when she went into the toilet later on 'It went all cold in there.'

THE MYSTERIOUS CAVE

There are two places where I have strongly felt a mystic, 'other-worldly' quality; one of them was on the top of Glastonbury Tor, the other was deep underground, at man-made Royston Cave, which was cut out of the 60 metre thick layer of chalk that lies under the town. Sited close by a 'sacred' crossroads and right on a major ley line, the strange beehive-shaped cave is unique in the whole of Britain, a work attributed to the Knights Templar who were based in Baldock and were famous for their enormous wealth and secret rituals. 'Their' cave itself remained secret for over 400 years before its rediscovery in August 1742, when workmen improving the pitch used by women selling butter discovered a large millstone under the surface of the road. Beneath the stone was a shaft leading straight down to the cave and it took a hundred cartloads to clear the rubbish that half-filled the interior.

My first visit here was several years ago, as part of a group of other sightseers, when I found myself profoundly impressed by this place. With its oddly shaped interior and chalk surface carved all over with images of saints and Christian symbols (which were once painted in various colours) together with eighteenth and nineteenth century graffiti, I knew that it was somehow 'special'.

The cave entrance may be found up an alley that leads off Melbourne Street where, in 1790 a builder had his premises. My second visit here was even more impressive, I was privileged to be given a private guided tour along with five friends on a chilly March Sunday afternoon in 2005. Donning a hard hat and carrying a torch I made my way up the scaffolding to the roof of the cave thirty feet above the ground, where the public doesn't normally have access. I didn't realise it at that moment but I was on a level where, hundreds of years before, a similar platform had existed. I had a distinctly creepy impression up there, as if I might not be alone, but I had to use the opportunity to explore this fascinating place. I had a strong intuition that the 'shelves' carved out high up in the chalk face had been used to store offerings in ancient times. I made my way up another ladder to a higher level. I soon reached the very top of the cave and as I stood on the topmost, and smallest, platform my head was only inches below the pavement of Melbourne Street and daylight filtered through a small grille, where flickering shadows told me when someone was passing by.

I made my way back to the main platform and my friend Louise joined me. Without knowing what I felt, Louise began voicing her impressions and told me that she could distinctly see an orb in a kind of chimney carved out of the wall in front of us. She shone the torch on the spot, I was unable to see the orb but I was not surprised as Louise is much more psychically sensitive than I am. Her impressions were very strong at this point and she picked up a young girl's presence. Human sacrifice had been carried out here; there was the impression of some poor unfortunate hanging suspended from the roof while their life's blood had slowly drained away from them to be collected in a chalice on the floor.

Back at ground level there were more surprises in store for us, my friends Andy and Sarah both distinctly heard a baby scream – it seemed to emanate from the very rock walls. The other five people present didn't hear anything but Louise and Paula were certain that this cave had been used both for good and for evil practices in its long history.

NUTHAMPSTEAD

Situated a few miles to the south-east of Royston is the delightful village of Nuthampstead, with its golf course and clay pigeon shooting grounds, which are sited on an old World War Two bomber base where American B17 'flying fortresses' used to fly. Not far from the former airfield is the Woodman public house which is haunted by what may have been a former airman. In 1980 the landlord had an eerie experience when a chair pulled itself up to his table as though an invisible guest had joined him. He looked around for signs of some trickery but there were none; this was something that had been experienced before by several different people. Regulars believe that 'something' sits in this chair and makes itself comfortable of an evening. This is not an isolated incident, people on their own in the pub often get the distinct impression that someone is watching them when in fact there is no one else there and a picture of a B17 bomber regularly falls off the wall. The bomber in question returned to base badly shot up, with a huge hole in the nose, the explosion which had caused the hole killed the bomb aimer. It is interesting to speculate if this man has returned to one of the places he visited before taking off on his final mission... the last place where he felt safe and happy in the company of his friends.

THERFIELD

The ancient village of Therfield lies a mile or so on the southern side of Royston and nearby Therfield Heath has long barrows that date back to the Iron Age. Therfield sits on the ridge of the Chilterns, just far enough off the busy A10 to retain its air of order, tranquillity and rural charm. Indeed it is not merely my opinion, because Therfield has won the coveted Best Kept Village in Hertfordshire award, organised by the Hertfordshire Society, on at least six separate occasions.

Once upon a time there were seven public houses in Therfield, now reduced to two, the Bell and the Fox and Duck. My wife and I tend to favour the latter, which is situated on the village green, as we particularly enjoy the food there. This hostelry hit the headlines in the local press during 1975, with both the *Royston Crow* and the *Herts and Cambs Reporter* taking up the story. Temporary managers had been brought in to run the pub and it seemed as though a former landlord (deceased) took exception to them. Lights were switched on and off by themselves, lamps were turned around and one time the light on the dartboard was found turned to face the wrong way. Bottles were rattled, toilets flushed of their own accord and footsteps ran across the landing upstairs. These events were witnessed by both bar staff and customers alike. In desperation the managers abandoned their bedroom and opted to sleep on a mattress in the lounge bar. Events culminated in a police investigation into an alleged break-in at the pub. They too, heard the footsteps overhead but upon investigation no trace of any intruders could be found. The sounds seemed to be coming from a room that had been used by the former landlord, but there was nobody there. Villagers remained tight-lipped about the weird goings on at the Fox and Duck and no explanation was ever forthcoming.

Chapter Six

STEVENAGE

Stevenage, immediately before the Second World War, was a large village of some six thousand souls. It achieved the status of becoming Britain's first 'New Town' in 1946, when it was originally planned as a satellite town for sixty thousand people, and now, some sixty years on, it is home to well over ten times that original population as envisaged by those early post war planners. They had divided Stevenage into six neighbourhoods, each housing ten thousand people, with its own facilities such as shops, pubs, schools and churches within easy walking distance.

Stevenage's history may be traced all the way back to Roman times. Six Hills Way, a major route through the town, was named after six 'hills' which are in fact tumuli, or the burial mounds of wealthy Romans who lived in the area around AD100 to 150. The town's name originated several hundred years later, from the Saxon settlement hereabouts called Sithenaece, meaning 'strong oak'.

Stevenage was referred to in the novel *Howard's End* as 'Hilton' by E.M. Forster, who grew up in the house known as 'Rooks Nest', where he lived with his mother until he was fourteen. Mrs Wilcox, one of the characters in *Howard's End*, was modelled on his mother's friend Mrs Poston who took the house after the Forsters left. E.M. Forster broadcast a talk in 1946 about the 'New Town' and he expressed his sadness at the great changes to the agricultural way of life in his old boyhood district. Rook's Nest is situated in the north of the town, up the winding lane above St Nicholas's Church. An earlier famous writer, Charles Dickens, also wrote about Stevenage in 1861. 'The village street was like most other village streets; wide for its height, silent for its size and drowsy in the dullest degree.'

Stevenage New Town has, of course, absorbed a number of villages over the years, places like Shephall, Shephallbury, Symonds Green (probably named after William Symonds who lived at Symonds Green Farm circa 1700) and Broadwater, known as 'Bradewater' by the Saxons, after the brook which runs past it. Many other place names retain strong historical links; there really was a windmill, dating from at least the seventeenth century, at Corey's Mill. It had four sails, a ladder, a tailpole and a timber roundhouse with a thatched roof, it burned down in 1878 but the mound upon which it stood remains behind the current public house.

THE GHOSTLY GROCER

Curious sightseers still make their way to the old National Westminster Bank premises in Stevenage for a viewing of Henry Trigg's coffin, which is perched high up in the rafters of the building. Certainly he was one of the oddest personalities who has ever lived in Stevenage, a quintessential English eccentric. Henry Trigg was a wealthy grocer during the 1700s, who sold meat from his own twin-gabled shop in Middle Row, which street had been home to market stalls in medieval times and it slowly developed into a row of permanent shops and dwellings.

Trigg was well known in the locality and a fairly important member of the community; a single man, he owned land and property, was a church warden and an overseer of the parish. When he died he caused his family much embarrassment due to the bizarre conditions contained in his will, copies of which were mass produced and sold to an eager public who read the details with amazement. Dated 28 September 1724, it instructed his Executor quite clearly that his body should be committed 'to the West end of my Hovel (barn) to be decently laid there upon a floor erected by my Executor, upon the purlin (roof beam) for the same purpose, nothing doubting but that at the general Resurrection, I shall receive the same again by the mighty power of God.'

What could have caused a clearly God-fearing man to have his coffin placed high up in the roof of a barn instead of being buried in the consecrated ground of a churchyard like everyone else? The simple answer is 'The Resurrectionists', the popular name, during the eighteenth century, given to those who illicitly dug up freshly buried corpses, which they then sold, for dissection in the medical schools. The fears aroused by the activities of the resurrectionists were out of all proportion to their real effect and led to the passing of the Anatomy Act of 1832. Henry Trigg had had a close encounter with these ghouls one night after a drinking session in The Black Swan with a couple of friends. As the trio passed through St Mary's churchyard they happened upon some grave-robbers at work on a new grave, but 'those unscrupulous vampires' (as Trigg described them) could be dangerous people to tangle with, so Henry Trigg and his companions slipped quietly away. The idea that his own body could fall into the hands of such loathsome creatures, to ultimately end up on a dissecting table somewhere, filled Henry Trigg with horror. His solution to the problem was to create his own highly unconventional final resting place.

It must have been difficult for Henry's brother, the Rev Thomas Trigg, to accept the strange terms imposed on him, but Henry had obviously anticipated any opposition to his last will and testament by naming Thomas as his Executor, however, if he objected to carrying out his duties everything was to go to brother George, and so on, down through the family. The estate was considerable, and so it came to pass that Henry Trigg's lead-lined coffin was hoisted up into the rafters of the barn at the back of the shop. The famous coffin, still seen in the present day, is neither the original coffin nor does it contain the mortal remains of the ghostly grocer...

In 1774 the former Trigg house and shop became the Old Castle Inn, and then in the great 1807 fire, when many thatched buildings in Middle Row were destroyed the old Trigg barn (along with its coffin) situated in the northern half of the street, remained undamaged when the wind suddenly changed direction. The pub's licence was not renewed after 1919 and it eventually became a branch of the National Westminster Bank. Henry Trigg's coffin though, had not been untouched during all these decades. In 1831, Mr Bellamy, landlord of the Old Castle Inn, could not resist the temptation to check on 'old Henry' and declared that 'the hair on the skull of the deceased is in a perfect state of preservation.' The coffin was a different matter, it was deteriorating badly. At some point in the 1800s a new one, bound with iron bands, was made, and Trigg's body was placed inside and returned to the rafters. When the East Herts Archaeological Society later inspected the coffin they found 'about two thirds of a male skeleton' – were grisly souvenir-hunters responsible? The peace that Henry Trigg had sought was not to be... At the time of the First World War Commonwealth troops were billeted in Stevenage and persistent rumours circulated that they had also opened the coffin and removed more of the unfortunate Henry Trigg's remains. Did they perhaps imagine that, like a saint's relics, the Trigg bones might afford them some sort of protection in the coming conflagration? It was also said at the time that these same soldiers sold some of these remains for ready cash and when the bones were at last all gone the resourceful recruits made up the deficiency by restocking with animal bones, obtained through one of the town's butchers.

A Stevenage resident later admitted, in a letter to the local press, that in 1917 she had, with some Army friends, raided the coffin, but the bones that were found turned out to be horses' bones! The fact that the coffin no longer contained any part of Henry Trigg was kept quiet because copies of his will were still selling steadily at sixpence per copy and revenue might well have suffered if it became public knowledge that there was only an empty coffin in the barn rafters. It is extremely ironic that the man who went to so much trouble to ensure that his dead body was kept intact at all costs, rather than having it stolen and dissected as he had feared, instead had it stolen piecemeal...

In 1964 renovation work was carried out on a building in Middle Row – a building that backed onto the barn that had once belonged to Henry Trigg. During the course of the project a workman named Fred Usher went into the storeroom one morning to fetch a crowbar when he came across a 'shabbily dressed' old man, 'in an overcoat and gaiters', coming through the doorway who 'must have been about five feet eight tall', so real was the apparition that Usher called out to him, but as is the way with ghosts, there was no reply and the figure 'seemed to drift past me.' What happened next though really shook the workman, 'I turned and nearly collapsed when I saw him disappearing through the solid brick wall.' Older residents who had lived in the area a long time were under no illusions and told Fred Usher that what he had seen was the spirit of Henry Trigg…

When it came to true ghost stories Stevenage posed one of the biggest problems in North Hertfordshire for me. There has been hardly anything written or reported concerning paranormal events in this particular town, and what little there is comes from ancient, handed-down tales, that date back a hundred years or more. What I wanted was more contemporary material.

After a lot of spadework I finally unearthed some modern spectral stories, I was contacted by Phyllis Ayres with a strange tale from the Roebuck area of Stevenage. It concerned her son, Ian Abernethy and his wife, Amber (they have since parted) at the time they were living together in a modern house, about 30 or 40 years old, in Forest Row, this would have been during 2002/2003. A variety of weird occurrences plagued the couple. Jewellery which had been left by the bed would mysteriously be moved to the window. A photograph taken of their West Highland terrier, Jim, showed a cloud around the dog and in the cloud a woman's face could be clearly seen. While the children, Holly and Jack were watching TV in the front room there was a crash overhead, from their bedroom, as though someone had jumped off the bed. Another time Ian was at home alone decorating the stairwell when he saw a lady in a long grey skirt appear at the top of the stairs. He was to see her on a couple of occasions. He had a bad back and used a special spray attachment in the bath to ease his backache. One day there was an almighty crash and Ian ran to the foot of the stairs to find that his sprayer had been hurled downstairs.

Running footsteps were heard overhead when there was nobody upstairs. Bath taps would be turned off only to be turned on again by some invisible entity and sometimes this would happen several times in a row. Ian's brother, Andrew, stayed over one night to look after the place. He too heard footsteps in the empty house, which came up the stairs and crossed the floorboards, then his bedroom door was pulled open, at which point he ducked under the covers…

The Grange is an old Stevenage landmark with a haunted reputation that goes back to 1965, when a caretaker and his assistant at the school first saw a ghost in broad daylight. One Sunday morning, as the two men crossed the playing field, they saw a figure staring at them from the garden. It looked like a man dressed in brown livery and when the caretaker called out to the 'stranger' he simply vanished. What is thought to be the spirit of a stableman has appeared on a number of occasions. It is believed that the Grange was once a coach house, which burned down in the nineteenth century, killing a stableman.

Other odd things have been reported by the caretaker at the Grange, such as what happened one night after he had left the building, having turned off all the lights, only to find, when he turned around, that the place was 'ablaze with light.' Over the years he has owned dogs of various breeds while he has been caretaker at the school. All of these animals, both large and small, have had one thing in common – none of them could ever be persuaded to enter the house.

One of the better-known haunted areas of Stevenage is around Monkswood, where many people have felt an unaccountable sense of unease while walking the tree-lined pathways. It is said that a monastery once existed there and that during the Reformation the religious order that was based here received particularly brutal treatment, including the burning down of their buildings and the murder of the monks, who are thought to be buried beneath these very trees. What is known for sure among local people is that phantom monks have been reportedly seen at Monkswood.

I recall visiting George W. King on several occasions many years ago in another life when, as a young man, I worked on the industrial magazine *Storage Handling & Distribution*. King's sold hoists and other engineering kit for a lot of years and was a regular supplier to many of the motor car manufacturers. Eventually the firm closed and the vast site was sold off to become reinvented as Stevenage Leisure Park. Soon after the Park opened an ugly incident occurred where a thug, masquerading as 'a doorman' (how do these people ever get employment?) kicked a man to death outside Smilin' Sam's. Afterwards people regularly reported seeing and hearing strange things in the vicinity of the slaying, usually at around 2am when the site was otherwise empty...

My friend Duncan Campbell once worked in security at the Leisure Park and about five years ago, on a summer's evening, he was walking the site with his friends Giles and Andy. It had been a hot day and it was a warm evening, it would have been around 7.30pm. The guys were quite relaxed as they chatted and strolled along. They came to a point by the bottom of the car park, near the railway line and close to Jigsaw's Nursery, which was just a shell, as it was under construction then. Out of the blue their mood changed, all three friends suddenly felt extremely uneasy for no obvious reason. It was as if they were being watched when, out of the corner of his eye, Duncan caught sight of a flitting shadow which he then saw head on. This black shadow was upright instead of lying along the ground as you might expect and it was man-sized, as he looked on the black shape appeared at the other side of him and the sudden darting around was quite uncanny. Duncan's friend Giles confirmed that he had had exactly the same experience.

Not too many people are aware that the British Aerospace site in Gunnelswood Road is haunted. I am obliged to former engineer Eric Hornby (now retired) for the following true tales. Over the past 60 years the BAE site has had various owners, including English Electric, Napiers and others. Prior to its industrialisation, however, a huge burial mound used to run from north to south almost to the full extent of the site. It was quite high and had to be levelled to accommodate the buildings. Since then, over a long period of years numerous reports have been received of Roman soldiers marching about three metres off the ground down the length of the former burial mound. Other mysterious happenings have been witnessed at night by the security staff in some of the older buildings, while a former member of staff was seen by a number of people, walking through a wall where there had once been a door.

Eric Hornby used to work for some time in the calibration department in 'C' building on the north side of the British Aerospace site in Gunnelswood Road. Adjacent to the calibration laboratory was a male toilet. The policy at BAe was to employ retired personnel to do the toilet cleaning and this block had an old man who attended each day at the same time. If Eric happened to use the toilets when the old man was there he would invariably be found sitting on a box in the corner, rolling a cigarette, having wetted the floor to give the appearance of cleaning. Eric's visits did not always coincide with the cleaner's except for once or twice a week, sometimes less. Whenever he saw the old man he always said 'good morning', but he never received an acknowledgement. The engineer had not seen the cleaner for about a fortnight when one morning there he was, sitting on his box as usual. Eric greeted him and was not surprised to be ignored. The next day he encountered the cleaners' foreman mopping the floor and asked, 'Is the usual fellow off sick today?' To which the foreman replied, 'He died of a heart attack two weeks ago.'

Jack's Hill, near Graveley, is just north of Stevenage and Daphne McCarthy was returning from Stotfold, passing through on her way home to Old Stevenage. It was early evening, around dusk in 1982, and she was 'thinking of nothing in particular' when she was surprised to see 'a soldier, standing motionless at a gap in the bushes', she looked back but the figure had disappeared. She described her sighting to me, 'He had a helmet with a visor and both hands were resting on a long pole he carried, which could have been a pikestaff, he was looking down.' This sighting made a big impression as it was still obviously most clear to Daphne, although it happened 22 years prior to her recounting it to me. I wondered if she had glimpsed the shade of some tired and lonely sentry, from the Civil War era perhaps.

WALKERN

Walkern is a village due east of Stevenage, where Eric Hornby lived some years ago. He was a close friend of John Bunce (now deceased) an ex army officer who had moved a few miles north to Walkern from Datchworth village after his wife was killed outside their home, called Rats Castle. John's new home was opposite the Robin Hood pub, at Fairview Cottage, which had once been a row of three small workers' cottages, about 300 years old. Having been converted the large cottage was full of nooks and crannies, uneven floors and it had bags of atmosphere and character. John collected antiques – clocks, furniture and numerous brass and copper implements, which he kept in the huge inglenook fireplace. There had been a number of prowlers in the garden and around the cottage so John would let his Labrador out to scare them off. He also installed lighting all around the cottage, linked to detectors. From day one the lights came on in the evening, the dog would be sent out, but no one was ever seen. This continued each evening and it became apparent that there was a pattern – the light would come on every evening at 9pm. After John asked Eric and another friend to investigate the history of the cottages it emerged that an ostler and his wife had lived in the end cottage, furthest from the drive, where access was from the rear, away from the road. He worked for a family who lived in a manor house over towards Bennington and the ostler was allowed to take the carriage and horses home in the evening and stable them in the grounds behind the cottages. It became apparent that he was a most punctual man, for he used to walk from the stables to his cottage each evening at precisely 9pm…

BOOK TWO

East Hertfordshire Entities

Chapter Seven
BISHOP'S STORTFORD

Bishop's Stortford is situated in the 'top right hand corner', 'the Far East' of the county, hard by the border with Essex, and is noted as a Medieval Market Town. The town's name is derived from the Saxon Manor of Esterteferd, which became Stortford, once owned by a Saxon woman, Eddeva Pulchrima, who sold it in about 1060 to the Bishop of London, and so it became Bishop's Stortford. There were settlements in the area at a much earlier date, both Stone Age and Iron Age men lived here long before the Saxons, who invaded Britain in 449AD. The town's importance as a river crossing influenced its growth, as did the flourishing market and the growing of cereal crops which resulted in it becoming a major supplier of malt for London's brewery industry. The most famous native of Bishop's Stortford was Cecil Rhodes, founder of Rhodesia (now Zimbabwe).

Hauntings in Bishop's Stortford are concentrated into a compact area, centred around the road that runs east/west through the town, from Wind Hill, which becomes High Street and then Bridge Street and these hauntings may be attributed to one ghost – 'the (ubiquitous) Grey Lady' of Bishop's Stortford. I paid a visit to the town in November '04 to see for myself, starting at the old Boar's Head on the hill (Wind Hill) opposite St Michael's Church. I spoke with Penny Haynes, who told me that just eight months prior to my visit the latest odd incident had occurred. It was late at night and her brother Patrick had been in the bar when several unexplained incidents happened. The PDQ machine, for processing credit cards, went off on its own accord, printing out paper, also there had been several loud bangs at the door but nobody was there and suddenly the optics above the bar began shaking violently. It seems that the exorcisms carried out thirty years ago had not entirely cured the ghostly problem.

During recent years the ghost of a child has been witnessed at Saplings Independent Nursery. This fair-haired girl has been heard crying and it is thought that she is the spirit of an infant who died in a fire on this site in the past.

STANDON

Standon lies about midway between Buntingford and Bishop's Stortford, from Buntingford you travel straight down the A10 then turn off along the A120 for a very short distance and the centre of Standon is just off on your right. The village is home to The Star Inn, a delightful small pub by the green, right opposite the church. It has a history dating back to 1550 and was known as the Maypole in the 1700s, when it provided accommodation for coach travellers. For the past four years or so it has been run by David and Isobel Underwood and visitors can read the story that made the pages of the *Mail on Sunday* on December 31st 1989, an article that I remember well, as it was of particular interest to me. The landlord at that time was Frank Spelling and his story dated back to a night in 1972 when he was awoken around 3am, by noises from downstairs. When he got down to the bar he was amazed to find a crowd of people in old-fashioned dress, laughing and drinking there, the men wore tri-corn hats, a striking Latin woman was among them, while flute-like music played in the background. As he went through the door to investigate further the room reverted to being silent, empty and as normal. He turned around to go back up to bed, then changed his mind. He decided to take another look as he could not believe what he had just seen, and peered through the small window in the bar door.

'My heart almost leaped out of my body', Frank was quoted as saying, 'Not only were they all back again, but this time they were joined by a buxom looking wench.'

He opened the door once more and instantly the scene changed back to an empty bar. Frank didn't share his weird experience with anyone until prompted to do so by a meeting with an old lady one afternoon several months later. This person claimed to have grown up in The Star and enquired if anyone had seen its ghosts lately. She remembered coming home late from a party one night, and as she crept through the back door she was taken completely by surprise to discover a dozen or so people in the bar. Unaware of the landlord's recent encounter and to his undoubted relief, she proceeded to corroborate Frank's experience in exact detail.

I spoke to the staff at The Star in November 2004 and was assured that the pub remains 'spook central'. When the very last customer of a session is engaged in conversation at the bar it is often noticed that 'someone else' gets up and goes out, 'someone' who wasn't there before... Footsteps are frequently heard running about on the landing at various times of the day or night. The sounds are noticed by customers and staff alike, when there is obviously nobody upstairs, and this can happen when the bar is full of people. It has even been known for the spook to visit the upstairs toilet. Those who work in this charming pub are quite sanguine about their other-worldly guests and feel that they mean no harm. Staff have been known to say, 'They (the ghosts) have been here a lot longer than we have and they'll probably be around for a lot longer too.'

Chapter 8

BROXBOURNE

Julie Salmon e-mailed me a strange tale from Broxbourne, in response to an article I wrote for the local press. She was living in a flat at Cozens Lane East in Silverfield, Broxbourne. It was in the summertime, around June 1989. The problems began with the light bulbs, which blew constantly. During my many investigations this is something that I come across frequently, when spirits are trying to appear they will use a handy source of electricity to manifest, and it is often drawn from light bulbs, so one mark of a haunting is bulbs that blow more frequently than is normal. Small unaccountable noises then began to be heard in the night. One morning Julie got up to discover knives embedded in the walls, as if thrown by someone with great force and anger. The kitchen door had been locked so that the children couldn't get at the knives, which were kept on a magnetic holder, out of reach of small hands.

More strange things started to happen in the night. Shampoo bottles would have their contents tipped out in the bathroom and cat food was found spread around the kitchen in the morning. Then something odd occurred in the daytime. One afternoon Julie's turntable had a cup of tea on it when all at once it spun around sending the tea flying. Shadows around the walls began to appear in daylight and the children's bedroom got so cold that icicles began to form. As she went to answer the front door the teddies that had been on the top of the children's clothes cupboard were suddenly 'Thrown off the top of the wardrobe in one sweep. I just ran into the living room and was panicking because I was very scared.' As Julie's friend Clare tried to calm her down the sound of bells could be heard from the bedroom. It was a walk-along toy with bells that rang when it was pushed and some invisible entity was now pushing it. Julie also noted that her cat had made itself scarce.

In an effort to understand what was going on Julie visited the library to try and find out the history of Cozens Lane East, but all that she could find was that there had been greenhouses on the site in the past. Her search for answers continued, with a visit to the vicar of St Augustine's, Broxbourne. By this time Julie's oldest child was making strange noises in her throat and insisting that she saw a strange man on her bed. The vicar came over one afternoon and blessed every room in the flat with holy water. Unfortunately, as is sometimes the case in haunted houses and flats, things actually got a lot worse after the blessing. Julie's daughter reported that 'the man' was in this corner and then that corner, going all around her room and various items were moved about the place too.

Now Julie was becoming so scared that she just wanted to move out of her flat. In desperation she called in a psychic that she knew from Enfield, called Teresa, who duly came to carry out a form of exorcism. She brought her husband and together they used a censor to spread incense, they also had a Bible and they recited prayers in every room. Before they left the couple advised Julie to stay in the house for 24 hours as they had 'put a seal on every door and window', figuratively, not literally, and Julie was to only talk about happy things. Julie's boyfriend Paul came and stayed over to add his support. The morning after the 'exorcism' little things were still going on around Julie, draughts and wall shadows, Paul said that he had seen lights in their bedroom. Teresa was brought back the following night, only to assure Julie that whatever 'it' was had gone now. Taking Julie into the children's bedroom, which had always been cold before, she showed her how warm and calm it now felt. Teresa's husband carried out healing on Julie, placing his hands over her. 'A kind of warmth ran down my body to my toes, it made all my fears go and I felt calm and relaxed like never before, I felt I could have slept for a week.' It was explained that the lights that Paul had seen were from the tunnel that had been given for the spirit to move back to where he had come from. Julie's awful two months' ordeal was finally over…

Julie came up with her own possible explanation for the paranormal disturbances in her home. She recalled that her 'ex' had been seeing a girl from Norfolk and at the time these weird events were unfolding Julie and her husband had parted; her 'ex' later told Julie that his Norfolk girlfriend had been a follower of the Dark Arts. Julie's feeling is that this woman had probably sent something other-worldly to plague her home. One thing is for sure, Norfolk has sometimes been called a 'witch county', due to the prevalence of witches there and witchcraft has been traditionally associated with Norfolk along with other parts of East Anglia.

Chapter Nine
BUNTINGFORD

When I drive into Buntingford along the Baldock Road and come up to the T-junction with the High Street it always feels like I am stepping back in time. Although my home town of Baldock is an ancient place, this neighbouring much smaller town somehow has an even older feel to it. Perhaps it is the many timber-framed houses, with their projecting upper stories mixed happily with more recent Georgian properties of eclectic designs, or maybe the narrow street with its various shops, or perhaps it's the numerous archways, but I can always easily visualise horses and carriages threading their way through High Street in place of today's innumerable motor cars.

A market was granted to Buntingford in 1360, signalling the start of the town's growth. One local businessman in particular lives on in our English language. Thomas Hobson was already a successful Buntingford carrier, working between London and Cambridge, when he decided to set up a sideline – a 'horses for hire' business. This innovative enterprise had no competition, thereby allowing its proprietor to completely disregard the whims of his customers. He imposed a strict rule – no picking and choosing of horses, clients either took the next one in line or simply went without, hence the expression, still in use today, well over 300 years since he died, of 'Hobson's choice', meaning no choice at all! He obviously loved his town for when he died in 1630, at well over 70 years of age, he provided for Buntingford generously in his will.

I went looking for Buntingford's ghosts in earnest in December 2004 and soon discovered that the town and its surrounding villages are, without a doubt, a Hertfordshire 'paranormal hotspot'. The obvious starting point was at the place known locally as 'the haunted house' – Bell House Gallery in the High Street. Situated in a building which dates back from 1450, Bell House Gallery is now a gift shop, where I met the charming Monika Bevan. She assured me during our friendly conversation that whatever had haunted the place was now long gone and she had lived here for many years with no hint of any paranormal events. A disappointing start, but I would soon unearth plenty of other true ghost stories surrounding the town. Before it became a gift shop Bell House Gallery was most definitely haunted, it began trading as the Old Bell Coaching Inn and by the late 1940s the owner at that time let out parts of the building to three separate families. All of these families witnessed strange, unexplained events at various times of the day and night. These included door handles turning but no one found on the other side, footsteps echoing in empty overhead rooms, a baby heard crying in great distress in an unoccupied bedroom and other noises, as of a woman sobbing as though in deep grief. More disturbing, however, were two events experiences by different male tenants. Tom Parker awoke to feel a great, invisible weight bearing down on him so that he was unable to free himself and he described his experience vividly, 'I struggled to get free, but couldn't. At last I had the idea of trying to roll from under the weight and after what seemed hours I managed to do it.' The other man was woken by the sensation that he was being strangled.

After two years of suffering with these frightening events the tenants spoke to the local press and two journalists from the *Hertfordshire Mercury* persuaded them to hold a séance. Using the traditional upturned glass and letters of the alphabet spread around in a semicircle, the group asked the spirits various questions. An entity contacted them and revealed her name – Hannah Bedwell. She explained that she had worked at the inn and was now searching for the baby she had killed (by laying on her) because she was frightened of losing her job and being turned out. Hannah told the investigators that she was 15 years old and the child's father, John Price, a porter at the inn, had been killed. Hannah had been arrested, imprisoned in Bedford gaol and later hanged at Newgate. Some of the people at the séance decided to research the story and parish records showed that Hannah Bedwell had indeed lived as a serving girl at the inn and she was hanged at Newgate for infanticide.

In the early 1930s two local residents were just young lads when they had an unexplained encounter with 'ghost lights'. Charles Edwards of Greenways and Samuel Clark of Bridgefoot often played out together in the evenings, with their friend Fred Lee. The boys were strolling along Chapel End towards some old barns situated at the top of the lane around 7pm one November evening when they suddenly saw something extremely strange. In the middle of the nearby river moving lights suddenly appeared under the water. The three pals stood rooted to the river bank in amazement, never having seen anything like this wondrous sight before. As they watched, the spark-like lights rose to the surface and moved to the river's edge. The lights climbed the banking, crossed the road and continued moving to the area known as 'Totties Ditch' before finally forming up together at the rear of The Crown pub in a rotating circle, at which point the boys took to their heels and pelted down the lane, their wonderment turned to fear.

The three lads told their story to friends and family and a crowd went to investigate but nothing was found. The odd tale spread far and wide, the police were informed and the gas and electricity companies checked local pipes and cables but found no faults to explain the weird light-show. Journalists picked up the story and carried out their own investigation but were also baffled. To this day the mystery lights remain just that – a mystery!

'Ghost lights' have been reported from all over the country and they are thought to be the first stage of a ghost's manifestation. To me this story is interesting for a number of reasons. Ghosts usually manifest by using the energy fields of the living and children have strong bio-electric energy fields. We don't know what ages Charles, Samuel and Fred were at the time of their sighting but I wouldn't be surprised to discover that they had been under the age of 10. Children up to the age of 10 are the most likely to see ghosts, out of people of all ages. The fact that there were three 'energy sources' available for the ghosts to draw from increases the likelihood even further of the children witnessing some sort of paranormal manifestation. Water also seems to promote ghostly activity and my dowser friends tell me that 'tingling sensations' which they receive when they locate water, may suggest some sort of force-field similar to that which surrounds an electric wire. It is possible then that the ghosts of Buntingford, that materialised as moving 'sparks', were first stage manifestations drawing their energy from both the water's 'force-field' and the boys' own bio-electric energy. I am reminded too, of the 'corpse candles' seen in rural areas, these dancing lights often followed the route taken by coffin-bearers of times past. This leads me to another possibility – that the three boys saw the spirit forms of some people who drowned in the river and whose bodies had once been laid out at The Crown pub, as was the custom in the time before hospitals.

A house in Buntingford High Street was the site of paranormal phenomena in more recent years; these incidents coincided with renovations being carried out at the time. The ghost made its presence felt one evening with the appearance of a young girl in a nightdress who walked into the dining room while the daughter of the house was safely tucked up in bed. When the parents went into the dining room it was empty and when they checked their daughter's bedroom they found her fast asleep in her bed. The young girl's ghost was never seen upstairs but was heard, footsteps sounded on the landing, latches lifted and doors opened and closed, always when the couple's own children were sleeping. Their daughter was most affected by the entity. On one occasion she climbed sleepily to the open window ledge (with quite a drop to the street below) but fortunately she was seen and when her mother asked her what she was doing the child replied that 'the lady in white' had told her to get out of bed. On another occasion this same daughter was pushed aside just in time to avoid being hit on the head by a heavy wall-mounted clock, which unaccountably fell from its mounting. The clock caught her on the shoulder, giving her a nasty fright.

The kitchen was also a centre for ghostly attention, whenever the ghost's presence was felt the Rayburn's temperature would drop low and then pick up again. The kitchen door was sometimes difficult to open in the morning and it was found to have been blocked by the children's wooden rocking horse, which had been moved there in the middle of the night. It would have been quite impossible for any member of the household to have obstructed the door and then got back upstairs again.

Happily the hauntings ceased with the end of the building work several months later, which is often the case when old houses are renovated. Then some new owners moved in and they reported that the Rayburn was up to its old tricks again during the first few months of their occupation. They didn't actually see or hear anything themselves but on a few occasions just after they moved in their small son came into their bedroom and asked to sleep with them because 'the lady in my room won't let me go to sleep.'

The old approach road to the Tudor Manor House, Alswick Hall, is said to be haunted by the sounds of a ghostly coach and horses on the anniversary of the terrible accident that killed Lady Leman. One night she was being driven home when the horses took fright, supposedly at the appearance of an apparition, and bolted. The coach driver lost control and the heavy coach toppled into a deep pond beside the approach road. The unfortunate Lady Leman and her coachman were drowned and allegedly their bodies were never found.

A small pool, which no longer exists, once held great fear for local children. It was situated, surrounded by trees, near Monks Walk and the apparition of a monk was seen by this pond, which seemed to be searching for something. The pond was associated with a story about a child who had been drowned by a monk.

There is yet a third ghost story concerning a drowning, at Aspenden Hall, where a nursemaid, out walking her charge, lost her grip on the perambulator for an instant. The pram rolled down a slope and the child inside was tipped into a pond. Despite the nursemaid's attempt at a rescue the child drowned and the area was reputed to be haunted by the spirit of the nursemaid, seen searching for her charge and also by the sounds of the ghostly child's cries.

A TALE OF TWO CHURCHES

People ask me if there is an equivalent church in Hertfordshire to the atmospheric 'Black Magic' Church (St Mary's) at Clophill in Bedfordshire, which I wrote about in *Ghostly Bedfordshire ...Reinvestigated* and which was the place that aroused the most interest amongst my readers. I can immediately think of two such sites and one of them is on the edge of Buntingford. Down a country lane at Layston may be found the 'brooding' site of medieval St Bartholomew's Church, which stands high on the eastern bank of the Rib valley. Buntingford once lay within the parish of Layston and this was Layston's parish church, which continued to act as the main centre of worship in the area, even when Buntingford had become a substantial settlement with its own church, St Peter's. Built in red brick in the shape of a Greek cross, St Peter's was begun in 1614 and it was originally intended as a chapel-of-ease for the deaconry, somewhere to worship for those unable to reach the parish church of St Bartholomew's. St Peter's stands in the centre of town, but it did not formally become the parish church until 1900. As late as the 18th century the faithful were still travelling up Church Street to St Bartholomew's, high on the hill. Fewer and fewer people supported St Bartholomew's, so it was not worth maintaining, and after the Second World War the dilapidated nave roof was finally removed. Only occasional services are held in the covered chancel in connection with the neighbouring cemetery.

Just like the church at Clophill, St Bartholomew's is atmospheric as it is also in a remote setting and in a similarly spookily ruined condition. A natural setting for ghost stories, and St Bartholomew's has one of its own. In the 19th century the peal of bells could often be heard in Buntingford, coming from the abandoned, flint-built church at Layston, which was known to be empty on those dark winter evenings. One night the bell-ringers of Buntingford gathered together and descended on the empty old church of St Bartholomew's, determined to catch those responsible for what they thought must be a practical joke. The party was shocked to find, as they neared the building, that the church was brightly lit and all the while the bells continued their tolling, as if for Evensong. The Buntingford bell-ringers approached the place cautiously, then screwing up their courage they entered the church, and with that the bells stopped ringing and everything was plunged into darkness. The bell-ringing at Layston remained completely unexplained.

ANSTEY

Three miles to the north-east of Buntingford is the village of Anstey. An interesting place, named after the Old English word anstiga, meaning 'narrow or lonely track'. It was 'bandit country', north-east Hertfordshire, during Norman times, a vicinity where quite a few Normans simply disappeared, victims of Anglo-Saxon outlaws who assassinated the hated French invaders at every opportunity. Evidence of mottes (castle mounds) and moats, which would have surrounded these fortified positions, can still be found at Anstey and other villages in the vicinity.

Anstey is an attractive place, with its ancient well, which used to be the centre of village life – and gossip. Where once there were five pubs there is now but one, the Chequers. Gone too are the old village landmarks – the blacksmiths, the post office, the general stores, the cycle shop, the dairy and the shoe maker/repairer. One tradition lives on though – Anstey Fair, which used to visit around the time of St Swithun's Day, ceased to come at the end of the 1920s. The villagers revived it and it takes place in the Old Rectory Garden.

Anstey is well known for its legendary 'disappearing fiddler', 'Blind George'. At Cave Gate, where he allegedly disappeared, there is an ancient chalk pit and on its east face there is an entrance to an underground passage known as the 'Devil's Hole.' The passage had never been explored as it was believed that anyone venturing inside would never come out alive. The cave was thought to lead up the long hill and under the moat to the dungeons of Anstey Castle, the infamous scene of many tortures, about a mile away and now just a tree-covered mound. The story has been around for several hundred years, but it continues to fascinate those who hear it for the first time.

One evening in the mid-eighteenth century the local farm workers were gathered in the Chequers, drinking, talking and listening to the music of George, the blind fiddler. As the conversation turned to the mysterious cave that still lay unexplored, the fiddler, in a fit of bravado, told the group that he was willing to take on the challenge and accompanied only by his dog he would walk the underground passageway to the castle. Many of the villagers accompanied the blind musician to the mouth of the cave and some of them tried to persuade him of the foolhardiness of his proposed adventure. Undeterred, man and dog set off along the underground chamber, George's final words on the matter being that he would explore it 'though the Devil himself were at the end of it.' Calling for the crowd to follow the sound of his fiddle he disappeared into the shadows. The villagers duly complied; they walked across the fields, listening for the sounds of the fiddle that came from underneath their feet until they were nearly half way to the castle. Without warning the noise of the fiddle rose to a shriek before... absolute silence. They hurried back the way they had come and stood at the mouth of the cave only to witness George's howling dog come bounding out of the cave, minus his tail and with his coat singed off. The animal fled into the night and was never seen again and nor was his master. Soon after Blind George's disappearance the cave entrance was walled up – to deter any imitators of such a foolish act or to contain the Fiddler's ghost?

Parish records show that at the beginning of the 18th centuries Anstey did have a fiddler whose last name was George, according to the register; however, he was buried in the churchyard...

In 1944 a B17 bomber crashed near the site of Austey Castle and the moat was drained in order to remove the aircraft. At the entrance to the tunnel some iron gates were discovered, locked shut.

Rumours persisted that the sounds of a fiddle could still be heard coming up through the ground on certain nights and some locals have maintained that no crops will grow on ground that lies above the tunnel and that when it snows it always melts first along the supposed line that the tunnel follows to the castle.

BENINGTON

Between Stevenage and Puckeridge lies the quintessential, 'movie set' English village of Benington, much admired for its vital village visions of green, tree-screened church, timbered cottages, Georgian stately home (The Lordship), folly, duck pond and pub, complete with its overhanging gables, black timbers and white pargeting – The Bell. Of course the pub has a ghost story, what did you expect? Just the one episode of anomalous phenomena was reported, but it is well worth recording. This story was related by one of the Area Managers for the Greene King Brewery. Some work was being carried out at their pub which necessitated taking off the front door. This was when the trouble started – a horrendous, putrid smell just by the doorway that could almost be tasted throughout the bar, but nobody could locate the cause, so the work was speedily done and the door was put back. During that hectic day the landlady was kept so busy that she hadn't been upstairs to her private sitting room. On entering it that evening she discovered every picture and mirror askew, as though someone had run around the room in a rage hitting everything that hung on the wall. The landlady put everything straight and shouted, 'You can stop it now, the work is done and we've put the door back.' It is sometimes a good idea to talk to your ghosts, especially when they are attracting your attention and being mischievous. This landlady had sense enough to realise that the disturbance was connected with the door. Maybe 'something' was let in that had been shut out while the door was in place. In times gone by 'witch bottles' were buried under thresholds to stop evil presences from entering, this practice continued up to the turn of the last century in remote corners of the countryside. It may be that this pub's threshold had been protected in the past by a charm against a local witch and the removal of the door temporarily 'broke the spell'. What we do know for sure is that when the door was replaced nothing further happened to disturb the peace of the Old Bell at Benington.

BRAUGHING

Braughing is, for me, synonymous with sausages; the place has long been famous for these particularly fine products from White's, the village butchers. Braughing (pronounced 'Braffing') is situated just three miles to the south of Buntingford along the A10. You reach it by means of a ford over the River Quin, where you may encounter ducks, and in times of heavy rainfall the ford has a tendency to flood. Downstream the Quin joins the River Rib and in the late 1970s part of the bank collapsed to reveal the foundations of a Roman villa. This was a reminder of Braughing's status in that era, when it was, after St Albans, one of the most important Roman centres in Hertfordshire. It's an easy place to fall in love with, as it possesses two greens, a main route through called The Street, a 15th century church with an interior that is full of interesting features and beside that some characterful old houses with slopey walls and gardens that lead down to the little Quin. A number of brightly washed cottages may be seen in Church End and one particularly fine example of pargeting in a blue and white cottage is another of the many architectural attractions.

The village also has a charming tradition that survives to this day, which began over 400 years ago. Every 2nd October the villagers celebrate Old Man's Day. A widower named Matthew Wall, was thought to be dead after suffering an illness and was duly prepared for burial. On the day of his interment the cortege was passing down Fleece Lane when a pall bearer slipped on wet leaves and the coffin fell to the ground, whereupon faint noises were heard from inside it, so the lid was prised open and Matthew Wall sat up and looked around him in astonishment. Matthew recovered from his shock and his illness to later remarry and to raise a family. Upon his death in 1595 his will was found to contain certain requests, one of which was a shilling for a poor man to sweep Fleece Lane from Wall's house to the church gate and there was a shilling to be paid for the tolling of the funeral bell. Those bequests continue every 2nd October, when the bell is tolled, village children sweep Fleece Lane and prayers are said at Matthew Wall's grave. The bells are rung out again in the evening to commemorate the happy event which followed Matthew Wall's close encounter with premature burial.

There are some intriguing ghosts in Braughing; one is a lady who appeared so life-like that Walter Martin, a local man who ran a taxi business, stopped to give her a lift in his vehicle only for her to disappear! This incident happened at Christmas time in 1954 and many years later Mr Martin could still recall the details vividly. He had been returning home after just dropping a regular fare at Cockhampstead Priory on a bitterly cold night, when his Landrover's headlights illuminated a tall lady walking along the drive ahead of him. She was about six feet tall, wearing an elegant grey two-piece outfit and her hair was drawn back in a bun. He noticed that her clothing looked very old-fashioned and he slowed to see if she wanted a lift, as it was so cold, but the next instant she was gone. Mr Martin was never able to explain his eerie encounter as the driveway was fenced on both sides, so there was no way the mystery woman could have disappeared from his view so abruptly. He went as far as to revisit the Priory to enquire about her, but nobody knew of any such person. Although he passed that way regularly, to pick up and drop off his client between the Priory and the station, he never again saw the tall woman in grey. A neighbour later confirmed to Mr Martin that she too had witnessed the appearance of a tall lady in grey around the same area; she just walked along, appearing perfectly solid until vanishing suddenly into thin air, this had happened on numerous occasions.

Friars Walk is said to be patrolled by a ghostly monk and five more monks haunt the lower end of Upp Hall Lane, known as Horse Cross which name was changed from Whore's Cross, after Anne Boleyn it seems. Several legends accompany the five 'brothers', one is that to see them is an omen of good fortune to come, but they only appear every five years, for just one night, the 10th May. It is also said that before the dissolution of their monastery of Braughingbury the five phantom friars were discovered eating trout (were they fish friars?) that they had caught from the River Rib without permission. The fish is alleged to have poisoned them and after their deaths they are doomed to make their five-yearly pilgrimage as an eternal penance – their next appearance is due in 2006.

An 'unpleasant feeling', as of an evil presence, has been experienced by some folk on the Dassels road, by the sewer farm. Before the sewer farm was in existence local legend has it that a man died a nasty death here, while in possession of some ill-gotten gains...

COTTERED

Cottered had a ghost called 'Old Charlie' that was reputed to bring good luck to those who saw it. Many years ago a farmer offered a 'gentleman of the road' a home in return for light work at the farm. Old Charlie gratefully accepted as it was a lonely life on the road and he was now getting on in years. He preferred to sleep in the barn amongst the straw bales, rather than being in the comfort of the house. He came and went as he pleased but his memory wasn't what it once was and he tended to wander off for days at a time but eventually he would return to the farm so everybody was used to him 'going missing' once in a while. While he was away the farmer visited a friend in the local hospital and was surprised to see the old tramp in one of the beds in the ward, looking so pale and weak that he might die at any moment. The concerned farmer asked if there was anything he could do and Old Charlie replied that he wanted to return to the farm and wondered if he would still find a welcome there. His farmer friend reassured him that his family were waiting for Charlie's return as this was his home, but privately he very much doubted that the old man would be leaving his bed. The tramp died peacefully in his sleep later that day, at 4.30pm and the farmer was greatly saddened.

With a lot occupying his mind the busy farmer forgot to tell his wife about his opportune hospital meeting with Old Charlie just before he passed over. He was, therefore, shocked to hear her telling him that Charlie had turned up out of the blue as usual that very afternoon. He told her that her husband had said it was all right for him to come and with that he'd gone straight to the barn where he usually slept and he hadn't been seen since. 'What time was this?' the farmer asked. 'Why it would have been around 4.30pm' was the reply...

The old barn became known as 'Charlie's Barn' thereafter, but it is now long gone and houses have been built on the site. Sightings of an old man shuffling along the street before abruptly disappearing continued over the years and those fortunate enough to have a sighting always seemed to have good fortune after the old tramp's appearance.

GREAT HORMEAD

Listed in the Domesday Book as three separate manors, Great Hormead, Little Hormead and Hare Street are now known as one parish – The Hormeads, which lie in a triangle about three miles east of Buntingford. Most of the houses in this community date from the 16th and 17th centuries. They were built alongside the main road and in most cases the church was built next to the Manor house, so that the lord of the manor could walk to church across his front garden.

Brick House in Great Hormead is reputed to be haunted by the ghost of a monk and in the 1980s a monk was reported to be wandering through the churchyard, as though searching for something. Local conjecture was that he may have been connected in some way with a murder alleged to have been committed hereabouts.

RUSHDEN

Situated half way between Buntingford and Baldock is the ancient village of Rushden. It is a tranquil, out of the way spot, and the area is beloved by ramblers for its fine walks. I have enjoyed some gentle strolls through the natural beauty of its surrounding woodlands and open fields, particularly up by hidden away Southern Green, which is a magical place to escape to, away from the roar of traffic and the ringing of telephones. There is a beautiful manor house here, Julians, which was visited by the writer Anthony Trollope. The Flemish Ambassador to the Court of Queen Elizabeth I owned a retreat in the neighbourhood, but this unfortunate diplomat was murdered by outlaws, who ransacked his home and threw his body down one of the many wells in the area. Legend has it that he buried a valuable ring, a gift from the Queen, under a walnut tree in his garden, so it would seem that he had a fear of being robbed at some time.

The village store and post office are long gone but the pub is still intact, as I can verify, having enjoyed the occasional meal and a few pints of ale there. The Moon and Stars is a characterful old pub, frequented by the locals and popular with summer visitors to the village. The resident ghost likes to turn off the beer pump in the cellar, which means that only hand-pulled beer may be served, which is fine by me as I'm a real ale fan!

One ghost of modern times was a well-known personality to some villagers, he was Tommy Chapman and he served as the village gravedigger for a number of years. It was his custom to sit on the bench near the phone box at the Green whenever there was a funeral. He was seen on at least one occasion by a Rushden resident, sitting in his accustomed spot on the funeral day of one of his close friends – but this was a few months after Tommy himself had died!

During the Second World War, when invasion by the Germans seemed a real possibility, an artistic character called Percy Portsmouth lived in the village. He kept a biplane in pieces at his barn, together with his sculptures and he was prepared to assemble the aircraft and fly it to Ireland in the event that the Germans arrived on English soil. Percy is dead now but there have been sightings of him in his garden. He is most distinctive as he sports side whiskers and wears a sculptor's smock…

In the centre of the village stands Barberry Cottage, which was once home to the spirit of an old lady who was seen many times, leaning on her gate in front of the cottage. The entrance was altered and the gate removed, it seems the ghost went with it because she was never seen again afterwards.

There are many other spooky stories told on dark nights by roaring log fires in homes around Rushden. They say that the Vicarage was so badly haunted in times past that the incumbent vicar, Reverend Roxburgh, was obliged to hold a ceremony of exorcism in response to the torment his daughter suffered by paranormal phenomena which occurred in their home. Local superstition maintains that anyone who is foolish enough to dig up or otherwise disturb the land at Broadfield Church will be dead within the year.

You are also not safe from supernatural encounters on the roads in the locality of Rushden. Some people feel uncomfortable when driving past Offley Green's telephone exchange at night. That may be because the exchange was built on the former site of a plague pit. The apparition of a small boy has also been reported on this road and he is believed to be the spirit of a murder victim.

The Village Hall has its own ghost story. Workmen were enjoying a break during renovations to the building when they were surprised by the sudden appearance at the doorway of a smiling woman, who carried a trug, as though she had just been doing some gardening. They were even more startled when she slowly dematerialised before their very eyes!

Chapter Ten

HATFIELD

Hatfield is a common name; there is a Hatfield and a Hatfield Woodhouse in Doncaster, a Hatfield in Herefordshire, as well as yet another Hatfield and Hatfield Broad Oak, both of which are in Essex. The name is derived from Old English, *haeth* and *feld* or 'heathy open land, or land where heather grows'. Hatfield, Hertfordshire can be traced back to Saxon times when King Edgar gave 5,000 acres of land to the monastery at Ely. Records are sketchy until 1226 when it was recorded that Henry III granted the rights to hold a market and a four day fair to the Bishops of Ely.

In later centuries Hatfield became a coaching town, before the coming of the railways in 1850, which effectively ended the coaching days.

Hatfield's Eight Bells pub will be forever famous as the setting for Bill Sykes' attracting attention by the bloodstains on his hat. He fled London after murdering Nancy in Charles Dickens' *Oliver Twist*, to make for the small pub at the foot of Fore Street, believed to be the Eight Bells. A plaque on the pub commemorates this distinction.

Nineteen-thirty saw the arrival of the aeronautical industry in Hatfield, in the form of the de Havilland aircraft factory. This illustrious company was responsible for designing and building such classic British aircraft as the Mosquito, Comet and Trident. British Aerospace had factories here too. The aviation industry's association with the town was to last some 60 years, but by the early 1990s the defence-related establishment at Hatfield Aerodrome had closed down and with the end of aviation operations it was recognised as a Key Employment Site. Out of the ashes emerged Hatfield Business Park, now home to over a million square feet of new business premises and provider of well over 3,000 jobs.

The disused British Aerospace site of almost 1,000 acres found a new lease of life as a film location. The mixture of vast, empty warehouse and office space, disused runway and huge 'backlot' area of grassland, hedgerows and woodland was ideal for films such as *Saving Private Ryan* and the television mini series, *Band of Brothers*, and I visited this set when the series was being made. The vast collection of World War Two uniforms, tanks and guns that I saw was hugely impressive!

The other connection that Hatfield has with the world of films is that it was home to Guy Ritchie, creator of *Lock, Stock and Two*

Smoking Barrels. The man who married the Queen of Pop, Madonna, and wrote a script for a movie that went on to take £11 million at the box office after its release in 1988, was not born in Essex or the East End of London, as many people believe, but in a rather good part of Hatfield.

Hatfield House is the most famously haunted building in the town and it has a fascinating history. It was formerly Hatfield Palace, built around 1485, and it originally belonged to the Bishops of Ely before Henry VIII exchanged it with them for other lands. It was convenient as a home for his children; the younger ones were educated at Hatfield. When Henry died, in 1547, the ten-year-old Edward VI was taken from Hatfield for his coronation in London, but he was only to live another six years before his half-sister Mary took the throne. During her reign Mary kept her young half-sister Elizabeth a virtual prisoner at Hatfield but eventually Mary was deposed and Elizabeth heard of her accession to the throne under the famous Hatfield Oak.

Queen Elizabeth the first's childhood things can be seen at Hatfield (when it is open to the public); her yellow silk stocking and her garden hat, as well as many of her letters are there, along with two famous portraits of the monarch.

Elizabeth's successor, James I, swapped the palace of Hatfield with Lord Burleigh's son Robert Cecil, the first Earl of Salisbury (who was the King's Chief Minister) for Theobald's, a Hertfordshire country house of legendary beauty which, alas, is no longer standing. In 1611 the first Lord Salisbury pulled down three sides of the medieval palace of Hatfield and built Hatfield House, the present palace, in what was then the most modern style. The cost of rebuilding was £38,000; a vast sum in those times and the Jacobean house was built in the shape of an E to commemorate Elizabeth's popularity. It was both extravagantly decorated and elegantly furnished and it boasted the most luxuriant gardens.

The Great Park of Hatfield House today has been restored to its former glory and is best visited in June if the roses are to be fully appreciated. The grand old house is owned nowadays by the 7th Marquess of Salisbury, ex-Conservative MP and former Leader of the House of Lords. Salisbury's fortune, estimated at some £250 million, makes him the richest man in Hertfordshire. His family company, Gascoyne Holdings, owns the Hippodrome nightclub, land in America, a London estate, two stately homes plus 10,300 acres as well as a vast and valuable art collection.

The Old Palace part of Hatfield House has a haunted passageway, where ghostly footsteps are heard, followed by the sound of a door opening then slow footsteps, indicative of a careful descent, down the stairs. On moonlit nights a shadowy woman's figure has been reported, passing through the Old Palace gateway, crossing Fore Street then entering the church.

In the main part of Hatfield House Queen Elizabeth I is rumoured to return in spirit form. The ghost of the first Marchioness was reported as recently as 1982 by both a visitor and a workman at the house. The dowager Marchioness was burnt to death in 1835, at the age of 85, after knocking over a candle in her bedroom, which started a blaze that destroyed the majority of the house's west wing. A certain 23-year-old Charles Dickens (later to become the famous author) was sent to Hatfield by the *Morning Chronicle* to cover the story. When alive the Marchioness was renowned for her hunting and gambling, which continued throughout her long life, and she would frequently travel to London in her coach, it is this same ghostly coach which is the best known and most impressive of the apparitions at the house. The phantom coach has been seen to appear at the gates, with its four black horses, before travelling at breakneck speed down the long drive and thundering on through the doors before continuing up the stairs where it dematerialises.

The University of Hertfordshire is based at its Hatfield campus, with other campuses at Hertford, St Albans and Watford. It has progressed a long way from being Hatfield Polytechnic to full university status. The Natural Sciences Facility has developed a strong reputation for its pharmacological work fuelled by Hertfordshire's position at the centre of the UK pharmaceutical industry. No doubt the next big development in the curriculum will be in favour of medicine, when the new super hospital, which is planned for Hatfield, is finally built. The Todd Building at the university is haunted, with several reports from night security staff of 'a misty figure' seen in the darkened, secure building and lights have been seen to turn themselves on and off.

Bush Hall House is a comfortable hotel in its own grounds on the edge of Hatfield that is popular for meetings and conferences. It was once home to Sir Robert Chester, who lived here in the early nineteenth century and was master of ceremonies to four different monarchs. There are persistent reports that he haunts his former home still, he is said to have appeared on the stairs and in various bedrooms. Another one of Hatfield's former residents drawn back to his lovely old home…

ESSENDON

Essendon village lies a couple of miles due east of Hatfield and is home to Camfield Place. I will never forget my first sighting of Camfield Place, an impressive, bright, white-painted, rambling Victorian mansion, surrounded by 500 acres, which stood alone on the hill amidst the surrounding green fields, overlooking a valley and the rise beyond it, so picturesque that it could have come straight out of a fairy tale and indeed it has inspired at least two authors who have lived here. The estate was in existence in Tudor times but the original building was demolished in 1867 to make way for the present rambling Victorian mansion. It has been home to two famous fiction writers, the first was Beatrix Potter, children's storyteller and creator of Peter Rabbit, who grew up at Camfield Place and spent most of her life here. She wrote the classic *Tales of Peter Rabbit* in the potting shed in the attractive gardens of this wonderful historic house. It was her grandfather who had the Victorian mansion built. The young Miss Potter said that one evening she had been sitting in the big lounge when she had suddenly felt very cold and one by one the candles unaccountably were extinguished, as if snuffed out by invisible fingers. The ghosts were said to haunt the hall and stairs and were known to have caused the young writer some fear.

In 1950 the romantic novelist Barbara Cartland, in real life Mrs Hugh McCorquodale, moved in with her husband, two sons and two dogs. A strong believer in the supernatural, Barbara's policy was to have the house blessed before she even moved in. This was in order to save any trouble with ghosts, and it seemed to work well until 1955. That year she had to put down her younger son's dog called Jimmy (a brown and white cocker spaniel with 'an attitude') after it developed a serious problem with its throat. She later noticed that her other dogs got jumpy at feeding time, responding to something that wasn't there by watching it and barking at it. One of the dogs, Murray, was particularly badly affected, he would back away from his food as if threatened by some invisible presence and even jump into the air and yelp as if being attacked. As time went on the 'ghost dog' (Jimmy) began to appear around the house. He was seen both by Miss Cartland and her maid, Miss Rose Purcell, lying in his favourite places. For some considerable time the other dogs continued to do battle for their food with the dead Cocker Spaniel's spirit.

Chapter Eleven

HERTFORD

Hertford is named after the Old English words *heorot* + *ford* meaning 'Ford frequented by harts or stags' and it achieved town status in the early 10th century when King Edward, son of King Alfred, had the stone castle built in this strategic spot where three Hertfordshire rivers meet – the Beane, Mimram and Lea. The Lea served as a medieval highway for people and produce between London and Hertford. After the Conquest, however, the town declined, decayed and reverted back to a village. The Normans used roads rather than rivers and so Ware, on the Great North Road, rose to prominence. There has been rivalry between the two towns ever since, with Hertford winning out eventually as county town but if you live in Hertfordshire, as I do, you have to declare for one or the other and I choose Hertford.

When I worked in Hertford County Town I got to know it quite well and discovered its charms by strolling its streets and alleys. The great outdoors lies all around the town, you can walk for miles through the flood plains. I particularly love the walk from Bull Plain, over the river bridge, along Folly Island beside the Lea and up past lovely old St Leonard's tiny Church at Bengeo, through the quiet woods and back down to the newly improved towpath into Hertford once more, via the open parkland. Hertford Castle now lies in ruins but it is a pleasant spot in the summer with its surrounding lawns and trees providing a relaxing ambience.

Hertford Town is full of interesting old buildings which lend the place so much contrast and character; they range from the solid Victorian family-owned McMullens brewery on the River Beane to the art deco styled listed building which was the former Addis plastic products factory. Then there are the many timber-framed, plastered and brick edifices of the 16th, 17th and 18th century houses, some small and pretty, others quite impressively grand, in the older parts of the town. Lombard House, near the river in Bull Plain, is one of many that I admire; it is the former home of Sir Henry Chauncy, Recorder of Hertford, this is where he wrote most of his County History of Hertfordshire in 1700. The house was built in the 16th century, the façade was added to in the 18th century and the house is now known as the Hertford Club, an excellent place for a meal or a relaxing game of snooker, but beware, the snooker room is haunted! Staff have reported the sounds of male conversation and laughter when the room has been unattended and snooker balls have been found scattered across the table as though a ghostly game has just been in progress. The phantom footsteps that are also heard when the place is empty have been attributed to 'old Henry' as the ghost is affectionately known in memory of the former historian. The Hertford Museum is not far away, housed in a 17th century building and well worth visiting but you may experience a chill in the air near the staircase and an uncomfortable feeling which has been reported by some people.

It has been said of the county town, 'Hertford is not an important town, as compared with other shire capitals.' This probably still holds true but it retains a strong identity despite 'relief roads' built in the 1960s which carve the town up to no good effect. The plentiful supply of water has meant that the area has long been associated with paper-making; Hertfordshire once boasted 20 paper mills in the 18th century. Thomas de la Rue, the company that printed banknotes, had a presence on one of the several industrial estates that edge the town. With paper-making went printing and Stephen Austin, which was founded in 1768, retains a print works in Hertford.

The county town of Hertford is another 'hot spot' for paranormal activity in Hertfordshire, much as Bedford is for Bedfordshire. Almost every corner of Hertford has a haunting and the most haunted street in this most haunted of towns is undoubtedly Fore Street. I worked for the charity Carers in Hertfordshire for nearly two years up till August 2004, and I was based at the Red House, a famously haunted house, at 119 Fore Street. It is over 400 years old and was once part of Christ's Hospital for the orphaned children of London. I was in the Red House on my own on a number of occasions, with not the slightest trace of anything paranormal ever occurring although I was on my guard for any trace of the former tray-bearing matron said to haunt the top floor staircase.

Just along the street at number 63–65 is Albany Radio, where I bought an excellent Miele washing machine and was delighted with the service I received when it was installed for me. I learned that the shop used to be a private house called Cupboard Hall and a woman who had lived there had her own ghostly experience when she awoke one night to find a lady dressed in fine clothes of the Georgian era.

On the corner of Fore Street is the Cafe Uno, which I know well, it is one of several dozen good bars and restaurants in the town centre, but this place also has a sinister reputation. Trouble started when the building was altered by shop fitters who converted the musty old charity shop into a new and trendy café. It was as if 'something' unseen objected to the radical changes to the structure and one phenomenon involved pieces of timber which were seen being moved across the room, but not by any human agency. Wires that had been clipped to the ceiling were unaccountably discovered ripped out of their clips and left dangling and bricks were found to have been moved overnight from where they had originally been left. A weird mist was also seen to rise up out of the basement. The staff bore the brunt of the haunting though, the women who worked here refused point blank to use their own 'ladies', preferring instead to walk to the public toilets, such was the intense feeling of evil surrounding the area. 'Marching shadows' on the walls were reported one night, and one day a cleaner, who was working alone on the second floor, was startled to hear a thunderous crash from downstairs, but when he investigated it no explanation for the noisy din could be found.

Threshers wine store is another Fore Street shop with a story to tell, it has been home to various wine merchants since 1933. Staff have often opened up the shop for work in the morning to discover a tap turned fully on and water pouring onto the floor despite the place being locked and unoccupied overnight. The cellar is reputedly a 'chilling place' that makes some people very uncomfortable. The strangest story of all concerns the loud crash that was heard by staff in the bottle store and on checking six bottles were found on the floor, tidily arranged into the shape of a star.

On the other side of Fore Street is Marshall's Furnishings where you can pick up a video about the hauntings of Hertford that was made some years ago, it features interesting re-enactments of well-known true local ghostly encounters. In 1996 the store had its own ghostly happening to report after a major fire in the warehouse at the back of the shop left the building vulnerable to looters. A police presence was maintained throughout the night of the 30th September by a woman police constable. During her solitary vigil she looked up at one of the windows to see a man with long curly black hair and a moustache looking back down at her. The WPC called for back-up but when some colleagues arrived and searched the place they could find no sign of anyone in the ruined building yet the policewoman remained convinced about what she saw. In recent years certain people have sensed a presence in the storeroom and it has been described as that of a 46-year-old man, but no further details have been revealed.

Also active in 1996 was yet another Fore Street spirit, a most communicative one as it turned out, which made its presence known at Sheffield's the Chemist. It started in May of that year when the pharmacist suffered an unnerving communication. He heard a knocking in the floor and wherever he moved to in the room the knocking followed him. Pat Blake, a staff member, was very forthcoming with details of the haunting. A bottle of Paracol D, a preparation for diabetes sufferers, travelled along the passage and smashed on the ground in front of startled witnesses before a shelf noisily crashed to the floor. One day there was an apport (when a physical object appears from nowhere and without any explanation. Often, as in this case, apports will be relevant to the spirit that delivered it and may give a clue as to its identity). It was a bottle of strychnine which 'came out of thin air and dropped to the floor without smashing', according to Pat. Interestingly this is classed as poison today but in times past it was used as a medicine. As well as an apport there was an asport (when a physical object suddenly, completely and inexplicably vanishes). One of the two hundred year-old prescription books was discovered on a toilet seat, opened at a particular page but the next day it had gone. Pat said that she asked out loud 'Can we have our book back?' and about an hour later it literally appeared through the wall and fell to the floor with a bang. But the strangest thing was it was still open at the page it had been open at before. 'It was like it was trying to tell us something.' By now Pat had established a means of communicating with the spirit; it would rap once for yes and twice for no. This was a case worthy of investigation by the Society for Psychical Research but when Pat tried to contact them stamps disappeared and the phone went dead when she tried to ring them so she tried the direct approach again with the spirit. 'One day I asked it if it had a story to tell and it tapped out yes.' A code of letters and knocks was worked out and eventually a message was deciphered by Pat, 'it had been killed by its brother in order to inherit the business.' With the successful communication the activity seemed to disappear...

On the same side of Fore Street as Marshall's, but up at the junction with Bell Lane, stands the attractive old Salisbury Arms Hotel which is home to more than one ghost. It is claimed that Bedroom 6 is haunted, the corridor is reputedly visited by a 'Cromwellian figure' and on the first floor a middle-aged man dressed in black has been seen to enter a small room and supposedly disappear.

Wiggintons toy shop is one of Hertford's most haunted locations, a building with over 500 years' history behind it. Many customers have sensed a presence in the upstairs room, which used to be a bedroom, and the proprietor's daughter Jane used to sleep in this back bedroom and often saw the ghost of a Victorian lady at night, who would stroke her brow while a feeling of love surrounded her, so she was never frightening. A man with white hair and a beard, wearing a morning suit, also stood at the end of the bed sometimes. A psychic investigator, the late Graham Wylie, who presented the film about the Hertford hauntings said, 'Immediately I entered the haunted room, I went cold. This indicates there is a presence here.

There is a feeling of grief in the room. A young lady nursed her dying father here, hence Jane's experience of the hand across the brow.' Graham had the impression of a benevolent spirit but in the attic store room there was something completely different. Dogs stay at the bottom of the stairs leading up there, growling and whining at an unseen intruder. I have always found dogs to be an unfailing 'paranormal barometer' in my investigations into haunted places. They are all psychically sensitive and will often react by refusing to enter rooms, by watching invisible entities moving around a room and by barking, snarling or growling a challenge to them. If in any doubt as to whether a place is haunted or not it pays to bring along a canine companion! Jane Holt also refused to go up there and Graham Wylie picked up distinctly negative energy, he was quite unequivocal, 'There is something nasty and evil in this room; I can't wait to get out. I got a choking feeling in my throat as soon as I entered. I feel it was about 1750 and a young man, on the run for murder and feeling the net closing in around him, came up here to hang himself from one of the beams, thus cheating the gallows. It is the evilness of this man's actions for taking another's life that remains in this room.'

Before they removed to new offices at the former Addis factory site, staff at the *Hertfordshire Mercury* recounted some strange experiences at their old premises near Fore Street. Hard-headed journalists like Gary Mathews admitted to paranormal encounters at their previous offices. One Christmas Gary was working alone late one night. 'I suddenly became aware of the lights flashing on and off. I checked my computer screen and that was OK, so I knew it wasn't the power. Then I heard the door handle moving and when I looked over at the door, the handle was indeed moving up and down.' He went to check the building to make sure no one was playing a prank, but the building was empty. As he returned to his seat the lights went out completely then came on once more and the door handle started moving again so Gary made a hasty exit.

Mike Poultney was another newspaperman who had a weird encounter when he had been working at the *Mercury* and was just locking up one Sunday. There was the noise of a door slamming above him, so he called the police as he thought it might be an intruder. A policeman arrived with a large black Alsatian and together they thoroughly searched the premises, the dog was even sent into the cellar to make sure nobody was hiding there. After a matter of minutes the badly frightened dog began frantically scratching at the door to be let out then tore out of the cellar with all its hair standing on end. They continued searching and came to an office which had a bunch of keys in the door lock, which were swinging as if someone had just closed the door. The policeman rushed into the room only to find it empty, he left the building soon afterwards with his dog. It subsequently turned out that the cellar had a reputation for being haunted – by the ghost of a kitchen maid who had been murdered long ago by the butler. Another story suggests that a machine operator died one Friday afternoon upstairs in what later became the newspaper offices.

The offices at County Hall in Hertford are extremely impressive, they are set in extensive tree-lined grounds and inside there are sweeping staircases, huge windows, high ceilings and cavernous rooms with portraits on the walls and plenty of solid wood and deep carpets. I attended a committee meeting there once and we needed the individual microphones to communicate with each other in the vastness of one of the council chambers.

So far as I know no ghosts haunt the interior of the main buildings but there is a haunted house in the grounds. This is Leahoe House, built in the mid 19th century for a medical man, Dr George Elin and acquired by Hertfordshire County Council in 1935 as a recreation and leisure centre. In the 1980s a volunteer worker called Tony Joshua reported a close encounter of the paranormal kind. He was locking up and as he walked through the snooker room he felt an unaccustomed and unaccountable fear stealing over him. He continued into the corridor and his eyes were drawn to the top of the stairs, where he saw a woman standing there wearing a long skirt and nun's habit. The fear was replaced by a feeling of great calm and he stared in fascination for some time before finally switching off the lights and as he turned to leave he saw that the nun was still there. On subsequent occasions Tony felt the nun's presence but never again did he see her.

Railway Street is a former slum area of Hertford and this is where Pearce's baker's shop can be found; many is the hot snack I have taken away from here in my lunchtimes, so I was surprised to learn that this friendly little shop had a ghostly reputation. Pictures fell off the counter for no reason and items would mysteriously fall from shelves. Sheila Woodford is one staff member whose experiences have been quoted – 'We're not allowed to smoke down there (the cellar) yet there's the distinct smell of cigars sometimes. I get a cold shiver when I have to go down there, it gives me the creeps.'

Mike Sage, who currently lives in Fishers Green Stevenage, told me that he lived, for three years, in the old Post Office in Ware Road, opposite the police station, in what is now the Value Centre shop. This was nearly 30 years ago yet he remembered his time there all too clearly. One room in the house always seemed damp, always seemed cold, at all times of the year. This was the main bedroom over the shops where his cat's fur used to stand on end, it was obviously terrified of the room and it would always run away from it. Although it was the biggest bedroom the awful atmosphere meant that Mike didn't use it, preferring to get a good night's sleep in the smaller bedroom but he still heard odd thumps and bumps from the haunted room. Mike later learned that a former postmaster who had lived there had got into terrible debt in the late 1960s and he had also been a very heavy drinker. One day he put a shotgun to his wife's head, dismembered their cat and used a revolver to shoot himself in the head.

In January 2005 a reporter from the *Guardian* visited Hertford and got talking to a young lady called Gemma, who was the manager of the Monsoon shop, they were discussing the rumour that there was a tunnel under the building. She insisted that there was no tunnel beneath the shop, 'Just the store room – but it's definitely haunted. When we have our sales meetings there you can hear someone walking over our heads, or doing the vacuuming. But upstairs, the shop's closed and empty.' Yet another site to add to the long list of haunted Hertford properties...

Chapter Twelve

HODDESDON

The Domesday Book mentions 'Hodesdone' or 'Hill of a man called Hod'. The name of Hoddesdon is inextricably linked with the notorious Rye House Plot of 1683, when the Earl of Essex, the first Duke of Monmouth, the first Earl of Shaftesbury, Baron William Russell of Bedfordshire and Algernon Sidney (the last two were executed for high treason) were implicated in a plan to assassinate King Charles II and the Duke of York (the future James II) at Rye House. Historians believe, however, that the plot probably involved far less prominent men and served as an excuse to dispose of the King's perceived enemies.

The town of Hoddesdon prospered, as it was on the Great North Road (later to become the A10) and many inns sprang up here to cater to weary travellers, as late as 1900 there were some 22 of them! Hoddesdon was a malting town with its own large brewery – Christie's Brewery (which closed in the 1920s), as well as being home to a popular market (a charter was granted in the 13th century). One of its most illustrious residents was James McAdam, the engineer who improved Britain's roads with his invention of 'tarmac', who lived here from 1825 for the last ten years or so of his life.

A phantom policeman has been reported at Holy Cross Hill, Hoddesdon, on a number of occasions. He stood in the middle of the road then vanished in front of startled motorists' eyes. The best documented sighting dates from the 1960s, when a couple stopped on seeing the authoritative figure in the road, illuminated by their headlights. They were convinced enough by his reality to wind down the window (no electric windows in those days!) only to see him fade away. They managed to get a good look at him before he disappeared, however, and later recalled that there had been something strange about his uniform – it had been distinctly old-fashioned looking.

Guy Playfair is an authority on poltergeists, having been one of the two main investigators of the famous Enfield poltergeist case. He was also part of a team of paranormal investigators who held a vigil at a pub, The George III, at Hoddesdon in 1982. The team was brought in after shelves had inexplicably collapsed, doors had been opened by invisible hands, ornaments were mysteriously broken, machines switched themselves on and off and the landlord's dog had refused to go anywhere near the cellar.

BRICKENDON

Due west of Hoddesdon is Brickendon village, sited around a large green which has five oaks, each one planted to commemorate either a coronation or a jubilee of five sovereigns, from Queen Victoria to our own Queen Elizabeth II. There is a village hall called Fanshaws Room, formerly a barn that belonged to Fanshaws Farm and there is a pub near the green, called the Farmer's Boy, scene of a haunting, but more of that later. The parish is known as the Brickendon Liberty, so called because Henry II gave to the ancient manor liberty from certain taxes around 1184. There are some fascinating mansions in the area, like Brickendonbury House, about a mile and a half to the north of the village, which I have had the pleasure of visiting on several occasions. It has an intriguing past, having been originally built on a moated site where Roman coins and pottery have been unearthed. At one time the lands belonged to Waltham Abbey, they were given to the church by King Harold around 1062, before his death at the Battle of Hastings and monks farmed the estate, then after the Dissolution the monastery and the manor of Brickendon were bought by Thomas Knighton of Bayford. The present Brickendonbury House was built by the Clarke family in the early 18th century and later became the property of the Morgan family. They gave their name to the splendid avenue of trees which stretch for almost three-quarters of a mile in length, lining the approach to the house from the Hertford side – Morgan's Walk. During the Second World War the mansion was used as a training base for secret agents of the Special Operations Executive and presently houses the laboratories of the Malaysian Rubber Producers Research Association.

Fanshaws mansion is home to the Institute of the Motor Industry and the estate at Bayford houses the ecology and astronomy centres of Hatfield University.

Blackfield Farm was the scene of a notorious 'supernatural' hoax in 1920, when a crowd of several hundred would gather at the farm, hoping for evidence of life after death. The fake 'spirit communications through rapping' fooled a large amount of people at the time, including villagers, local Councillor Mr Searles, national and local newspaper reporters and even the famous writer and Spiritualist Sir Arthur Conan Doyle himself. It emerged, many years later, that the young girl, Dorothy White, who was the focus of the so-called poltergeist activity, had colluded with her brother, Norton, in producing supposed 'phantom rapping noises' by means of wires, hidden in the front garden, which ran into the house!

The Farmer's Boy case, by way of contrast, is a genuine haunting with ghostly happenings reported in almost every part of the old inn; staff have witnessed the complete repertoire of manifestations associated with haunted pubs, including beer pumps turned off and beer kegs rearranged in the cellar overnight, objects moved around the kitchen and things falling off the walls. It has sometimes been impossible to open the dessert freezer as though there was a great weight on the lid, keeping it firmly shut. Staff became used to asking the spirit, believed to be a small girl, to remove itself from the freezer then they could open it once more.

Knocking has been heard from one of the pub bedrooms and sounds as of someone trying to enter it, also a figure was seen to pass through the wall of this same room. One girl who worked here claimed to have been waiting outside when she saw the lights go on in the pub, but everyone was in bed at the time. Then she saw a stranger, a man in his 40s with dark scruffy hair, take a drink from the optics before coming to the window, where he stared intently at her, whereupon she quickly drove off in her car!

Chapter Thirteen

SAWBRIDGEWORTH

The origins of the unusual name of this small Hertfordshire town may be traced back to 1086 and the Domesday Book reference, when it was known as Sabrixteworde, meaning 'Enclosure (later in Old English called *worth*) of a man called Saebeorht'. It was once dependent for its prosperity on the River Stort, with its associated industries of malting and milling, but Sawbridgeworth today is a shopping town for well-to-do local villagers from places like Much Hadham, Green Tye and Standon. There can be little doubt that the town's most famous and exotic residents live at 'Beckingham Palace' – as David and Victoria Beckham's palatial home on the outskirts of the town is known to one and all, but so far no news that it is haunted…

Haunted Hyde Hall hit the headlines in the 1980s when it was the home of the singer Suzie Quatro, who was convinced that her home hosted a spirit called Richard, 'the ghost of the guest room' and a little girl's ghost was also said to wander the house. Hyde Hall is now a girls' school but once it belonged to Sir John Jocelyn, an eccentric Nonconformist in a land of Quakers, who was Lord of the Manor. He insisted that he be buried along with his favourite horse in the churchyard and argued with the local Vicar, who refused this bizarre request to bury both man and animal in consecrated ground. Sir John's will stipulated that he be buried, instead, without a coffin or shroud and his horse should be slaughtered and buried with him, in the grounds of his home. In November 1741 Sir John died, childless, and as per his instructions he was buried in a circle of yew trees on the avenue leading to the Hall, without benefit of any stone or memorial. History does not tell us however, if the knight's steed was interred with him… His ghost was later seen galloping along the avenue near the church on his beloved charger.

Bell Street gained a brief notoriety in the mid 1990s from the old flat above a shop that had once been three cottages thought to date back to the 17th century. The occupier, elderly Freda Byers, claimed to share her accommodation with four ghosts! One was a little boy with a wound over one eye, two were women in Romany garb and the last was an unknown wild animal. These visitations were regular, always in the afternoons and in the same room over a period of two months and they left the old lady quite mystified as to who were her spectral visitors and why they had appeared to her. It is not uncommon for very old people to report strange apparitions before they themselves pass over – were these spirit guides or messengers, bringing a warning of impending death?

Warren Farm provided an intriguing sighting, by a man driving to work, this incident was also reported in the mid 1990s. Standing by the roadside, close to the farm's front gate, was the apparition of an American pilot, wearing his flying clothes. The airman was also seen by the man's wife and the couple claimed several sightings of the mystery flyer on their regular drives while commuting. Attempts to put a name to the ghost proved interesting, it was discovered that on the 3rd April 1943 an American pilot was killed when his P47c Thunderbolt fighter crashed after engine failure, in a field near Green Tye. The pilot's name was Lieutenant Smolensky – did the couple encounter his spirit more than fifty years after his fatal accident?

A few miles south of Sawbridgeworth lies the village of Gilston and its local, The Plume of Feathers is a pub which has a seriously spooky reputation. The inn looks out over Pye Corner, at the crossing point of three roads, where executions were carried out at the gallows which stood on this spot. In the event of bad weather the public hangings were alleged to have taken place upstairs at the inn itself. In recent times an electrician who was working in the attic suddenly fled the building looking terrified. He would not, or could not, tell about what he had experienced in the roof space of the pub. Down in the bar glasses have mysteriously been moved and a fruit machine has been found in the middle of the room when nobody was around to move it away from the wall where it is usually located. Locals refuse to use one seat by the fireplace due to 'a strange atmosphere'. There is a story that a stagecoach pulled up one particularly cold night at the inn with a dead passenger on board who had frozen to death. Attempts were made to revive him by sitting him next to the fire, but it was too late for the unfortunate traveller. Were the man's last thoughts fixed on The Plume of Feathers, his only hope of salvation on the long, cold journey that night, and did he leave a part of his spirit forever lingering at his final destination?

Raban Court, Baldock   (Vicki O'Dell)
A Baldock landmark – where ghostly aromas of tobacco have recently been reported.

Ashridge Manor House, Little Gaddesdon   (Vicki O'Dell)
Home to the ghost of William Jarman?

Lady Anne Grimston's grave at St Peter's Churchyard, Tewin   (Vicki O'Dell)
Evidence of life after death?

Henrick's Hairdressers, Royston   (Mark Head)
Note the light in the top left hand window (not visible when this picture was taken) and the orb
(up and to the extreme right in the photo). The ghost of William Armatage claimed
responsibility for causing the light effect.

The International University (formerly The Royal Masonic School) Bushey   (Vicki O'Dell)
Tragic Hillary Sinclair is one of the child ghosts that haunt this former school.

All Saints Church, Datchworth   (Damien O'Dell)
Shadowy figures and strange chattering sounds have been reportedly seen and heard here.

Hitchin Priory   (Mark Head)
Ghostly inhabitants include a grey lady, a Cavalier, Roman soldiers and Carmelite monks.

St Albans Cathedral   (Vicki O'Dell)
Invisible choirs and restless Benedictine monks are part of the fabric of the building.

Chapter Fourteen

WARE

Ware is mentioned in the Domesday Book as Waras, or 'The Weirs', derived from the Old English 'waer'. Ware long enjoyed strong trade links with London as a malting town, in the mid-eighteenth century there were seventy malthouses supplying London as well as many local Hertfordshire breweries. Surprisingly the most widely-known haunting in the area does not involve old maltings, nor even an alehouse, but a most unusual haunted bed…

SLEEP TIGHT

When I think of Ware hauntings I always think first of Ware's unique origin – home to the most haunted bed in Britain… Carpenter Jonas Fosbrooke, in 1463, so it is said, created a bed fit for a king, in this case King Edward IV, to whom he presented the Great Bed of Ware as it became known. It certainly was great in every way, measuring almost eleven feet square with posts eight feet high and having a richly engraved bedstead, it was described as a 'rare specimen'. In grateful recognition of the gift the King supposedly granted the carpenter a pension for life. The bed was intended for the sole use of 'princes or nobles of gentle blood to sleep in', but when Edward's son disappeared from the Tower of London the bed was sold and it was to pass through many changes of ownership.

Certainly the Great Bed of Ware became famous, even being mentioned in Shakespeare's *Twelfth Night* and in the 16th century it was the property of the Lord of Ware Manor, Thomas Fanshaw, the alternative history being that it was actually built for him in the first place, around 1500, before being sold again in 1575 and travelling around Ware's inns, where it was reputedly shared one festival night by twelve married couples when the inn was full. It is not recorded if they had a restful night, they would certainly have spent an overcrowded one, for this bed was haunted and others who tried to find sleep in the Great Bed of Ware were pinched and scratched so badly that they ended up seeking an alternative place to retire. Harrison Saxby, Master of the Horse to King Henry VIII didn't take the warnings seriously and was reportedly found next morning, covered in bruises and exhausted, on the floor beside the bed. It was assumed that Jonas Fosby's malevolent spirit was responsible for disturbing the sleep of those he felt unworthy of using the bed he had created for kings and princes. These ghostly intrusions were acknowledged by guests at the inns, who customarily drank a toast to Jonas and his bed before they themselves sought repose for the night.

And so the Great Bed moved around and it was, at various times, in the Bull, the Crown, the George and finally the Saracen's Head, where it was put up for sale in 1864. By then it was much defaced, by dates and initials which had been carved into the woodwork, before 1864 when it was bought by the owner of Rye House (near Hoddesdon, Hertfordshire). Its new home was to be the alehouse in the Rye house pleasure gardens and many thousands of visitors saw it before its removal, in 1931, to the Victoria and Albert Museum in South Kensington, London, where it has remained ever since and it continues to be one of the top tourist attractions here.

TAVERN TALES

The busy A10 London to Cambridge road was an ideal situation for a coaching inn and a little way north of Ware, at Wadesmill, the Prince's Arms, which dated back to 1615, did a roaring trade in the seventeenth century. In 1670 it changed its name to the Feathers Inn, as it is still known to this day. This attractive, ivy-clad old tavern holds a secret – it is haunted by the ghost of a fair-haired child, said to have been a young girl who was run over by a London-bound stagecoach, for even in those far off days travelling by road was not without its dangers.

HAUNTED HOUSES AROUND WARE

Local people still talk about the New Road haunting which happened in recent years. A family living there was subjected to the familiar ghostly routines, with taps being turned on and doors being opened without human assistance as well as the inevitable phantom footsteps being heard on the stairs.

Another haunting is at Amwellbury House, it has a reputation for monkish antics, with cowled figures seen in the grounds and chanting heard inside the building.

High Cross, just north of Ware up the A10, featured in the *Hertfordshire Mercury* in March 1995, when paranormal activity was reported at a private house. This included dogs barking at some invisible entity and objects disappearing, but strangest of all was the photograph taken of a mirror in the kitchen. The image that was captured here appeared to show a skull and a caped man. Many psychics believe that mirrors act as portals to the spirit world and ghosts can and do use them to materialise in our world…

THE GHOSTS OF FANHAMS HALL

A Short History of the Hall:

Fanhams probably derives its name locally, from Brandefanhams, by which title it was known circa 1420, when it was no more than a cluster of farm buildings. The Old English 'Brande' was used in the Middle Ages to describe blighted or infertile land or crops. Fanhams is also Old English, used to refer to fen or marshland, while 'ham' was commonly a contraction for 'home' or 'homestead'. The original farm may have been built on fenland which was cleared by burning the scrub vegetation it supported. A date of 1412 is carved on a brick at the house; but in England brick making only began to revive slowly during the beginning of the fifteenth century, after dying out with the Romans' departure, so it is most unlikely that valuable bricks would have been used in the construction of an obscure farmhouse. The date is likely to be a later commemoration of the supposed antiquity of the original farm.

The next major reference to Fanhams is in 1651, when John Nash, yeoman of Ware, is recorded in possession of the property. He died in 1663, when William Weld, 'gentleman', of Widberry Hill, Hertfordshire, purchased the estate. It is possible that Weld built the first brick house on the site, another brick bears the date 1666 and when he died, in 1699, Fanham was sold for a vast sum – £1,810.15s.0d. The buyer was John Evans, cloth maker and citizen of London. The Queen Anne house that he had built here was to stand for nearly 200 years. In 1715 he commissioned John Lane of London to survey and value his estate at Ware. Lane produced a coloured map of Fanhams Hall, showing the two-storey Queen Anne house with its impressive central chimney (a third storey was added, circa 1800). The frontage would have stretched from the present lounge to the dining room door in White Hall, but little remains now, save for the elegant White Hall staircase and an old metal bell-pull in a wall in the courtyard.

While the house was taking shape a garden and orchards were planted, the garden still exists, dominated by quince and medlar trees – varieties quite rare these days – but there are also figs, peach, nectarine, walnuts, mulberries and morello cherry to add colour and variety. The paths that wind through the garden were only added last century; using bricks from an original wall that used to conceal the garden from the house and about this time the pleached lime alleys were set out around what used to be a tennis court, but is now the croquet lawn.

John Evans died intestate, in 1729, and the property, now known officially as Fanhams Hall, passed to his younger brother, George, who died here in 1747, also without leaving any will. First his cousin Elizabeth Phelps inherited and later her son George Phelps who sold it in 1771, for £4,000, to the immensely wealthy and influential William Plumer of New Place, Gilston.

Described as 'one of the most opulent country gentlemen in the kingdom besides possessing the most extensive property of any gentleman in this country, his additional estates in Essex, Middlesex and Suffolk make up a clear income of fifteen thousand pounds per annum' by *The English Chronicle* of 1781, Plumer was not so lucky in love. He became, at 27, MP for Lewes in 1763 and represented the Sussex town until 1768, when he represented Hertfordshire right up to 1807 and then finally Higham Ferrers, from 1812 to his death in 1822. Sadly the wife he married in 1760 died a mere seventeen months later. His second marriage, to his cousin (and thirty years his junior), Jane Hamilton, the grand-daughter of the 7th Earl of Abercorn, was a disaster. Gradually she took over the administration of his estates which she proceeded to mismanage. Plumer didn't stay at Fanhams Hall, preferring to reside at his house in Gilston, so the farmland was let out to local farmers, while the house was occupied by tenants of independent means, as was common in the eighteenth and nineteenth centuries. The grand old man of Whig politics was completely under the sway of his young wife and when he died, aged 86, he left her all his considerable array of worldly goods. Jane Plumer promptly put Fanhams Hall up for auction. It was purchased by a prominent citizen of Ware, Samuel Adams, barge owner and banker on 31st October, 1822. In 1834 Adams died and the estate was inherited by his son, also called Samuel, who continued the family barge business but also set up as a maltster in Ware. He had the estate, including over 138 acres of land, valued in 1847 – it had a worth of £6,750. When Samuel passed away in 1850 his heir, Thomas Bell Adams, put the estate up for auction but it didn't finally sell until 1859. Once again its new owner, astute businessman Henry Page, who had accumulated a substantial fortune as a maltster, didn't live there, preferring to let it out instead.

The great house saw some improvements in the early 1870s, by Henry Page on behalf of his daughter, Anne Elizabeth, who had married Lieutenant Richard Benyon Croft in 1869. This bluff, outspoken Royal Navy officer with over ten years' experience had seen service in the West Indies and China. Born in 1843 he could trace his family's roots back to Croft in Hertfordshire, which place gained a mention in the Domesday Book. After his marriage he resigned his commission to join his father-in-law's malting business, of which he eventually became head. Croft became a local celebrity, involving himself in local affairs and occupying Fanhams Hall until his death in 1912. He was elected to the Ware Board of Guardians, to Councillor for the Ware division of the Hertfordshire County Council and, in 1892 he was made High Sheriff of Hertfordshire. One of his passions was education and he was largely responsible for creating the Ware Grammar School for boys. He was Chairman of the Board of Governors and was made an Alderman in 1906.

In March 1900 Anne Elizabeth Croft commissioned estimates for the complete rebuilding of Fanhams Hall. The architect chosen was Mr W. Wood Bethell and the builder was a local man, Mr Thomas Hunt. Bethell's design was in the Jacobean style, with extensive alterations and additions for the structure of the property and its complete encasement with stone from the Stancliffe Estates Quarry at Darley Dale. One of the hallmarks of Bethell's style was minute attention to detail; he even drew up designs for the individual hinges, door latches and grates used in the building. Most of the interior work, including the beautiful Italian walnut panelling with its inlaid mother-of-pearl in the lounge, the oak panelling in the Minstrel's Gallery, the tiled fireplace in the Great Hall and the elaborate plaster ceilings, as in the Long Gallery, are the work of Lawrence L. Turner.

During 1900 and 1901, while the house took shape, Anne Elizabeth Croft concentrated on the redevelopment and improvement of the gardens. Being particularly interested in Japanese culture she entrusted a Mr Inaka to draw up designs for a traditional, beautiful and delicate, Japanese Shin garden, one of the three main types of Japanese garden designs. His plans set out an elaborate and undulating landscape with hills, waterfalls and lakes, each physical feature having some intrinsic significance in its relationship to the others. Mr Inaka called the garden Koraku, after a famous garden in Tokyo. The word Koraku recalls a Japanese saying which translates as 'Start worrying before others, and afterwards rejoice in the advantages of foresight!'

Professor Suzuki and two professional gardeners were given responsibility for creating Mr Inaka's vision. Every year before the start of the First World War they came over from Japan to spend the summer months in the 'Jap cottage' (now demolished), tending and expanding their horticulture, much of which can still be seen today. This includes the tea-house, Sei-shin-tei (House of the Pure Heart), sent over from Japan and erected in 1900; Kitsune-ike (Fox Lake) crossed by Shin-Kyo (Spirit Bridge), the mound known as Fuji-Yama (the soil for which was taken from the large lake in the garden) and the 'Small House' which represents a Shinto shrine. The bamboo fence which originally surrounded the garden has disappeared.

Other improvements were made to the gardens, The Queen Anne Garden was restocked and the shape of the lime alleys was improved by the addition of numerous young lime trees. Variety was added to the banks of the lake in the shape of the Austrian House, purchased at the 1900 Paris Exhibition. An Italian garden was planted in 1905, which contains some fine specimens of roses, particularly Paul's Scarlet Climber.

Once the house was completed Mrs Croft turned her attention to its furnishings, a vast number of illustrated Dutch tiles were incorporated into the new house. The Arts & Crafts Movement is represented by Morris & Co's stained glass window and tapestry curtains.

All eight of the Croft children (two sons and six daughters) were brought up at Fanhams Hall. Their father, Richard Benyon Croft died in January 1912 and their mother died nine months later. The estate then passed on to the second son, Henry Page Croft, who was educated at Eton and Cambridge. After completing his education Henry entered his father's firm as a partner and married Nancy Borwick, daughter of Sir Robert Borwick, of Berkeley Square, London, in 1907. A few years later he became a Conservative MP and was eventually created the first Lord Croft.

The history of Fanhams during the 1930s and 1940s, however, is associated with Lord Croft's third sister, Anne Page Croft, who married Charles Alexander Nall-Cain, First Baron Brockett of Brockett Hall. She lived for a number of years at her husband's ancestral home at Welwyn, but was determined to return to her roots at Fanhams Hall, where she remained until her death in 1949 (her brother Lord Croft died two years earlier). Anne inherited her mother's passion for the gardens and took great pleasure in opening them to the public during certain summer days, so that all could enjoy their beauty.

During the war years Lady Brockett shared her house with many young people, as it served as a hospital. The Cheyne Hospital for Children evacuated its charges to convalesce at Fanhams, around 1941, under the care of Matron Miss E.M. Price, SRN. The military also had a small presence at the Hall, as documented at the Hertfordshire Records Office and Ware Museum; we know that the RASC (Royal Army Service Corps) had a supply depot and administration unit (in the basement area to one wing, which was out of bounds to the Hall's employees).

With Lady Brockett's death, the days of Fanhams Hall as a private residence effectively ended. The cost of running a building this size was now prohibitive, and her heir, Major R.A. Page Croft, decided to sell the property and auction the contents, which were sold in 1950. The building was sold to the Westminster Bank, who turned it into a staff training centre. During the 1960s a number of alterations were carried out, including the demolition of the old stables, harness room and loose boxes in 1965, so that a two-storey accommodation block could be built on the site. In 1971 Fanhams Hall was purchased by The Building Societies Association, who in turn sold it to J. Sainsbury PLC in February 1986.

The Haunting:

The ghosts of Fanhams Hall are particularly interesting because of the variety of their manifestations, they are sometimes seen, at other times heard, touched and even smelt! Not only that but they include partial apparitions and full-body apparitions. On a bitterly cold day in February 2005 I had a chat with some of the staff who have worked at Fanhams Hall over a period of many years and none of them are in any doubt as to the authenticity of the hauntings. Christine is a cleaner here, and has worked at the Hall for sixteen years and is an authority on the ghostly activities. Just last Christmas, after a party, she was staying the night with some friends. They complained about the noise – 'a lot of running about, up and down, by someone in high heels'. There had been nobody occupying the rooms above them, in the almost deserted Hall, at that (usually) quiet time of year.

Christine explained that one of the 'hot spots' for the hauntings definitely seems to be around rooms 205 to 212. Some three or four years ago a lady called Joy Lyons was staying in room number 207, while on a pre-retirement course. She was certain that she had heard music next door and thought that someone had left their radio on. It turned out that the next door rooms were unoccupied, but in times gone by, directly above 207, there had been a music room. In the corridor outside, both a cleaner and a conference delegate had reported seeing a reflection in the mirror of 'something' that wasn't actually there.

Some years back, at the time of the eclipse of the moon, Christine had an eerie experience in the drawing room while she was alone, first she had felt someone behind her then next instant she felt freezing cold hands around her neck, but on turning round she saw an empty room. Another cleaner, Betty, had reported an odd encounter to Christine; she had clearly seen, reflected in the mirror on the main staircase, a figure reminiscent of Guinevere, with long, flowing dress and a large pointed hat. Christine has also heard in the same area, of the main staircase, the sound of children crying. 'It seems to be coming from under the stairs, near the library.'

Upstairs, in the corridor near rooms 205–212, Christine has heard talking when nobody else is in sight, it's always indistinct and the words can't be made out. One word has been clear though; Christine has heard her own name called out, quietly, when nobody else is about...

Shirley is another cleaner who has worked at Fanhams Hall for a long time, she has had some fascinating poltergeist experiences, although she remains quite phlegmatic about them, they don't frighten her in the slightest. She recalled working in the Hitchin Conference Room, eight years ago when she noticed her polish sliding across a perfectly level table, all by itself, onto the floor. She replaced it only for the same occurrence to be repeated for a second and then a third time. As she was locking up the room her hair was pulled, hard, from behind by an invisible hand... Shirley has noticed that weird things happen in the Long Gallery, particularly when she feels a bit down or unwell. On one notable occasion, as she turned to look back into a room where she had been setting things up for a meeting, on the large u-shaped table all the notepads and pens were crazily spinning around on the table.

Probably Shirley's most spectacular encounter with the ghosts of Fanhams Hall happened one evening, around 7pm, when she had laid out a table for 58 people, hearing a tinkling noise she returned to the room to witness all 58 glasses hovering about six inches above the table! At the same time she felt an extreme chill, 'like a cold blanket round me.' She is also one of the witnesses to 'the grey lady' who haunts the main staircases and wears a short, grey cap and a big grey dress. The lady leans over the banisters as though looking for someone or something. Shirley has had a couple of sightings, the most recent about a year ago. There are other apparitions that she has come across, like the man in the Long Gallery, who looks out into the gardens. He wears a waistcoat and observers only ever see the top half of him, he is never seen as a full-body apparition. Shirley's one-time manager, James, was always dismissive of her reports, until he went up to the Long Gallery alone one time – and got quite a fright – it felt, he said, as he entered the Long Gallery, 'as though people were rushing towards me.' The Long Gallery is also host to phantom aromas – a strong smell of tobacco smoke is inexplicably detected here and in the Knebworth and Welwyn Rooms.

As Shirley was wheeling her trolley along to room 15, she looked up as 'a lady passed me, wearing a cream coloured dress, with brown markings on it, she had dark hair and I followed her as she went into room 15, but when I checked I found the door locked, so I opened up room 15 but it was quite empty.' This happened in broad daylight just last year – she had seen yet another one of Fanhams' ghosts. Shirley ended our conversation by telling me that radios are often switched on and off by themselves and that she, too, has heard her name called when she's been alone, usually in the Long Gallery and the Hitchin Room.

Joyce was another lady I was able to talk to, she works in the coffee area. One morning, while putting the cups away, as she stepped backwards, having completed her task, she stepped on someone's foot and she felt 'someone, putting out two hands on my back as if to stop me falling over, at the same time I went cold.' When she turned around there was no one behind her, there was only her colleague Audrey, who was still cleaning the floor, some distance away. Joyce was quite matter-of-fact about her strange experiences, but not so Adam, a waiter, who insisted, nervously, one early evening, around December last year, that Joyce should accompany him down to the cellar as he had to fetch something. 'It was freezing cold down there and my hair stood up.' Adam told Joyce that he had seen 'someone' walk through the empty basement and she thought it odd that all the fuse boxes had been left open. On checking they learned from the maintenance man that he had been certain that the boxes had all been kept firmly shut. The ghosts of Fanhams Hall seem to know all the staff's names; Joyce was the third person I spoke with who remembered having heard her name called, about two years ago, when there was nobody else about, in the Atrium.

Sarah Murphy, Duty Manager, told me of her own weird experiences. Towards the end of 2004, while working in the Atrium Bar, she heard, along with her colleague, the sound of breaking glass; although they searched the bar thoroughly they could find no breakages. A couple of minutes later the guest in room 40 phoned down, to say that just after entering his overnight accommodation he had found broken glass in his bedroom. Upon investigation it was found that the glass had not fallen, it was still on its tiled shelf, there was nowhere for it to fall, but oddest of all it appeared to have just 'exploded' into tiny fragments, while the room was empty. Last Christmas Eve Sarah was alone on duty at the reception desk, but she could hear doors opening and closing in the otherwise deserted Hall, it was so unnerving that she felt impelled to unlock and open the big front door, just in case a quick exit was necessary...

I was not surprised to learn from Steve Lomas, the Duty Manager, some days after this, that one of the night porters, who, understandably, preferred to remain anonymous, had a story to tell. Several years ago he used to take his break in the Drawing Room, but as he kept hearing laughter from behind the sofa he stopped, since he found the experience completely unnerving. It was only fairly recently that he managed to build up the courage to start going back here for his break.

MORE WARE WRAITHS

I was intrigued by Rebecca's factual accounts of two ghostly experiences that she had in Ware. These happened in 1998, when Becky was working as a mobile care assistant, visiting the elderly in their homes. 'I was driving in the early evening towards Stanstead Abbots and had just approached the roundabout at the end of Ware High Street, opposite the Waterfront pub. Although it was dark the street was well lit by the street lights and there were a few cars on the road. I looked right to proceed across the roundabout and saw, at the furthest point to my right, an old-fashioned car approaching but about five seconds' distance away. I judged this to be ample time to cross over and put my foot on the accelerator. In an instant the car was in front of me but completely stationary for perhaps two seconds. I was shocked as I had always judged myself to be a safe driver yet I had, apparently, completely misjudged the distance. I cringed as I waited for some kind of gesture from the driver, a man of between 25 and 45. As I looked at him he remained motionless, just staring straight ahead, with a very serious expression in profile. This was a man on a mission, who was totally unaware of my presence, and I noticed that his car had no lights on. Then as suddenly as it had appeared it vanished, leaving me feeling bewildered. It was fortunate that there were no cars immediately behind me as I had been forced to make an emergency stop in my efforts to avoid hitting this car. I cannot find any explanation for this event other than that I had seen a ghost. I didn't tell anyone about this incident for years and even then only a couple of trusted friends.'

There is a well-known phantom car reported in Hertfordshire, but it is usually associated further south, near Welwyn, at a place called Ayot Green, where sightings have been reported of it parking under some trees before vanishing. It is alleged to be the car of murderer Albert Rouse, a handsome, smooth-talking ladies' man who kidnapped a tramp on the night of the 5th November, 1930. He drove up to Northamptonshire, where he murdered his victim and then set the car on fire in an attempt to make it appear that Albert Rouse had died in a fire in his own car. He forgot to attach his identity disc to the body, however, and left it in an attaché case in the car, which led to his arrest. Could it have been Albert Rouse's car that Rebecca saw? It is just possible, as Albert Rouse was a married commercial traveller, with a 'complicated' love-life, who worked all over Hertfordshire...

Rebecca's work as a care assistant took her to one of the council houses in Tower Road, Ware, opposite the flats marked 100 onwards. This particular house was occupied by a tiny lady called Dorothy, who has since passed away and her home seemed to have an inquisitive presence. 'As a care assistant I was nervous of going upstairs since I felt a female spirit right behind me all the way. By the time I was upstairs I would be panicking and Dorothy would often remark on seeing the entity which would almost always be behind me. I do not feel it was malevolent but a sense of unhappiness pervaded the atmosphere there. One care assistant collapsed within minutes of entering the house and I wonder if the uneasy atmosphere could have contributed to her funny turn. No doubt there are new occupants in the house but I wonder if the spirit remains.'

STEVE'S STORY

Before we leave Ware I must include a haunting which happened to a good friend of mine called Steve Webster. Steve is a careful and considerate person and extremely rational, indeed he is one of the most credible witnesses I have ever interviewed. In the 1970s he had left his native Widnes to study economics at the London School of Economics and Political Science. After graduation he was offered a one-year temporary contract to work in Hertfordshire. As the employment prospects back in Widnes looked decidedly unpromising Steve didn't have a difficult decision to make. He accepted the temporary position and set about finding lodgings in Hertfordshire. The young graduate considered himself fortunate when he discovered a room to rent with a family in nearby Ware, but he was later to regret ever moving in to this particular house. I will let Steve tell the rest of his story in his own words…

'The house was a Victorian one, in Watton Road. Father and mother both worked. There were three children. The eldest (a boy) was in his early teens, the middle child was a girl of eleven and the youngest was a boy of seven.

The couple (we'll call them the Smiths) had their own bedroom and the two boys shared another room, the girl had her own room and I was given the fourth bedroom. The family hadn't had lodgers before and as far as I know they didn't ever have any again after I left.

The geography of the bedrooms was such that there was a flight of stairs up to a right angle landing of about a yard square, up a few more steps and my bedroom was on its own on the left, off another mini-landing (itself another right angle turn). There were a few more steps and then entrances to the other three bedrooms and a bathroom.

My bedroom was on its own and overlooked the rough ground at the back of the house, which was being worked as a quarry, with much earth being regularly moved. Since those days a housing estate has appeared.

I lived there between late September 1974 and late January 1975. It was particularly dark there at night. I should say at this point that I am not given to remembering dreams, sleepwalking, and flights of imagination, have no history of mental illness, was not on any medication, did not use any illegal drugs and drank alcohol rarely and in small amounts. Even after more than thirty years since the events I am about to describe I cannot recall any dream that I have ever had.

I didn't question why the youngest boy preferred to share his brother's room rather than to sleep in his own room. The Smiths told me that he'd slept, for a short time in the room I was now renting, but preferred to share with his older brother; the room was standing empty so they had decided to take in a lodger.

It was the cold which started to wake me up. Again, let me say that I'm not prone to this either. At night in bed I tend to roast. It always occurred about 5.15am to 6am. I began waking up shaking with cold which went right through to my bones. It would last until 6am at the latest and then revert to normal temperature. This was the first sign. It wasn't every night, but it was very regular. Then, another detail was added. The room was a rectangular one and from the bed I would look down at the door, which was kept closed at night, as were all the doors. I'd see light under the door as well as shadows and hear the footsteps of someone walking to left and right on the landing behind the door. At this point, after it had happened a few times, I queried it in my head. The landing was too small for more than one or two steps at most and it didn't lead anywhere else, so why would someone be walking it, and why was the light on? I couldn't find any answers so I determined to open the door the next time it happened and get a rational explanation. I duly did this – but there was no light on and nobody there. Once I looked out the footsteps stopped. Back in the room it didn't start again. I looked out on several occasions and got the same result each time but the intense cold would still be felt until 6am and then it would dissipate.

Then, another detail was added. The steps would come into the room (without the door opening) and walk up the room on my right hand side. I'd hear the footsteps come up and down but there was nobody there, or at least, no one that I could see. Much as I tried in the hard light of day, I could never make my footsteps make any sound on the fully-carpeted bedroom floor. The cold now seemed more intense than ever.

I began applying scientific method. I needed to prove that I was awake when the manifestations occurred, so I began to put my wristwatch and the alarm clock together on the bedside cabinet. Then, when strange things started to happen, I would wind one of them forward or backward in random fashion by two hours, five hours, 23 minutes… After 6am I'd go back to sleep for an hour and then wake up and be able to confirm to myself that I'd been awake and done this. I added something else. I began putting the alarm clock underneath an upturned metal waste paper bin on the floor. No one else could touch it without my hearing it. I proved to myself that it was really happening but that left the big question, what exactly was happening? I did ask several times if there was anybody there and what they wanted from me. That didn't stop the footsteps coming and going – they didn't even pause.

All this time I never mentioned it to the family – that is until my mysterious visitor added another effect.

One morning, at the same time as always, the cold was even more intense than usual. I was shivering and shaking and my teeth were chattering. I put my head below the duvet cover seeking any spot of warmth I could find. Some moments later my unwanted visitor grabbed my left upper arm in first one and then in two places and shook me vigorously. He (she, or it) said nothing. In any other circumstance, wouldn't somebody address the person in bed by their name, or say "It's 5.45am, it's work today…"? My visitor remained silent.

To my regret, I dived down into the bed and stayed there. In due course, I heard the footsteps going away from me and then out of my room, but without the door opening and closing. I stayed undercover until the temperature returned to normal and then I looked out.

With hindsight, I should have responded, perhaps my visitor wanted my help with something. Maybe he or she had manifested but I didn't even ask a question or take a look, just automatically went into "scared" mode. In hindsight I should have made a positive response, however, my visitor didn't try to contact me subsequently. The light, moving shadow, intense cold, visits to my room and the footsteps happened a few more times, rather less regularly but they didn't stop altogether.

In as matter of fact fashion as possible, I asked the Smiths if there was anything odd about the room. I gave them no detail of my experiences and on the first couple of occasions, they laughed away my query. When I persisted and they could sense there was a reason for my asking I gathered a few more details. They had travelled a long way to this neighbourhood in their search for work and then they had started house-hunting. The young couple viewed several properties but for one reason or another turned them down. Then an estate agent told them about this house, which was "a bit unusual" as it had stood empty for two years and remained in exactly the same condition in which the previous occupants had left it. There had even been a half-eaten meal on the table and a tomato sauce bottle was also left behind with its cap off. It was as though the occupants had just suddenly fled the place in terror. The owners had subsequently instructed their agents that the house should be sold. They refused point blank to go back to the house to give any instructions for the sale or to make any arrangements for it to be cleaned up and had left all these arrangements in the hands of their estate agents.

The Smiths bought the house some two years after it was so hastily "abandoned" and then moved in. A few days later they had all been downstairs when they heard a loud crash upstairs, as though a chandelier had fallen from the ceiling and smashed to pieces. They had gone upstairs to investigate; there was no chandelier in place and no sign of anything smashed on the floor. The seven-year-old boy had started sleeping in the back room but had said that he "didn't like it" and had moved into the front room with his brother.

I went on from these lodgings to stay in a caravan in Bayford Wood for a few months. In my new home I would hear scurrying inside the caravan at night, which later proved to be the sounds made by some mice. I heard a thud on the roof and scratching sounds, which turned out to be an owl. But at no point did I ever think that the caravan might be haunted. I didn't experience here, nor anywhere else that I subsequently stayed, any periods of that ephemeral yet intense cold that always heralded my unwelcome experiences in Ware.'

Chapter Fifteen

WATTON AT STONE

Watton at Stone, originally Wattun (969) later Wodtone (Domesday Book 1086) then Watton atte Stone (1311) meaning 'Farmstead where woad is grown'. Derived from the Old English 'wad' and 'tun', and the 'at the stone' derives from an old stone here. In the 21st century Watton at Stone is a prosperous east Hertfordshire village handily placed for commuting to places like Hertford and Ware, with its mixture of fine old character houses and suitably expensive 'executive' new-build housing.

Watton at Stone has two well known ghosts. The first belongs to a former café on the Great North Road which was run by a couple for many years until the wife, Lydia, died of cancer. Lydia's ashes were buried beneath a tree in her beloved garden. Her husband tried, unsuccessfully, to carry on the business and eventually he sold it and the building was converted into a private residence. Lydia's ghost, however, remained and subjected the new owners to poltergeist activity of the damaging kind. Items were broken in a particular pattern. A glass was seen to break in front of several witnesses, another time a teapot lid rose into the air and broke on the ground, again in front of more than one person. Irritatingly things like handbags and make-up vanished from upstairs bedrooms and later reappeared elsewhere. The disappearances were instantaneous – one second an object had been put down, the next moment it had vanished.

On one occasion the husband of the household felt a distinct push as he made his way downstairs. The ground floor toilet and bathroom were always cold, even in the height of summer. Both rooms face the spot where Lydia's ashes lie buried, under the tree. Lydia's chief domain, however, is the kitchen. It seems clear that the spirit is resentful of new people being in 'her' territory. Incidents reported include hair pulling, a visitor's belt undone so that her clothing dropped to the floor, objects seen moving out of the corners of the eyes, glasses flying out of a particular cupboard and even a misty figure seen by one of the children living there…

Frogmore Hall, currently the headquarters of Jarvis Plc has multiple hauntings and is populated by an unknown quantity of ghosts – a lady called Edwina, a clergyman, the Reverend Hudson, a phantom coach and any number of children. The Hall was originally sited much closer to the river Beane but it was demolished in 1860 and the present building was constructed further up the hill. The lady of the house, Edwina, was in the habit of standing at the highest window, keeping a watch for the return of her husband from the French Wars. When he did not return she is alleged to have hanged herself in a tower at the top of the house. Her ghost, accompanied by the phantom smell of lavender, has been seen on the staircase. Outside, a ghostly coach and horses have appeared many times, driving past the main entrance.

Former owner the Reverend Thomas Hudson has made his presence felt to an ex Jarvis employee and to a security guard. The cleric died in 1889, in his 85th year, and he returns, dressed in his cloak and dark priestly clothes, to slowly walk the gallery above the hall where there was once a chapel. A cleaner was scared in the 1980s by a different phenomenon – she heard the sounds of children chattering and laughing, the sounds moved up and down the staircase before eventually fading away in a room off the main hall...

Chapter Sixteen

WELWYN GARDEN CITY

The name Welwyn originally meant 'Place at the willow trees' and Welwyn Garden City developed much later, as one of the New Towns. In recent times it has gained the reputation for being one of the most expensive places to live outside London as it is easily commutable – King's Cross is a mere 25 minutes away by rail.

Most of my visits to Welwyn Garden City, particularly when I am with my wife, have involved a trip to our favourite department store, John Lewis, where I have had an account for about twenty years. It is an imposing building which was completed just before the Second World War, when it was called the Welwyn Department Store. I have a soft spot for the place because my first job on leaving school was at the Partnership's Oxford Street branch. What most shoppers are unaware of though is that the Welwyn shop is haunted. In January 2005 I was talking with one of the beauty consultants who was the latest person to have an in-store paranormal experience. The young lady was on her morning break in the old part of the building, which used to house the squash courts, now there is a smoking room and some toilets. The girl went into the ladies and heard noises from the next cubicle, which unnerved her as she knew she was alone at the time. She came out to check the next cubicle and noticed the toilet seat was down and it had been up. I spoke with her colleague, who also works as a beauty consultant, and she told me that her friend 'was shaking all over' when she returned from her break. The young lady told me that she was never going to use those particular toilets ever again. She had never had such a strange experience in her life. Other staff members have had similar experiences, saying that the toilet area is always cold and that there is a decidedly creepy atmosphere about the place.

TEWIN

Tewin village, just east of Welwyn Garden City, off the A1000 Hertford road, is known locally as the long-term home of singer Marty Wilde, father of Kim Wilde, who also found fame as a pop singer before turning to her garden designing. Tewin is well known in the world of the paranormal for its quite famously haunted pub – the Plume of Feathers in Upper Green Road, which may well qualify for the title of 'Hertfordshire's most haunted pub'. It is a Grade Two listed building, dating from 1596 and was once a hunting lodge for Queen Elizabeth I. Paul Sims has been the manager here for some three and a half years and he had a weird experience of his own, as reported by a writer called Gerry Gingell in *Hertfordshire Life* magazine in January 2004. One morning at around 9am, when he was alone at the bar, two butterfly corkscrews, kept on a hook in an upright post suddenly started 'swinging violently for no good reason!' The manager has heard numerous stories from the pub's regulars and the catalogue of phenomena is extensive...

Anyone who is the slightest bit psychically 'sensitive' is likely to pick up 'something' in the area of the ladies' toilet, where many people have admitted to 'a creepy feeling'. Before it was a toilet this used to be a quiet reading room, a small, out of the way nook, with some books and newspapers available for customers to peruse. Hard by the toilet is the entrance door to the cellar, scene of a frightening episode for an unfortunate female member of staff back in 1999 when she found herself trapped in the cellar, unable to open the swing door, which eventually 'just opened'. A mysterious occurrence given that the door had no handle which could have been held against the lady's attempts to open it. The cellar used to be servants' quarters long ago, but they have been bricked up now. The ghost of a little girl has been seen at the top of the cellar steps but her origin remains unknown.

There is a persistent story concerning a murder at the Plume of Feathers, dating from the 17th century, when a woman's body was discovered behind a bricked-up fireplace. It was said that her husband had been away at sea for two years and on his return he had found her pregnant. He murdered her and disposed of the body by bricking it up behind the fireplace, which was subsequently filled in. Close by the former hiding-place is the notorious table 8, where a former manager, Mark Thomas, reported hearing a noise while he was alone one afternoon and on turning round, discovering that the candle on table 8 had relit itself. The phantom of an old man has been reported, sitting at table 8, perhaps he is also the candle-snuffer? In the same restaurant area a lady with long grey hair has been seen and heard by staff at the pub. She haunts a long table behind table 8, wears a see-through dress and cackles at observers.

I heard, from an ex member of staff, that sometimes, when he was laying the tables, the cutlery would be swept onto the floor so that he would have to relay the tables again. Nearby there is an outside door and an old fireplace, this area is the original, much smaller building and some few hundred years ago this outside door would have been the main entrance, when the present bar area formed part of a smallholding at the back of the building.

Bar staff have also witnessed an old man who leans on the bar 'facing the wrong way', but in his time the bar would have faced the other way, so much has been altered over the centuries, as is evident from the quirky floor layout. Some staff have felt that the many ghosts that haunt their workplace influence them in some subtle way, making them feel awkward and clumsy, prone to dropping things.

In the kitchen the Chef is not immune from the pub's invisible residents, the oven regularly switched itself on and when his back was turned the gas was often turned up so that quite a lot of soup has been burned. Lights have a habit of switching themselves on and electrical items generally can be troublesome. Beer taps which open and close by themselves and shadows that are frequently spotted flitting about the place are just a regular part of life in the ghostly Plume of Feathers...

St Peter's Church at Tewin is reached via a long straight driveway at the bottom of which may be found the small, squat, flint and brick church with its large clock face dominating the square tower. Inside the church there is a marble tomb in commemoration of General Sabine, a former Governor of Gibraltar, who died in1739. A figure wearing a black cloak with a hood is reputed to haunt the vicinity and it is thought to be the spirit of Lady Hester Sabine, the general's former wife. As recently as the 1980s two visitors spoke of hearing crinoline skirts rustling in the aisle and of feeling a female presence in the bell tower. St Peters stands on a small rise which affords panoramic views over miles of open countryside. A great variety of trees have been planted in the churchyard, some in remembrance of those people who lie buried here, I noted oaks, acers, firs, a red chestnut and even a tulip tree amongst them. A number of once-prominent and influential individuals rest in this graveyard, including members of the famous aeronautical family the de Havillands. It is certainly one of the most attractive and peaceful churchyards which I have ever visited.

Behind the church one grave stands out, with its wrought-iron fence, it contains the last mortal remains of Lady Anne Grimston, who was said to be a Sadducean. This was an ancient Jewish priestly sect that flourished for about two centuries before the destruction of the Second Temple of Jerusalem by the Roman legions in AD 70. As she was a non-believer in the Resurrection of the Dead the vicar felt obliged to make an attempt to save her soul by making her recant her heresy. When the Lady Anne lay dying, in November 1780, she refused to change her beliefs and wouldn't even let the priest administer the last rites. 'If, indeed, there is a life hereafter, seven trees will render asunder my tomb', she is reputed to have challenged him. My visit to her grave indeed confirmed that several trees have sprung up through her tomb, causing it to lift slightly and breaking off large pieces of mossy masonry onto the nettles and brambles inside the wrought-iron fence which guards her final resting place. My wife's photograph, which is among the illustrations in this book, is testament to the fact. The ghost of 'a lady' has been seen at night time by church bell ringers on a number of occasions, she wanders alone amongst the gravestones and it is assumed to be the shade of Lady Grimston.

AYOT ST LAWRENCE

North-west of Welwyn (which is Welwyn Garden City's smaller neighbour), lies the village of Ayot St Lawrence, a tranquil small community, with its Queen Anne manor house, ruined old church and its replacement, St Lawrence's, which was built in 1779. Ayot St Lawrence will be forever associated with George Bernard Shaw, the acknowledged twentieth century genius of literature who was an immensely successful playwright. He lived at Shaw's Corner (as it was affectionately called by the villagers) from his middle age right up till the ripe old age of ninety-four (from 1906 to1950). I was intrigued as to why he chose this particular part of Hertfordshire to live out the rest of his days. He was visiting St Lawrence's churchyard when he came across the grave of Mary Anne South, who died at the age of seventy. 'Her Time Was Short' read the inscription on her tombstone. If longevity was associated with life in the village then this was the place for Shaw. He arrived with his wife Charlotte in 1906 and rented the village rectory, which had been recently built, in 1902. They continued to rent for about twelve years before buying it outright, as a wealthy playwright he could now easily afford it. His means of transportation was similarly upgraded with his improving fortunes. When he first lived at Ayot St Lawrence he used a bicycle and a motorcycle to get around, and later graduated to a huge Rolls-Royce. He employed a chauffeur, Fred Day, but often drove the big car himself around the narrow, twisty lanes, which led to some close shaves. Ayot St Lawrence can only be approached by way of lanes so narrow that two cars cannot pass one another and even a moderate snowfall has been known to cut the village's connections with the outside world..

After George Bernard Shaw's death both his ashes and Charlotte's were scattered in the garden of Shaw's Corner, in the home where they had known much happiness together. Soon after Shaw died Alice Laden, his housekeeper, heard a knock on the kitchen door and, without thinking, from force of habit, invited her employer in. Framed in the doorway stood Shaw, 'I heard a noise and thought you may have had an accident,' he said. As the housekeeper started to explain that she was only sorting out her cupboards she realised that she was alone in the kitchen. The deceased playwright made one final visitation to his trusted housekeeper some days later. While she was standing at the foot of the stairs she clearly heard his footsteps on the landing, then he called out 'Are you there, Mrs Laden?', before his footsteps faded away again. His former home is one of the smallest, but brightest jewels in the crown of the National Trust, an organisation of which I am a member and which I wholeheartedly support.

Shaw's Corner regularly draws many thousands of visitors, from all over the world, every year. The house itself is not intrinsically beautiful, one visitor described it, not inaccurately, as 'a very ugly, dark red-brick villa', its attraction lies in the secluded nature of the place and the original features of the great man's home, left intact, preserved as it was during his lifetime. What struck me during my visit was the fact that it was not hard to imagine that the Irishman had just popped out for one of his strolls, his hats and walking sticks are in the hall, his typewriter and books still await Shaw's return to his study. The 'time capsule' extends to the gardens, which remain as he would have known them, with enviable views and at the end of the grounds is the little 'summerhouse', a simple, tiny little shed, plain and unadorned, following the theme of the main house, and containing the minimum of useful items – a desk, a telephone and a day-bed, the writer's own 'desert island', where he could create his imaginary world, uninterrupted by the intrusions of the noisy, rushing material world. Even without the kudos of its former owner's name, this wonderful property would probably be worth around three million pounds on today's market. Shaw's benign presence can still be strongly felt by the staff that care for the house and new custodians are traditionally greeted by the alarms going off all by themselves when they spend their first night at the place. Just a short stroll down the leafy lane he would instantly recognise, although he was a teetotaller, The Brocket Arms, which has its own hauntings.

The Brocket Arms dates back to 1378, when it was the monastic quarters for the local church and in the twentieth century it was part of the Brocket estate. The proprietor of the Brocket Arms since 1980, Toby Wingfield-Danby, has admitted to having a ghostly monk for company. There have been problems with alarms going off in the early hours of the morning when nobody was around, yet when checked the alarms have had no faults found with them. Other noises have been heard from the first floor, including mutterings, thumps and footsteps. Tony has experienced unexplained feelings of panic and claustrophobia in parts of his inn. The first report of an apparition, however, was not until 1969, as recounted by Betty Puttick in her book *Ghosts of Hertfordshire*, when Teresa Sweeney, a part-time barmaid, witnessed the appearance and swift

124

disappearance of a monk, 'a little man with his head bent', while she was on her way to the dining room one evening and she sighted him again, this time in the morning, 'a thin, old face, rather hazy', he was wearing monk's robes, and he was seen in the dining room. Teresa also heard little tapping feet following her downstairs one night which quite unnerved her. Guests have also encountered the frightening friar – one woman awoke to discover mysterious burn marks on her feet and another visitor reported seeing a monk staring at him, while apparently the friar was on fire!

A monk was allegedly hanged in this very place, during the Reformation of the monasteries. Legend has it that Henry VIII's men came to the village to escort the King's last wife, Catherine Parr (who lived in Ayot St Lawrence) to London, when they happened on an unfortunate monk. They decided to hang him and he was duly dispatched, from a beam alongside the bar in the Brocket Arms, which can be seen to this day. Visitors may also read the poem in the same bar, written in 1940, which concerns history from the Spanish Civil War to the Second World War, and the ghost has a mention:

'…A monk had ridden as he fled from the mob
of howling villains who feared no god.
They slung him up to a beam in the bar
Declaring he should not have ridden so far.'

It was said that the locals wouldn't go back in the bar for three weeks afterwards. The monk continues his haunting nearly five hundred years on and the most astonishing story regarding this famous phantom friar was recorded by Gerry Gingell in the December 2003 issue of *Hertfordshire Life*. Toby Wingfield-Danby told the journalist, 'I've had one guest staying overnight, the only person staying upstairs that particular night, who told me in the morning that he had met this chap in a brown robe or dressing gown, and how this person was so interesting because he knew so much about the village, and how they had chatted away. I thought as he was telling me his story that I couldn't possibly tell him that he was the only one staying that night, as it would have frightened the living daylights out of him. But there was no question about it; this guy had had a conversation with the monk!'

Lemsford

Lemsford is a village that lies just to the east of Welwyn Garden City and the A1 corridor. The Brocket Arms, from the previous story, takes its name from Lord Brocket, of *I'm a celebrity get me out of here* television fame, whose country seat used to be Brocket Hall, for my money one of the most striking stately homes in the entire county. Situated opposite Lemsford Church, the property was built in the late eighteenth century, a square mansion in the most attractively landscaped and well-maintained grounds, with the River Lea running through the surrounding parklands and an artificial lake (spanned by a small bridge) which was created directly in front of the house. It has been the country retreat of two of Queen Victoria's Prime Ministers. The first was Lord Melbourne (William Lamb, 2nd Viscount Melbourne) who was a favourite of the Monarch since he guided the new Queen and acted as her mentor. Melbourne was married to the notorious Lady Caroline Lamb, the beautiful, highly-strung rebel who fell madly in love with Lord Byron. Unfortunately the poet tired of his mistress and Lady Caroline later learned of Byron's death in the most terrible circumstances. She was driving out from Brocket one summer's day in 1824 when she saw a funeral cortege, and after enquiring whose funeral it was she was told it was her former lover's. Lord Byron's cortege had been travelling back to his old family home at Nottingham. Lord Melbourne died in 1848 and the story is that he passed away in the billiard room, after vigorous sexual intercourse!

Viscount Palmerston (Henry Temple) was a later Prime Minister, famous for his 'gunboat policy', when British overseas interests were threatened. He, too, served under Queen Victoria and he also lived at Brocket Hall.

Now Brocket Hall is a conference centre, hotel and golf complex that still has echoes of its past in hauntings of the present. Lord Brocket always maintained that his home wasn't haunted but I beg to differ. I believe that the house has its ghosts but Lord Brockett was unable to see them for himself, which is a different matter altogether. The odds are against it not being haunted in the first place, since you are as likely to see a ghost in a historic house as you are in a pub, together these two locations probably represent about 50% of all reported hauntings across the U.K. It has been further estimated that 80% of all historic houses in Britain are haunted, so that made it even more likely that Brocket Hall would be home to paranormal phenomena.

I decided to put my speculation to the test and some few years ago I visited Brocket Hall and spoke with one of the maintenance staff, a down-to-earth young man who confirmed what I had suspected, something unearthly still resided at the Hall and he had direct personal experience of it. On numerous occasions he had locked up for the night and knew that there was no one else in the place. One instance he mentioned was when he had distinctly heard someone cough, just as he was about to leave the empty building. This doesn't sound too scary in the cold light of day but when you are alone on a dark night and you are certain that there is nobody else in a mansion but yourself... He also smelt perfume when there was no one to account for it and he told me that he was quite convinced, as some others were, that this was the ghost of Lady Caroline Lamb. He told me that the mansion had been visited by many celebrities, including Nicole Kidman, John Thaw, Michael Winner, Ronnie Corbett, Timothy Dalton and Kim Wilde and it was used for filming on occasion, being particularly favoured for period dramas. Back in the 1950s a famous black and white horror film, *Night of the Demon* was made here. It was based on *Casting the Runes*, a great M.R. James short story. As a horror film fan (the best ever made in my opinion being *The Exorcist*) I was familiar with the movie, particularly the scenes where the invisible demon stalks its prey through the woods, leaving smoking footprints as it moves along. In more recent times the pop group Steps shot a video in the mansion. Their 2001 shoot was a decidedly eerie experience for the band, temperatures would suddenly drop in certain places and objects would move about by themselves.

In April 2003 permission was granted to a paranormal investigation team from Ghost Investigators UK, a Hertfordshire-based group, to conduct a vigil at Brocket Hall. Perfume was briefly smelt on leaving the Prince of Wales Room and in the Dining Room one of the mediums felt someone touch her side and then her lap, while another witness clearly saw, for an instant, a 'broad-shouldered silhouette'. In the Library a camera, which had been set for 'on', was found to have its manual switch turned to the 'off' position, but not by anyone on the team! A tape recording picked up an indistinct human voice, which sounded as though it had spoken very close to the microphone and a minidisk recorder seemed to suffer a battery drain. One of the mediums also conversed with the spirit of 'Lucy', a six-year-old girl with fair hair, and her brother was also contacted, his name was thought to be Phillip. This investigation further enhances the haunted reputation of Brocket Hall and helps to confirm my long-held opinion that paranormal phenomena most definitely do manifest at this site.

BOOK THREE

South Hertfordshire Spirits

South
Hertfordshire
Spirits

WEST HERTFORDSHIRE

EAST HERTFORDSHIRE

GREATER LONDON

Sarratt •

RICKMANSWORTH

Leavesden •

• Croxley Green

• Abbots Langley

WATFORD

Bushey

• Aldenham

• South Oxhey

BOREHAMWOOD

Chapter Seventeen

ABBOTS LANGLEY

THE CURIOUS CASE OF THE HAUNTED FIREPLACE

Abbots Langley is associated with a haunting that centres on St Lawrence's Church (built in 1150) as well as the graveyard and the nearby vicarage, by the ghost of housekeeper Mary Anne Treble. I visited the church of St Lawrence in May 2005, in order to take a photograph of the old vicarage and discovered a charming, tranquil place. There was a verdant lawn set in the middle of an attractive, well-kept garden and there was plenty of shade to be found beneath several large trees in the foreground of the house. The nearby, pretty country church is small and square. I don't think I have seen a vicarage that was so close to its church before, it is merely a few yards apart, most conveniently sited for its vicar.

Rumours surrounded Mary Anne Treble's death at the rectory in 1914 and her previous alleged mistreatment by Mrs Parnell, the vicar's wife. The tragic servant was, it was said, probably murdered by Mrs Parnell (variously suggested as either being shaken to death while in her sick bed or by being pushed down the stairs) or else she committed suicide. She had been a popular figure in the village; noted for handing out sweets to the little children. One unique aspect of the haunting is that Mary Anne's spirit seems to have focussed her angst on the fireplace in her former bedroom at the vicarage. It was repaired on several occasions but would then be found to be mysteriously damaged again.

Ghost-hunter Peter Underwood personally investigated this most unusual case. In his book *The A-Z of British Ghosts*, first published in 1971, he tells how he tracked down a former rector who recalled consulting a local builder about alterations to the Queen Anne vicarage. The builder had pointed to the damaged fireplace which was sticking out from the wall in the haunted bedroom and said, 'Not much use repairing that; it will be out again within six months.' When the vicar asked what he meant the builder explained, 'Annie it was; died a horrible death in this room and the place will never be free of her.' The fireplace was, however, repaired but within a few months it was out again. This was the second occasion when the vicar's attention had been brought to the fireplace, for soon after he moved in at the vicarage he met a parish priest who had been assistant curate at St Lawrence's church. The parish priest told him that during Mass on All Souls Day ten years previously he had seen a stranger, a woman who vanished as he turned to give the Invitation, a woman that his wife had not seen. The curate gave a full description of the mysterious woman, a description that was subsequently found to match that of Mary Anne Treble. After the service the curate and his wife accompanied the rector back at the rectory where they discovered the fireplace to be freshly cracked.

There was much more than this in the way of evidence for a haunting. After Mary Anne's death villagers who lived in cottages on the other side of the road from the rectory confirmed that they had seen Mary Anne's shade looking out of the window of her former bedroom and she was also seen walking from the vicarage to the graveyard. Another curate was praying alone in St Lawrence's one Halloween night when he heard footsteps approaching from the west end of the church and then clothing brushed his face, but he could see no one there and the ghostly footsteps echoed on towards the east end before ceasing. The ghost was seen several times on All Soul's Day and it was seen again on this day, a year after the curate's report, when an Irish vicar saw the same woman in his congregation and witnessed her abrupt disappearance. He was concerned enough to give the details of the supernatural events to his bishop. This resulted in Bishop Michael Furse carrying out the full Service of Exorcism and things quietened down for a while at the church and the vicarage, apart from some 'unaccountable noises' from Mary Anne's old room, which caused the vicar's wife to keep the room locked.

Writer Betty Puttick later carried out her own enquiries for her 1994 book *Ghosts of Hertfordshire* and she discovered new information from the Reverend Andrews, the vicar at the time, who came to the parish in 1979. He was convinced that Mary Anne Treble had fallen down stairs and died as a result of that accident, possibly of pneumonia. His sources did not hint that she was pushed or that she committed suicide. Rev. Andrews did admit to some electrical anomalies at the vicarage soon after he moved in with his wife. An electric toothbrush had switched itself on as they were going to bed one night and another time an electric kettle switched itself on in their kitchen.

At the antique shop owned by a Mr Dobson in Abbots Langley, Betty Puttick managed to trace a photograph of Mary Anne Treble. It had been kept by the shop owner, who had come by it via a (deceased) close friend of the former housekeeper. Mary Anne's friend had been certain that there was a mystery surrounding the housekeeper's death.

So why did the spirit of Mary Anne single out the fireplace for special attention? And why was there persistent gossip and rumour in the village that she was at the least ill-treated as a servant and at the worst murdered? Why, indeed, was her close friend convinced that 'mystery surrounded her death'? Perhaps it was a coded message to the living from the dead, in the form of an old adage – no smoke without fire – the ghost's way of telling us that her death had been the result of foul play. So the perpetrator, most likely Mrs Parnell, would seem to have got away with murder... or did she?

Chapter Eighteen
BOREHAMWOOD

Borehamwood is very much a part of Britain's answer to Hollywood, for Los Angeles, California, USA read Hertfordshire, Great Britain, where our main, home-grown movie-making industry is based, with huge studios located at Elstree and Leavesden. A cluster of studios, permanent production bases and film locations are centred on south west Hertfordshire and some 85% of the industry's skilled workforce live within a 25 mile radius of these 'dream factories'. Elstree merges with Borehamwood, the town of some 10,000 inhabitants, where the BBC studios are located. Filming in Elstree dates right back to 1914 when the first studio was built. It was rapidly followed by six more, thereby establishing the largest production capacity outside Hollywood. Three original studios remain and there is a visitors' guide available for the area. Elstree Film Studios, owned by Hertsmere Borough Council is where the original *Star Wars* trilogy, *Superman* and the *Indiana Jones* trilogy were made in the 1970s and 1980s, all films that I found hugely entertaining. The tremendously successful television programme *Who Wants To Be A Millionaire?* is permanently based at Elstree and big hit *Big Brother* is also produced here. I was fortunate enough to visit the site some years ago and parked in Chris Tarrant's designated parking bay (he wasn't filming on that day). The Spice Girls and Cliff Richard have also used the studios. Some years ago they were extensively renovated, to offer the best in on-site facilities and have provided pre-production facilities for a movie that I particularly enjoyed, *Saving Private Ryan*, filmed at Hatfield, as well as the development of special effects for yet another of my favourite movies, *Tomorrow Never Dies*.

Close to the Elstree Film Studios in Borehamwood are the Millennium Studios, which were a production base in the early 90s, but now they offer a full service from sound stages, power and lighting through to make-up and props. Work includes commercials, music videos, documentaries, TV drama and even films for television.

The BBC Centre at Elstree is sited on what was probably the first film studio in the UK, which opened in 1914 – the old Neptune Studios. The BBC Centre is the permanent home to *Grange Hill* and *Casualty* and *East Enders* and *Holby City* are also filmed in the area as well as *BBC South East*, *Newsroom South East* and national and regional weather forecasts. To this already impressive list may be added programmes like *On the Buses* and *Inspector Morse*, which were Elstree products. In Tescos at Elstree there is a large mural of *Moby Dick*, the legendary movie that starred Gregory Peck. This reminds shoppers that they are on the site of the studios where that great film was shot.

Borehamwood's Gate Studio, which dates back to 1928, was the smallest of the local studios. It has been described as a 'glorified aircraft hanger' and it was originally used for the making of silent movies. With the advent of 'the talkies' its proximity to the railway station made it a less than ideal location for movie-making and a man with a flag and loudhailer was employed to warn of the impending arrival of trains so that recording could be delayed till the train had gone again. Probably the most famous film associated with the Gate was *Odette*, about the famous Second World War French Resistance heroine, starring Anna Neagle. British film entrepreneur and flour tycoon J. Arthur Rank owned the Gate for a time and he made several religious films here. He found that there was another fortune to be made in photocopying machines when he joined forces with an American company to form Rank Xerox, which still has a presence today in Welwyn Garden City.

The Gate seems to have been haunted by several ghosts; the apparition of a former make-up artist who committed suicide in one of the offices is just one that has been seen in recent years, nearby the cinema screen. A workman's shade has also been observed; he died in a fall from one of the roof walkways in the room where cinema screens were made.

The Borehamwood & Elstree Times covered the Gate Studios story in 2003 and quoted Steve Oake, the maintenance man at the site, who had a sighting at the end of the previous year: 'I was working on the floor looking up at the cinema screen and I saw someone, out of the corner of my eye, walk up the gangway and go behind some piles of foam. Usually the person comes out the other side, but nobody came out. I went to look and there was nobody there.'

Simon Jones was another studio worker to have a similar experience with his colleague at the time, Dave Blake. The pair reportedly beat a hasty retreat after locking up late one night, when they saw a figure move from one corner of the building and exit through a doorway.

In April 2003 the *Edgware and Mill Hill Times* also ran the story and they interviewed a personal assistant for Macevoy mailings, Sue Carpenter, who noticed the air go cold in her office one day. She described her encounter as follows, 'I felt someone standing there and I looked round and there was this man. I did a double-take and he disappeared.' Her description was quite detailed; the man was smart, tall, aged in his 40s to 50s with a large beard and he wore a white shirt and black trousers. This was not her only sighting, she reported two other appearances while she was working late at night organising exhibitions. Sue spotted the bearded man in the corridor, this time he wore a long jacket. She said, 'When he went, he faded. He did not make any movements, he just went.' The other time she did not see the apparition clearly as she reported, 'I felt this rush of air. A plastic bag hanging on the door was swinging. This shadow, the form of this man, went whoosh past, outside the office door. It all happened in seconds. I walked out of the door and he had gone. There was a very distinctive wind. I had never felt that rush of wind before.' At the time of the interview Sue was looking forward to moving to smarter offices, with the imminent prospect of the Gate Studios being demolished. She believed that there might have been a link between the uncertain future of the studios and the apparitions, 'My mum always said if you are moving or changing things, they get upset.' She mused about the fate of the ghost, 'I just feel sad. Where is he going to go?' Sue admitted that the ghost's identity remains unknown although she had heard about the accident in which a man was killed in a fall from some rigging, 'People have said someone died here. There is definitely something.' Interestingly another female employee described an encounter with the same apparition, because her description tallied with Sue's, despite the fact that Sue had given her no details of her own sighting…

At time of writing, in May 2005, the Gate Studio site has been acquired by Bryant Homes and is due for demolition any time soon as it has been empty for a very long time, so I had to take a photograph of it before it disappeared from the skyline for ever, even though it is an ugly old building. It lies neglected now, with its many broken windows, separated from the railway station by a brick-built building directly in front of it, then a road and a car park. But film studios are just giant 'sheds', freezing cold in winter and baking hot in the summer, merely factories for making movies. There is nothing glamorous at all about them as structures.

Recent ghost hunters have mistakenly attributed the busy working environment at Elstree Film and Television Studios as the site of the hauntings that have, in fact taken place at the much smaller, derelict old Gate Studios, a couple of miles further down the road in Borehamwood. Soon they will be gone, taking a piece of history with them, to make way for many new houses, so we will probably, but not necessarily, have heard the last of the Gate ghosts…

Chapter Nineteen

BUSHEY

Bushey is called Bissei in the Domesday Book, meaning 'Enclosure near a thicket or hedged with box trees'. Life was based on agriculture in this part of the county until the railways came in 1841, when the growth of the place really began. Bushey's story can be traced back in its excellent Museum and Art Gallery and the reason may be found as to why over the years some 1,000 artists have been associated with the area. It began with Sir Hubert von Herkomer, who set up his art school in 1883, when the population of Bushey would only have been a few thousand. Many artists who went on to achieve great success learned here, including Lucy Kemp-Welch and Marguerite Frobisher.

Bushey's most famous son, however, was born of Greek-Cypriot immigrant parents, the Panayiotous, who settled in the town in the mid-seventies. They called their son Georgios and when he was old enough he attended Bushey Meads School where he became great friends with Andrew Ridgeley, who was to change his life. Andrew persuaded Georgios that they could set up a band together. Their live debut was at Bushey Methodist Church in 1979 but the early years were a struggle and Georgios took various jobs to make ends meet, including labourer, cinema usher and DJ. By 1982 the boys had a new name for the band – Wham! They also had a new record deal and, in time, hit records followed. Eventually the partnership broke up. The boy Georgios grew up and metamorphosed from a bespectacled, overweight teenager with frizzy hair and acne, to become an adult heart-throb, solo singing superstar, George Michael.

One of Bushey's landmarks is the now defunct and empty International University building, with its huge clock tower. It is an impressively large place, a spooky old edifice, set well back from the road in its own extensive grounds. Originally built as the Royal Masonic School, it has been in great demand as a backdrop by film and TV companies for use in their movies, commercials and feature programmes, like *Silent Witness*, *Midsomer Murders*, *Holby City*, *Judge John Deed* and many others over the years. Sometimes various TV crew members have had to stay overnight in this Grade Two Listed building and have been pleased to leave when the shoot was over as the former students' residential area can be quite a creepy place after dark. Electrical problems, particularly with the lighting, have plagued the building, a typical sign that a place is haunted, as the ghosts seem to draw their energy from the electricity supply in some way as yet unexplained. There is an upstairs room which is allegedly always cold and it was said that a little girl died here after an accident when she was thrown by her pony. The little girl's shade reputedly haunts the stairs of the school. The security men confirmed that the Royal Masonic School was haunted when I paid them a brief visit some years ago. I had been curious as to why such a huge place, which could provide living or office quarters for hundreds of people, was left empty. Some of the guards were uncomfortable when patrolling the corridors and grounds alone at night. I was told that there are vast underground tunnels beneath the old school, which have to be checked out from time to time and they are definitely not an inviting place to be, especially after dark. One security man that I talked to, who didn't want to be named, was absolutely certain that the place was haunted. He was reluctant to say much, but I managed to prise out of him that he had heard a lot of unexplained noises here at night, like phantom whistles being blown and loud sobbing noises, as of someone in great distress. He also said that when this had been a school there had been some children who had died in accidents but he couldn't, or wouldn't, go into any more details. It also transpired that some of the television people who had worked here had been 'freaked out' by odd occurrences in the building, like doors and windows opening of their own accord, strange noises being heard and objects mysteriously moved around when nobody was about.

I renewed my acquaintance with the former International University in May 2005 and I was fortunate to meet one of the custodians of the sprawling complex of buildings, Stephen, a young American who was an ex-student at the University. He was aware of the ghost and even knew her name, which he told me was Hillary and that she had been the daughter of the former headmaster during the time of the building's original use as the Royal Masonic School. There were various colourful stories about her premature death; some said it was suicide and that she had thrown herself from one of the towers in the school, others maintained that her death was the result of a fall from a horse. Stephen related a strange incident that had happened to him during his very first week as a student, when he was studying alone in his room on campus. He distinctly heard the sound of galloping hooves passing by his window, yet when he looked up there was nothing to be seen. He had a good look around but there was no trace of a horse and no horses were kept on the grounds then. He didn't know it but I later discovered that a former headmaster had regularly used a pony and trap for his transportation.

So what is to become of this imposing structure? Stephen confirmed what I had heard years before, this grand old piece of history was due for redevelopment as luxury apartments – just what Bushey needs, more expensive housing! The present owners are wealthy Irish property developers so it would be happening soon; I am just surprised that it has not happened sooner and that the place has remained empty for so many years now…

My next contact was with Gordon Metcalfe, who was a former art teacher at the Royal Masonic School. He told me that there is an *Old Masonians* magazine which is circulated to 1100 former staff and students. He was a teacher at the RMS from 1960 till it closed as a school, in about 1975. He was also able to confirm that the former headmaster, Norman Sinclair, had indeed lost his sixteen-year-old daughter Hillary, not in a tragic riding accident, but more prosaically as the result of 'an infection'. This happened in 1947, some thirteen years before Gordon joined the staff. He was aware that Hillary's ghost had been seen wandering in the chapel and at least one security guard refused to set foot in the place. When the chapel was being prepared for a film some years ago the electrician had taken a series of photographs of his handiwork with a digital camera. He had taken about 10 or so exposures as he made his way up to the altar without noticing anything unusual yet the final photograph showed a strange, smoky image which could not be explained…

In conversations with other security guards Gordon learned that they had seen young boys 'larking about' on the playing fields, turning somersaults and playing football. Determined to catch the intruders the guards had formed a pincer movement to cut them off but as they rounded the corner there was no trace of any trespassing children, they had suddenly just disappeared and the guards could only conclude that they had seen some of the ghosts that haunt the site.

I arranged to meet Gordon Metcalfe on Friday 20th May 2005, exactly one hundred and five years, to the very month, since the foundation stone was laid at the school by the Duke of Connaught and Strathearn. I was most privileged to be given a guided tour of the fascinating sixty-acre site. Comer Homes had scheduled the redevelopment into luxury apartments for August 2005, so there wouldn't be many opportunities like this. We met in the entrance hall and made for the chapel, a short walk away past the headmaster's large house. We entered the detached building and I was struck by the musty smell associated with disuse and damp. When the Royal Masonic School had been built in 1900, with Charles Keyser as the Chairman of the Building Committee and Treasurer of the Board of Governors, it had cost £96,950 and as the money began to run out the ambitious chapel was scaled down in size from the original grand design. It seemed somehow forlorn but atmospheric inside and I felt sure that an overnight vigil would have produced some interesting results. Except for one day each week the school day began here, and at the back of the chapel I was shown some lovely Victorian oak 'Herkomer' screens which had been rescued from the former home of artist Sir Hubert von Herkomer, mentioned earlier, by headmaster Norman Sinclair. On another wall was a plaque to the memory of a former headmaster T.R.N. Crofts MA, head from 1915–1938 who died in his 76th year. Gordon mentioned that this headmaster was the one who used to travel about in a pony and trap, which could account for the phantom hoof beats heard by the American, Stephen (whom I had spoken with earlier) when he was a student at the International University …

As we made our way out of the chapel my guide pointed out some of the brass memorial plaques set into the wall, which were dedicated to the memory of former boys who had died either at school or during school holidays. One tragic story was about a lad who died on the playing fields when a hockey ball hit him in the chest. It transpired that he had a heart defect and the sudden blow had killed him. It was, therefore, not surprising that the playing fields were witness to the apparitions of ghostly children, as seen in recent times by security patrols.

I reflected on how fortunate I was to be accompanied by an ex-teacher, one who had spent seventeen years at this special place. Gordon, who was originally from Yorkshire, had taught art at the RMS from September 1960 until its closure in July 1977, a large part of his life had been devoted to the fatherless boys who had benefited from the finest free education that this unique public school could offer. The art teacher had met his wife here; Sally had been in charge of the housekeeping staff. I was astonished to learn that every boy who attended the Royal Masonic School had lost his father and his education was paid for by his deceased father's fellow Freemasons. In fact the Freemasons are a most generous society, major players in the league table of British charities. It was satisfying to be able to set the record straight on the good deeds carried out by this secret society which has generally suffered a bad press due to uninformed and biased reporting. Indeed the Brotherhood has a history of persecution, but here was a shining memorial to their charitable works, which also once included the Royal Masonic Hospital in North London, which is now closed, and various old people's homes across England as well as a girls' school in Rickmansworth, all of these institutions exist due to the patronage of Freemasons. Nowadays only a small proportion of the girls at Rickmansworth are 'petitioners', paid for by the Masons as a society.

The vast majority of the 765 girls at the school are from non-Masonic parents, but of course there are those girls who are daughters of Freemason families whose family pay fees as they would do at any other private school. Moves are afoot to make Masons' meeting places, their Lodges, more open to the public and less secretive, which should help to redress the balance in favour of a more positive image of Freemasonry.

We continued on to the 'Big School' as it was known in RMS days, where school assemblies were held in the past. I peeped around a curtain to see the actor Martin Shaw dressed in his robes filming an episode of *Judge John Deed*. We hurried through the quadrangle and saw one of his co-stars, Jenny Seagrove, deep in thought, obviously mentally rehearsing her lines. I am not in the slightest star-struck but it was quite exciting to suddenly and unexpectedly come across two well known stars of the small screen hard at work. I was informed that a popular series for young people, called *Hex* was simultaneously in production on this site.

Our tour led us through the dining hall where teachers and pupils used to eat their lunch together and then we made our way into the masters' dining hall, where teachers would meet to have their breakfast and evening meal with their colleagues. It had an impressive stained glass ceiling and Gordon pointed out the symbols of Freemasonry on it – the level, the set square, the square and compass and the mallet. The large fireplace had the words 'audi vide tace' carved into the stonework, which my schoolboy Latin translated roughly into 'I see, I hear, I take note'. I learned from Gordon, that a 'lewis' (a piece of lifting equipment) was the term for the son of a Mason and the daughter of a Mason was known as an ashlar (a piece of masonry).

From the masters' dining hall we made our way outside again, where I was shown a number of different buildings around which television company vans clustered with their attendant generators, cabling, sound and lighting equipment. I saw the tuck shop, Gordon's old Art and Craft Block, the observatory and the swimming pool, which had a set under construction inside its empty depths. Gordon led me on to 'Croft's Piece', an impressive swathe of green belt landscaping that was completed in 1938 after eight years' worth of toil by the school's own Pioneer Corps. Working with hand tools, such as picks and shovels, the boys had created their own rugby pitch. The side of a huge bank of earth had also been excavated by manual labour alone. The resultant space was turned into a cricket pitch, surrounded by a 400 metre running track. This is situated at the back of the school, bordering Finch Lane. Croft's Piece land will remain verdant, as it is green belt acreage, and any new buildings will be built only on brown-field sites where there are already existing buildings. As we strolled around Gordon pointed out various landmarks – the old laundry, the sanatorium, the infirmary. He recalled a flu epidemic that had once kept the resident nursing sister, the nurse and the other staff extremely busy. There had even been a mortuary at the school, it was now used as a store. Many Irish girls had worked at the RMS, where they had been employed variously, in the dining hall, as domestic maids and as cleaners. In South Drive there once resided a number of tradesmen, carpenters, electricians and plumbers, as well as a chef. My guide also told me about some famous Royal Masonic 'old boys', the actor Anthony Andrews, the senior executive Sir Stuart Hampson of the John Lewis Partnership, who had achieved considerable academic success at school and later on at university, and Sir Dick Evans who had become Chief Executive of British Aerospace despite leaving the RMS with no 'O' levels.

After our tour we sat chatting in the entrance hall and I asked Gordon about the 'underground tunnels' I had been told about years ago by a security guard. There are subways, he explained, that led under the cloisters to each house and to the laundry. The subways carried the hot water and gas services, they were big enough for a man to walk along them standing upright and they had come in useful during the Blitz in World War Two when they had served as temporary air raid shelters where masters and boys had taken refuge; they had eaten and slept and apparently 'got rather smelly' down there. As the school lies in a basin the firewatchers on duty in the clock tower could see the huge fires of London reflected in the clouds at night. The school was deprived of its headmaster for part of the war when Norman Sinclair was reclaimed by the Army as he held a regular commission in the reserves. He served with the Officer Training Corps; where he held the rank of Major and was called up from 1938 to 1940, but a campaign to restore him to his beloved school was eventually successful and he went on to serve his school right up till 1957.

I was fortunate that Steve Smith, the electrical contractor who took the ghostly photograph in the chapel, phoned while I was on site, and Gordon directed me to the electrician's house and introduced us. Steve's place is only a stone's throw away from the school and when we got there I found a friendly, pragmatic tradesman with a keen interest in photography. He had been searching for an answer to his puzzling picture but nobody had been able to offer any logical explanation as no fault could be found with his camera. He was certain that there had been nothing like a mist or vapour present when he took his photographs yet it was plainly visible on one of the exposures. After carefully studying his picture I explained that the image I believe he captured was what paranormal investigators call a 'stage three' manifestation. This is at the stage where a ghost has utilised enough energy to assume a sub-physical form using plasma (once commonly known as ectoplasm). Plasma is not solid, nor is it a liquid or a gas – a good example of plasma would be a candle flame. This sub-physical phenomenon is often invisible to the naked eye, but videotape and photographs can capture the ethereal presence as a bright blue or dull grey swirling indistinct shape, as illustrated by Steve's photograph. Typically the outline or silhouette of an apparition is created but it may also resemble the shape of a figure or a face. If Steve had been psychically sensitive he would have sensed the presence of a ghost particularly strongly at this stage. Temperature monitors and electro-magnetic field meters would have confirmed this. Stage three manifestations' movement is smoke-like and may occur at slow speed or in sudden brief and irregular bursts. At night-time torches and camera flashes frequently highlight entities at this level so that they become clearly visible to the human eye, but they can sometimes be seen without the aid of photography.

Over the years the Royal Masonic School has provided the backdrop for a multitude of both cinematic and television productions. During the last five years alone it has been estimated that well over 200 episodes from a variety of films, popular television series and commercials have been shot here. The entertainment industry can be a hard taskmaster with up to a day's filming proving to be necessary to produce as little as five seconds of actual screen time. Many members of these film crews have found Bushey's Royal Masonic School to be an eerie place, especially in the wee small hours of the morning when a phantom ex-school matron is just one of the ghosts who allegedly patrol the school block…

Chapter Twenty

CROXLEY GREEN

Scotsbridge Mill was once a paper mill, but around 1988/89 it was scheduled to be converted into a Beefeater Steakhouse, much to the annoyance of some local residents, who were quite vociferous in their objections. The ghosts of Scotsbridge Mill also seem to have objected, as there was an outbreak of hauntings which were verified by surveyors and brewery staff who worked on the site. Unearthly moans and groans were heard and a variety of objects mysteriously appeared and disappeared. One local clearly recalled seeing a headless horseman galloping through the grounds when he was a child. The case came to the attention of the Society for Psychical Research, who held a vigil in October 1989 but although they recorded various cold spots in the area, suggestive of a haunting, they experienced no manifestations that Halloween night. Plans were eventually dropped for the Beefeater Steakhouse but in due course the building was converted into a restaurant anyway although it was not a Beefeater. Since then there have been no reports to suggest any further haunting.

A private residence in Croxley Green briefly hit the headlines in May 1970 when it was subjected to poltergeist activity. The lady who resided there saw 'something' follow her down the stairs and she quite regularly heard footsteps upstairs when there was nobody on the upper floor. Workmen arriving to fit a new bathroom discovered all their tools 'flung on the lawn' despite all the doors being locked at the property. This unexplained activity also caused the lady distress in the form of her china and glassware being broken when it was hurled out of cupboards and smashed against walls by unseen forces. Poltergeist activity of this kind can be most distressing but fortunately it is, more often than not, a short-lived affair and such phenomena usually ceases in a matter of months. Such was the case in possibly the most famous poltergeist incident ever recorded, in December 1716 to January 1717, at Epworth Parsonage in North Lincolnshire, birthplace of John Wesley, the founder of Methodism. For two months the devoutly religious family was plagued by all manner of paranormal phenomena including John's father, the Reverend Wesley, who was physically pushed three times by some invisible force, there were also knocks and loud rumblings heard regularly and the sounds of 'something' running up and down stairs. A neighbour, Mr Hoole, was witness one night to some of these various unexplained noises. Latches were lifted on the doors and even as Emilia, the parson's daughter, held down the latch she found the door pushed violently against her. Weird animal-like shapes were seen both by Mrs Wesley and by a serving man. The Wesleys bought a dog, hoping to either track down or frighten away the cause of their disturbances, but of course the poor animal was itself terrified by the strange noises. All of these reported incidents were collected together by John Wesley and the entire material was published after his death in 1791.

Chapter Twenty-One

RICKMANSWORTH

A frozen food supermarket isn't the most obvious site for a ghost to frequent; nevertheless there have been reports from one such establishment in Rickmansworth where staff have been touched by ghostly hands in the staff room and have felt a presence around the toilets in the upstairs part of the building. The supermarket stands on the site of the Swan Hotel, which was haunted by the shade of an old man who was seen upstairs in the past by a number of staff and guests at the hotel. It seems that he is still attached to this site and with the passage of time he has become sensed and felt rather than being seen.

SARRATT

The village of Sarratt, lying north of Rickmansworth, is a village of curiosities. The first curiosity concerns its place name. Over the centuries the place name has changed probably more times than any other in Hertfordshire. It was originally known as Syret, later becoming Syreth in the 11th to the 13th centuries. It did not rate a mention in the Domesday Book, which implies that the land did not produce any profit for the King, there is a clue which may be derived from the Old English word 'steret', meaning 'dry or barren place'. In the 16th century, after three more variations to the name, it became Sarrett, only to change yet again, in the 17th century when it finally became Sarratt.

It is believed that the village lay on a drover's route, Sarratt was where the drovers could rest their sheep and their animals could feed on the grass and drink from the ponds that were sited on the village green.

Gradually Sarratt has embraced the modern world, in the early 1920s a water supply was laid on and in 1932 electricity arrived. The 12th century parish church, is another curiosity, standing a mile south of the village at Church End, rather than at its heart. It is situated where there was once a Roman cemetery, amidst a maze of field-paths, close on the Buckinghamshire border. Near at hand lay one of the village's two pubs, the Cock Inn, a manor house and a row of early-nineteenth-century Gothic style almshouses.

Tradition has it that the 12th century builders found it impossible to construct the church near the village green because each morning, after work had begun, the stones and other building materials were found moved down the long hill, a mile away. Eventually it was decided that perhaps a 'higher authority' was trying to make a point, so the church was finally erected in its present position.

The attractiveness of Sarratt in modern times was recognised with the award of Best Kept Village in 1982. It retains a long, wide village green with houses surrounding it and there are a blend of cottages, council houses and flats, modern bungalows and old and new houses to be found in the village. There is still a pond, a dell and old water pump that have all been here for many generations. The May Day Fair is another strong link with the past, it continues, as it has done for hundreds of years, to fill the village with visitors, music and noise.

Sarratt's Rosehall case deserves special mention because it is the first haunted place to come to the attention of Britain's undisputed, number one ghost-hunter himself, Peter Underwood. He heard his first ghost-story when he was still a child, as Rosehall, a 17th century farmhouse which stood on the site of a 12th century manor house, it was occupied then by his maternal grandparents, so it is a particularly well-documented story. The President of the Ghost Club wrote about it in his autobiography, *No Common Task*. The story goes that in November 1897 a traveller was taken in by his friends after braving a horse-ride of several hours duration, which included travelling through a bad storm, all the way from London. After his cold, damp and tiring journey he soon fell asleep only to be awakened by the barking of dogs. He heard his host in the adjoining bedroom opening his window then calming the animals. The traveller went to sleep once more but woke up again to feel heavy pressure on his feet. By the dying embers of the fire he saw the smartly dressed figure of a man who was stooping and supporting himself on the bedstead. The man was dressed in a blue coat with shiny gilt buttons, but the man's head could not be seen as it was hidden by the curtains of the four-poster bed. The traveller had dropped his clothes at the foot of the bed in his haste to get into it and he wondered if it was his host who was visiting his room, in the act of picking them up, although it seemed unlikely. He raised himself upright and was just about to address his nocturnal visitor when the figure passed on and disappeared. He got out of bed and searched the room, found the door locked as he had left it earlier and finding himself completely alone made his puzzled way back to his bed. It was now ten minutes past two in the morning, he tried to get back to sleep, but, perhaps not surprisingly, sleep evaded him for the remainder of the night.

The following morning the visitor was asked how he had slept, so he told his story to his hosts, who agreed that the room was allegedly haunted by the spirit of a headless man, although they themselves had not seen the ghost. They were sorry that their guest's sleep had been disturbed but there had been no other room available.

A short time later, the traveller was telling his tale to some ladies that he was dining with, as they were from Hertfordshire, and he was interrupted by a lady who had also stayed at the farmhouse. She corroborated his story, having had the same experience and it was her belief that many people had witnessed this same ghost, the spirit of a man, murdered in that very room some years before, who had been decapitated.

Peter Underwood's investigations revealed that in the 19th century a prayer meeting had been held in the house, to 'lay' the ghost, as it had been particularly active at the time. An unusual feature of the case was that the apparition was never seen by the owners, only by strangers to the farmhouse. The owners at the time of the enquiry rubbished the story, but they would wouldn't they, as they were never likely to witness the haunting? When the Ghost Club's President revisited Rosehall in 1962, along with some other members of his society, three of them correctly identified the haunted bedroom without prior knowledge of which room it was reputed to be.

The appearances of the headless gentleman ceased many years ago now, but recent occupants of the property declared that the place remained haunted, the vestiges are 'an uncomfortable feeling' about the place and the disinclination of animals to venture upstairs.

Chapter Twenty-Two

SOUTH OXHEY

My friend Lynn lives in Oxhey and she describes herself as a 'psychic consultant'. She is clairvoyant (from the French 'clear seeing') which, in its highest sense, means that she has been born with the ability to view the non-physical planes, the spiritual worlds and the beings that inhabit them. Like many clairvoyants Lynn's ability overlaps her other psychic faculties such as her clairaudient (also from the French, 'clear hearing') gift, an ability to hear spirit communication, but primarily she sees spirits and to a lesser extent (which she tells me she is developing) she hears them and also feels their presence (which is known as clairsentience or 'clear sensing'). We may all have some clairsentience to a greater or lesser degree as it is closely linked to intuition or 'gut feeling', which can so often prove useful in steering us in the right direction when it comes to making difficult decisions, for instance. It can be comforting to have the psychic's rare gifts, as was the case when Lynn returned from a friend's funeral and was invited by the deceased's son back to the family house. As Lynn turned to look at the son she clearly saw his dead mother behind him in the kitchen, making a cup of tea, a white-haired old lady wearing a powder-blue tracksuit and looking exactly as she had been in life.

Lynn uses her psychic abilities to help others, and one recent case that happened around March 2005 involved a lady who lived in Oxhey village. She called on Lynn's help because she was having problems with her lights, a favourite target for spirits' attention. One light in particular would suddenly switch itself on; it was the type that you had to pat three times to bring it to its full intensity. The home was a lovely old cottage which had been built on to and the current owners had extended it once again. Building work can sometimes attract the attention of spirits, they can be resentful that 'their' home is being altered. With her remarkable faculties Lynn was able to clearly see an elderly couple, first a lady appeared, with white hair, wearing a pinafore dress and carrying a duster, then behind her was a man and they were clearly shocked that she was able to see them! They seemed to be caretakers of the old cottage rather than previous owners and they were from the north of England, Lynn described them as a hard-working pair. She asked them to stop playing with the lights as it was upsetting the present lady occupant and her child. The trouble ceased; the 'caretakers' are still about

according to Lynn, but they no longer trouble the current residents...
That is the thing about apparitions, if you are clear and firm and tell
them not to bother you because they are frightening you,
inconveniencing you or otherwise being a nuisance, that is quite
often enough to do the trick and they will leave you alone.

Over the years I have found that there are many, many claimants
to advanced clairvoyant and mediumistic (communication with the
dead) abilities. The vast majority of these claims are greatly
exaggerated, by the self-deluded, by attention-seekers and/or
money-grabbing charlatans who are intent on parting vulnerable,
often newly-bereaved people, from their cash. Happily there are a
small minority, like Lynn, who have genuine psychic abilities and you
can recognise them by certain characteristics. They are usually
'giving' rather than 'taking' people, who don't charge inflated sums of
money for their services. Indeed they can often be reluctant about
asking for any money at all for their help, or if they do it is at a level
that is easily affordable to everybody. Often it will be found that the
less genuine the abilities the higher the charges that will be
demanded by the greedy, untalented majority who give all psychics
a bad name. This is nothing new; during Victorian times, with the
sudden, vast explosion of interest in the supernatural, unscrupulous
mercenary 'mediums' flourished in a bid to fleece trusting, desperate
and lonely victims. Fortunately many were exposed by investigators
like magician Harry Houdini and scientist William Crookes.

Genuine psychics tend to be down to earth, not 'showy' or
'theatrical' (we have come across quite a few like this during the
course of our Anglia Paranormal Investigation Society cases and
they can be a right pain in the neck). The real psychic is usually very
matter-of-fact concerning his or her gifts, like Chris Robinson, the
'Dream Detective', whom I wrote about in *Ghostly
Bedfordshire...Reinvestigated*, and they are surprised that more of
us aren't aware of our own latent psychic potential. They are also
keen to develop other people who are interested in the subject and
will volunteer their advice, training and encouragement without
thought of financial gain. Above all they don't see themselves as
something 'special', they are not 'divas', indeed it is their very
'ordinariness' that is extraordinary!

I have learned to trust a few of these 'sensitives' and we are
exceedingly fortunate to have some truly gifted psychics as
members of APIS, since, unlike some investigation societies, we do
not rely on the scientific methods of paranormal investigation alone.
From the outset I have been convinced that the spiritual and
scientific approaches are mutually compatible as we are all working
to the same end, to try and make sense of the paranormal
phenomena that we encounter on a regular basis. Psychic

investigators have just as important a role to play in an investigation as our technical consultants. The former use their sixth sense, the latter rely on the most advanced electronic measuring devices that quickly detect temperature drops, orb appearances, unexplained breezes, electromagnetic field fluctuations and other signs of ghostly activity.

The downside of using 'sensitives' to help us in our exploration of the paranormal is that we are using one unexplained phenomenon to explain another. When we have compared notes of one psychic's impressions with those of another psychic, sometimes gained many years previously, the results have, on occasion, been astonishing. The Chicksands Priory case is a good example, this was also documented in *Ghostly Bedfordshire...Reinvestigated*. Self-confessed sceptic Roger Ward, the Priory's historian, was given many psychic impressions by well-known medium Marion Goodfellow, during her visit in 1999. When he compared these statements with the notes he had made during the visit by another sensitive in 1975 he made an incredible discovery, 'It was as if the first clairvoyant had returned after 24 years,' he told me.

In order to get the best out of the working partnership with our clairvoyants at APIS we give them no prior information about the haunting we are currently investigating. We do make notes in our logbooks about their impressions e.g. 'I feel a great sadness' or 'I feel frightened', which are very real to the witness at the time and these need to be compared with impressions gained at subsequent investigations in the same locations. I strongly believe that this information is just as worthy of being logged as temperature and humidity fluctuations, EMF activity, sounds recorded or unexplained smells detected.

Chapter Twenty-Three

WATFORD

Watford is first mentioned around the year 945 and its Old English root is in 'wath' or hunting, so Watford was the 'ford used when hunting'. It has developed into Hertfordshire's largest town, after rapid growth in the nineteenth and twentieth centuries. Watford wraiths come in all varieties…

Garston has a 'smelly ghost' which made the pages of the local press in July 2003 when the story of two families living on the Bramfield Estate was revealed. A series of unexplained occurrences left the families with the conviction that the events were paranormal in nature. Worst of all was the pervasive stench of urine. It was found that prior to the building of the terraced houses there had been some garages on the site. A tramp was burned to death in a fire at the garages about eight to ten years previously.

Newspaper offices are out of the usual run of haunted locations but one of the exceptions is the offices of the *Watford Observer* where the canteen is the focus for some quite nasty paranormal effects. Catering staff who have arrived early for work in the morning have been pushed and prodded by an invisible assailant; one woman was knocked to the ground by the force of the ghostly onslaught.

An employee was working alone in the canteen late one night and heard something banging on the window, upon investigation, however, nothing could be found to explain the noises. The sounds continued and in addition a strange whistling seemed to invade the building as well. The badly scared man's response was to turn his radio up so loud that it drowned out the weird noises.

Cassiobury Park was once a palatial Elizabethan house with magnificent and exotic gardens situated just north of what was to become Watford station. Cassiobury's name can be traced back to the pre-Roman King Cassivellaunus and the house was the seat of the Earls of Essex. The house was demolished in 1927 and its staircase found its way to the Metropolitan Museum in New York. Most of the former magnificent estate is now beneath pavements and tarmac but part of the grounds, with a lake and a section of the Grand Union Canal, form the public park that is now Cassiobury Park. It is here that the ghost of Lord Capel, of Little Hadham Hall, is said to wander the pathways at night, particularly on the 9th March.

Lord Capel raised a troop for King Charles I and was recognised as a brave, capable commander and enthusiastic supporter of his King during the Civil War. He was eventually forced to surrender to the Parliamentarian General Fairfax, who was a man of great honour, a most successful professional soldier and an outstanding general of horse. Lord Capel was sent to the Tower of London and he escaped, but he was finally beheaded in1649, in the same year that his King was executed. Capel's heart was placed in a box in the muniment room of his house at Little Hadham Hall, and at the Restoration it was presented as a memento to Charles II. Lord Capel's ghost, however, continued to haunt Cassiobury Park, where it was variously described as either headless or with long hair and a full moustache.

The Grove, built around 1756, is a stately home just to the north of Cassiobury which was more fortunate than its near neighbour; it still stands, now in use as a hotel, and Watford's ring road borders its land. The mansion was home to the Earls of Clarendon until the 1920s and lavish parties were held here, guests included King Edward VII. It is haunted by Lord Doneraile, who leads a pack of hounds on ghostly fox hunts during certain nights of the year, usually during stormy weather. Legend has it that Lord Doneraile was condemned to endless hunting as punishment for converting an ancient chapel in the mansion's basement into a kitchen, when he built the Grove in the mid-eighteenth century. A building existed on this site long before the Grove and investigations revealed the fact that the foundations are over 500 years old. A man who was a warden at the house spoke to the *Watford Observer* in 1974 and he claimed to have seen the ghost many times. He also recalled the alterations in 1957 when builders removed plaster from what is now the entrance lounge to uncover a pale blue font, built into a three foot thick wall.

Copperfields was once a restaurant in Watford but was later converted to offices, in a building that dates back to the fifteenth century. A ghost in Elizabethan dress was regularly seen walking through the restaurant after the customers had left. One employee arrived early for work one morning and was greeted by the ghost, who promptly disappeared. The restaurant owner, Albert Fiedler, didn't see the spirit for several years but one day, as he was working in the kitchen, he became aware of someone in the restaurant. He went out to see who it might be but there was only a grey mist to be seen. Some days later there was a scream from the restaurant and a frightened employee ran into the kitchen. She said that she had seen something like a grey mist moving across the room and she didn't want to return there. Mr Fiedler hadn't told anyone of his experience at that time. On another occasion Mr Fiedler was on his own, and the restaurant was closed, when he saw the grey mist again, but this time it resolved itself into a human form. The restaurant owner was able to give a detailed description of a man wearing a tight-fitting tunic with puffy sleeves and a ruff. Mr Fiedler's father-in-law saw the 'Elizabethan' on one occasion; the ghost ascended the stairs and moved through the restaurant before vanishing near the outside wall.

When the restaurant became offices the installation of an alarm system seemed to trigger unwelcome ghostly attention and workers felt an atmosphere about the place. Staff who arrived early were often greeted with a spooky 'good morning' by the presence, which also adversely affected computers and set the alarm off once, and no one could switch it off.

The Palace Theatre, Watford, was built in 1908 as a music hall and is famous as a venue where Charlie Chaplin performed before his great Hollywood success. It has also become well known as one of many haunted theatres in Great Britain. During one incident, at 3am in the morning, while workmen were erecting a new set, members of staff were startled to see the curtains covering a door part, as if someone had just walked through, they then heard footsteps cross to another door and with that the curtains were once again moved aside although there was nobody to be seen. At another time an usherette locking up the gallery saw an apparition that walked down the aisle and then leapt over the barriers before disappearing.

Backstage workers have sensed an invisible presence and heard ghostly footsteps. One room in the theatre is particularly susceptible to paranormal activity, with strong feelings of a presence, also an icy cold atmosphere is felt and footsteps that stop at the door have been heard. For some reason, lost in the mists of time, 'the ghost' of the Palace Theatre is known as 'Aggie' but it is more likely a multiple haunting as at least three people have died here, some as the result of accidents, during the long history of this old building. One death was a follow spot operator who fell from the gallery, another was a dresser (also killed in a fall) and the third fatality was a former stage hand.

Most outstanding of all paranormal stories ever associated with Watford is the one that took place in France in 1901, indeed it has been called the most famous ghost story of all time. One of the two witnesses, Eleanor Jourdain, was the headmistress of Corran School for Girls in Langley Road in Watford at the time. Born in November 1863 Miss Jourdain was one of the first women to go to Oxford, where she studied modern history at Lady Margaret Hall. This was during a time before sexual equality was achieved in education; females were not allowed degrees and were only permitted to attend lectures if no one objected, as long as they were accompanied by knitting chaperones! Eleanor Jourdain was nearly 30 and had taught for six years before she established her school at Langley Road, in 1892, with just six pupils.

Miss Jourdain continued to improve Corran School for Girls. New classrooms were added, playing fields were purchased and two boarding houses were built. The establishment quickly achieved the local education board's approval and by the turn of the century there were over 100 students and 18 members of staff. As the school prepared girls for Oxford its headmistress kept in touch with the women's colleges, where she came to the attention of Miss Annie Moberly, principal of St Hugh's, who was seeking a deputy. That summer of 1901 Eleanor invited Annie to stay at the flat she had acquired in Paris, in order that they could get to know one another better.

On August 10th 1901 they decided to visit Versailles as neither of them had been there before. Eleanor and Annie were like any other tourists, neither had any particular interest in Versailles, or French history in general at this time and they had displayed no interest in, or knowledge of, the supernatural. The two Englishwomen looked around the main building before heading for the Petit Trianon, the small palace in the grounds that was a gift from Louis XVI to his wife Marie Antoinette and which had become a favourite place for the Queen. The teachers soon realised that they were lost and felt that something was not quite right, when they met two men that they took to be gardeners, who gave them directions, but the women thought their odd dress – long grey-green coats and tricorn hats, seemed very out of place. The ladies continued walking when a strange feeling of oppression stole over them. Eleanor was later to write: 'I began to feel as though I were walking in my sleep.' They both felt that their surroundings seemed flat and lifeless, the atmosphere intensely still. Ahead of them was a small bandstand or garden kiosk surrounded by trees. On the steps stood a man wearing a black cloak and a large hat. There was something disturbing about him, his dark skin had been ravaged by smallpox; there was an evil and unseeing expression to him. Suddenly a running man approached, Eleanor observed that he was young, agitated, and red in the face, he had long dark hair and he wore buckled shoes and a cloak. He directed them towards the house before hastening away. Eventually they reached the Petit Trianon and were about to join the tour when Annie noticed a woman drawing in the garden, but Eleanor did not see her. Later Annie described this lady as wearing old-fashioned clothes, wearing a white hat on top of a mass of fair hair. They entered the Petit

Trianon, saw a wedding party in the distance, and after their tour returned to their hotel for tea.

It wasn't till the following week that Annie wrote a letter home describing her visit when she suddenly felt the same oppressive feeling return. When she asked Eleanor if she thought the Petit Trianon was haunted they started talking to discover what each of them had seen. It was the first time they had compared notes and both ladies concluded that something mysterious had occurred on the afternoon of their visit to Versailles.

That November, at home in England, Annie Moberly invited her future deputy head to Oxford to compare notes again on the strange incident at Versailles and she undertook to thoroughly research into the history surrounding the French Revolution. Miss Jourdain then detailed her own account of events and asked her French mistress, Mademoiselle Menegoz for any details relating to the haunting of the Petit Trianon. Mme Menegoz told her that on a certain day in August Marie Antoinette and her courtiers could often be seen in the gardens.

On a cold and rainy afternoon in January 1902, Eleanor Jourdain returned alone to Versailles. It was to be another strange feeling for her – 'it was as if I had crossed a line and was suddenly in a circle of influence.' Two labourers in bright tunics and hoods were loading a cart, but when she looked back a second later there was no sign of them and there was a clear view in all directions. Around her she heard voices and the rustling of silk dresses but could see no one. Later that same year Miss Jourdain handed over the management of Corran School to Miss Wishaw, the Fifth Form mistress, and took up the post of vice-principal at St Hugh's.

Three years later Miss Moberly and Miss Jourdain returned to the gardens at Versailles and were shocked to see that everything had changed. The trees, a rustic bridge, a 'kiosk', a ravine and a cascade had all vanished. The teachers became certain that the surroundings that they had formerly seen belonged in the period of Louis XVI and Marie Antoinette. After studying a multitude of history books they were convinced that they had seen real historical pre-Revolution figures and Charlotte Moberly's 'sketching woman' was, in all likelihood, Marie Antoinette herself. Their book was published in 1911, under the pseudonyms of Elizabeth Morrison and Francis Lamont, and it was a sensational best-seller. It fired the imagination of the general public and intrigued academics and sceptics alike, who were as puzzled as the participants in the affair over what it could all possibly mean. After publication several people who had lived in a house overlooking the park at Versailles confirmed that they too had witnessed similar scenes so often that they had come to accept it. Eleanor Jourdain died in 1924 and it was only then that the authors' true identities were revealed. This aroused further public interest when it became known that the witnesses were women of such impeccable character and solid social standing. Miss Jourdain's school was eventually demolished but the educational connection is maintained on Langley Road through West Herts College.

Sadly the remarkable book, *An Adventure*, is now out of print, but the participants never altered their story. The two teachers' researches satisfied them that they had been privileged to see the park as it was in 1789. That year the French Revolution was reaching its climax as the Bastille fell, on July 14, and on August 4 the nobles agreed to surrender all feudal rights. The two academics satisfied themselves, after years of painstaking research, that the exact date when they had gone back in time was August the 5th 1789; Marie Antoinette's final day at Versailles. The 'running man' had been the messenger who brought the news of the mob's advance, while the 'gardeners' were in fact two Swiss Guardsmen on duty that day. The man at the kiosk was identified as the Compte de Vaudreuil, a pock-marked Creole and actor-friend of the Queen. As for the 'sketching lady' she was Marie Antoinette herself. In all probability every one of the ghosts encountered by the two English ladies had died a horrible death at the hands of the French mob.

On August 10 the Tuileries was sacked, the Swiss guards were murdered and the King and Queen were arrested. In her final days at Versailles, with news of the ever-worsening crisis developing, Marie Antoinette must indeed have been anxious and frightened. The King and his courtiers must have shared that fear – enough to produce a kind of 'group terror' so strong that it left its 'psychic imprint' which was picked up by a 'sensitive' over a hundred years later? Miss Jourdain was certainly psychic, with powers of second sight, as attested by Miss Moberly but her friend refused to develop her abilities as she disapproved of 'occultism', considering it morbid and dangerous, a view shared by her long term colleague and friend.

In 1938 an English psychical researcher named R.J. Sturge-Whiting reinvestigated the case and he claimed, through his researches, to have located all the places the women had described in their account and concluded that they had followed the paths that still exist on their first visit and failed to find them on their subsequent visit. Further fuel was added to this particular fire when Philippe Jullian published a biography of Count Robert de Montesquiou describing how this dandy took a house near Versailles in the early 1890s and often spent whole days in the park, and his friend Mme de Greffulhe organised a fancy-dress party in the Dairy. Philippe Jullian surmised that the two English schoolteachers possibly mistook some costumed guests for 'ghosts'. It was pretty damning stuff at the time and still influences some modern writers on the paranormal today, who dismiss the whole amazing Versailles adventure as 'explained'. I am not at all convinced with this rather glib 'explanation', which I also find insulting to the memory of two remarkable educators. I am certain that they did not either suffer from over-active imaginations or selective memories, nor did they mistake anyone's identity. These were two highly intelligent, respectable women in full command of their faculties, who were certain about their encounter, sure of the details, and with no possible motivation to concoct such a remarkable story.

Leaving aside the characters of the witnesses, the later theorists didn't attempt to explain the dramatic changes in the physical features of the area – like the missing kiosk, the ravine and its bridge and the small cascade, that were all seen during the first visit of Miss Jourdain and Miss Moberly.

During 1903 and 1904 the Watford Headmistress returned many times and became quite familiar with the layout of the park but always found it 'modernised' in comparison with the 1901 visit. It should also be mentioned that the 'fancy dress' theory didn't hold up either, since Count de Montesquiou moved to Versailles in the early 1890s and moved to Neuilly in 1894 so any fancy-dress party rehearsal would have taken place seven years before the English ladies' visit.

There can be no doubt that this particular 'adventure' remains a classic case in modern psychical research, and one of great rarity. It continues to fascinate readers who discover it for the first time, and it has been the basis of a great British television adaptation, also shown in the USA in 1983 and 1984. It has been described as an experience of retrocognition of the past and certain modern parapsychologists have labelled it an 'immersion timeslip', that is where the percipients are immersed in another era yet remain able to physically interact with their environment. The Versailles 'adventure' is one which defies explanation, a deeply puzzling and strange incident that will continue to be debated by students of the paranormal for many years to come.

ALDENHAM

Aldenham is close to Watford, lying east of Hertfordshire's largest town, and it is perhaps best known for its reservoirs, as well as the canal that runs through it. An affluent community, Aldenham boasts a lovely golf and country club, and one of its private schools has its very own ghost, seen in the old part of Edge Grove Preparatory School, which was once a country house. It is in this vicinity that there have been various sightings of a 'grey lady', in the rooms and corridors of the former house. The spirit is thought to be that of a former resident who broke her neck after falling down the staircase.

Aldenham holds fond memories for me, from my younger days back in the 70s, when I used to visit the teachers' training college at Wall Hall, memories of discos held here and of driving back to Finchley, North London in the early hours of the morning, in my MGB roadster, ah carefree days! I didn't see anything out of the ordinary back then but Wall Hall Mansion certainly has a haunted reputation. It is a place that certainly looks like it might be visited by ghosts, with its impressive, solid-looking Gothic frontage, which has been used in a number of film and television shows.

I found out that there had been a Wall Hall on this site as far back as the 13th century, and in the 1700s it was built as a farmhouse and the present building's exterior dates from 1802, when it was called Aldenham Abbey. By 1812 it was owned by Admiral Sir Morice Pole and after 1910 the fabulously wealthy Pierpoint Morgan family, American bankers and steel mill owners, acquired the property. By 1945 Wall Hall had passed on to the University of Hertfordshire and it became one of their campuses. A woman's ghost, thought to be of a former housekeeper dating from the times when the mansion was in private hands, was seen in the Philosophy Block on more than one occasion. As recently as a winter's night in February 2001 there was a confirmed sighting, by the housekeeping manager, Lynne Bright, who turned out to be an excellent witness. There was a most detailed description of 'a woman with grey hair, wearing dark shoes and a long grey dress, nipped in at the waist, with a bodice that had a white collar and long sleeves.' So real did the apparition appear that the manager had a conversation with the ghost, though as is usual in genuine hauntings it was a one-way conversation. The ghost made no reply, her (spirit) body language said it all, and she merely frowned hard, initially put her hands on her hips and later folded her arms while continuing to frown. The message was clear; the ghostly housekeeper disapproved of the modern cleaning regime. When Lynne explained to her fellow cleaner that she was talking with a lady in grey, the other woman hurriedly left the room. The 'grey lady' had not been visible to her colleague, and it was then that Lynne realised she had encountered a ghost!

Children's laughter is another phenomenon that has been regularly reported by the security staff at Wall Hall and one room in particular has been singled out for its odd atmosphere – M7, a lecture room, where it is always cold even on the sunniest of summer days. Various staff members have attested to other psychic disturbances, lights have been switched on and off by invisible agencies and the swishing sound of a long skirt has been heard.

Wall Hall is yet another site which has fallen into the hands of the developers. In summer 2005 work was progressing well and would soon be completed – the campuses and the mansion being converted into a massive development of executive homes by a company called Octagon.

LEAVESDEN

Leavesden is synonymous with the British movie industry, it is home to Leavesden Aerodrome, where the large-scale studios' complete facilities for major film production attracted the Millennium Group, owners of the Millennium Studios at Elstree, and they bought the site and established Leavesden Developments Ltd in 1995. Since then the company has established world-class studios and film-making facilities with over one million square feet of studio space and over a hundred acres of clear horizon backlot. Leavesden has attracted top production firms including JAK Productions with the *Star Wars* prequels, directed by George Lucas.

Goldeneye, one of the most successful James Bond movies ever made, was filmed in Hertfordshire by EON Productions at Leavesden Aerodrome. Some of the interior scenes of *The Beach*, starring Leonardo Di Caprio were filmed at Leavesden and one of my favourite horror movies, which won an Oscar for Art Direction, *Sleepy Hollow*, was made almost entirely here.

There is a ghost story attached to Leavesden, which dates back to an accidental death during World War Two, when an RAF corporal tried to open the hanger door on number two hanger, using a ratchet which operated the chains to lift the door. Unfortunately gale force winds were blowing through the county at the time and a sudden gust caused the heavy door to come crashing down on the airman and he died from his injuries. It is said that on windy nights the sound of rattling chains can still be heard, though both chains and hanger are history now and the ghost of an RAF corporal in World War Two uniform has been seen in the area where the hanger used to be.

BOOK FOUR

West Hertfordshire Wraiths

Chapter Twenty-Four
BERKHAMSTED

The five hundred-year-old Crown Inn at Berkhamsted is probably the best known haunted location in the town. It is home to the ghost of an old lady of unknown origin. The old lady was seen in a rocking chair in an alcove of what is now the cellar. She seems to be resentful of the intrusions of the staff, demonstrating her displeasure by tampering with barrels, causing bottles of wine to shatter and making light bulbs jump out of their sockets. Her presence has been detected by dogs, which refuse to go near the cellar.

The *Berkhamsted Gazette* carried a report in December 1969 about a cottage in Picotts End which had been subject to the unwelcome attentions of a poltergeist that slammed doors and caused rapping noises and footsteps to be heard in an empty upstairs room. Crockery was broken as it sat on the shelf, pictures were thrown off walls and objects appeared and disappeared.

A few miles to the east of Berkhamsted is the village of Little Gaddesden and Elizabethan Ashridge Manor House, haunted by the ghost of churchwarden William Jarman, who died in the 18th century. Locally the structure on top of the chimney stack at the manor house is referred to as 'Jarman's coffin'. The unfortunate Jarman lived in a house close to the Manor House, which was destroyed by fire some time around 1870. He was in love with the heiress of the Earls of Bridgewater's Ashridge estate, but it was an unrequited love and the churchwarden committed suicide. His death was variously attributed to drowning himself in the pond just across the Green, hanging himself in the house or hanging himself from a nearby oak tree. The latter is believed to be the more likely version of events. His ghost has never actually been seen in the house but was glimpsed by the pond. Jarman's spirit, however, was felt around the house, as candles would dip or go out and later on electric lights were similarly affected.

On one occasion two people who were talking in the drawing room remarked on the fact that all the lights, one after another went out. This report echoes the story of the seven parsons who came to exorcize Jarman's shade in times past. The seven candles they carried were extinguished one after another until just the one remained. It stubbornly refused to be snuffed out by the ghost, which was subdued after the exorcism but still occasionally showed its presence.

In the 1960s Miss Dorothy Erhart lived at Ashridge Manor House and she experienced her standard lamp being switched off by some unseen presence but she regarded Jarman's phantom as benevolent and friendly.

In 1963 there was a Ministry of Housing enquiry which mentioned the building of a new house nearby as a possible influence on the resumption of the haunting at Ashridge Manor House…

An interesting fact concerns the monastery which used to exist on the site of the Ashridge estate. An old manuscript was discovered here, entitled 'Johannes de Rupesscissa', and it was all about occult rituals, with advice on burning incense in order to rid a haunted house of evil spirits!

Chapter Twenty-Five

HARPENDEN

Harpenden's origins as a farming and agricultural community are illustrated by the fact that the small town (currently populated by some 30,000 residents) is home to the world's oldest Agricultural Research Centre – Rothamstead Experimental Station, situated to the south west of the town. It covers a vast area with numerous greenhouses and administration buildings, and I have visited it on several occasions. It was founded in 1864 by John Bennet Lawes. Its farms, covering 400 hectares, are based at Rothamstead and Woburn in Bedfordshire. The research station is justly famous as a centre of excellence for science, supporting sustainable land management and looking at environmental issues relating to biochemistry, soil, landscape and the ecosystem.

Harpenden's name originates from 'Valley of the Nightingales' and there is still a lot of evidence of its village days in the Common and the High Street. The Common covers 96 hectares to the south of the town and has a County Wildlife site designation as well as containing a cricket, football and golf club. The attractively tree-lined High Street is a conservation area and boasts many fine 17th and 18th century listed buildings and the town is also a consistent winner in the Anglia in Bloom competition. The coming of the railways in the 1860s and the 1880s was responsible for the rapid growth of the community and this is explained in the Railway Museum. Perhaps the most famous celebrity resident of 'The Village' (as Harpenden is known to its inhabitants) was top comedian Eric Morecambe, who lived here for many years and his widow, Joan, is still a resident. Not far away lived the reclusive film director Stanley Kubrick of *2001, A Space Odyssey* fame, who brought Tom Cruise and Nicole Kidman to live in Hertfordshire, while they were starring in the last film that Kubrick made before he died, *Eyes Wide Shut*.

There are at least two haunted pubs in this West Hertfordshire commuter town, the Cross Keys and the Silver Cup. The Cross Keys is a well documented case. In the 13th century there was a guest house on this site, which was owned by Westminster Abbey and the cross keys are the insignia of St Peter, hence the tavern's name. The main bar has two brass crossed keys set in the floor. In 1960 the relief manager reported a strange incident. After locking up he was disturbed by a number of voices coming from downstairs. He crept down, as quietly as possible, to discover three figures crouching over a bar table. As the door swung open, three faces turned towards him. He was later to describe them as shaven-headed men wearing dark, heavy robes like those worn by medieval monks. He was not afraid to admit to running upstairs and locking himself in his bedroom.

Some years later the Johnson family, who were the Cross Keys' licensees at the time, also witnessed strange goings-on, like the ashtray, which weighed several pounds, that was unaccountably found 'spinning like a top' in an empty bar one Sunday afternoon, after hours. Mrs Brenda Johnson also discovered a favourite skirt missing from her wardrobe one day. Three months later this same skirt reappeared back in her wardrobe as mysteriously as it had disappeared. Mr Johnson went to pick up a clothes brush on another occasion, only to find that it wasn't where it had been left. This time the brush reappeared three days later, near the fireplace.

The Silver Cup is a 17th century inn near the Common which was owned by the Archer family for many generations. Roy Mills was the landlord in 1985, when he talked about his encounter with a 'grey lady', with 'pulled-back hair' in the corridor of his pub, who smiled at him before disappearing through a closed door. Was she an Archer family member?

Rose Cottage in Church Green is another haunted building in the 'Valley of the Nightingales.' Some people believe that a suicide in the 17th century is connected with events that occurred around 1985, which led to three young men abandoning their tenancy to the ghosts. The men were no longer able to put up with the strange noises they repeatedly heard during the night.

The eighteen-year-old woman who lived at Rose Cottage 300 years earlier was alleged to have travelled to London to seek her fortune but returned home in shame. She killed her illegitimate baby before taking her own life and was then doomed to wander the cottage in her nightdress, moving furniture and searching for the child. Rose Cottage was blessed by a local priest but after a short time the noises began to be heard again…

WHEATHAMPSTEAD

A few miles to the east of Harpenden is Wheathampstead, which is believed by historians to be the likely former capital for the Catuvellauni tribe, Celtic for 'expert warrior'.

An unsolved murder is reckoned to be the source of a well known Wheathampstead haunting, at Marshalls Heath Lane. In December 1957 seventeen-year-old Ann Noblett disappeared after getting off a bus in the Lower Luton Road and her frozen body was found the following month in a wood at Whitwell. Detectives established that she had been strangled and stripped then redressed in the same clothes before being hidden inside an industrial freezer for about a month. She was discovered with her hands across her chest, still wearing her glasses and with no money missing from her purse. No motive for the killing was ever found...

Seventeen years later, in 1974, Anne's ghost was making its presence felt at a plant hire business situated on the former pig farm near where she had once lived. Workers at the plant hire firm were plagued by odd incidents – locked doors would somehow open themselves and one man saw a young girl playing at the end of the sheds and he approached her to have a talk, but by the time he reached the sheds she had simply disappeared. He was certain that there was nowhere for the girl to have gone but past him. Another man reported that 'something' unseen touched his head while he was feeding the cat and this animal was noted for arching its back and hissing, threatening some invisible 'enemy' at the premises.

Another strange Wheathampstead story concerns the haunted B651, where a woman motorist, returning to Wheathampstead from St Albans, reported seeing a column of Roman soldiers, led by a standard-bearer, marching along the road. They were illuminated by her car's headlights and she had passengers, but her companions didn't see the soldiers, although they confirmed that they, like the driver, heard the eerie sounds of marching feet and jingling metal. It is often the way with hauntings that not all of the witnesses actually see the apparitions simultaneously.

MARKYATE

A couple of miles to the west of Harpenden lies Markyate, at the north-west corner of Hertfordshire, in close proximity to the Bedfordshire border. In fact the name Markyate is derived from the Old English *mearc* and *geat* meaning 'Gate at the (county) boundary'. This area has some fascinating history. Not far away is Flamstead, where Thomas Pickford, famous founder of the removals firm, was born. He died in 1811 and had a road named after him in the town. The first ever reported hit-and-run accident happened in Markyate, when a four-year-old boy was knocked down and killed in the High Street in 1905. Ironically Sir Alfred Harmsworth, owner of the *Daily Mail*, offered a £100 reward for information and the owner of the car turned out to be Harmsworth's brother. The brother was not in the car at the time; it was driven by the chauffeur, who was later sentenced to six months' hard labour.

By far the most interesting piece of history about Markyate, for me, concerns the legend of Katherine Ferrers (aka the Wicked Lady), lady of the manor by day, 'highwayman' by night. There used to be a saying in the 'old wild west' of Hertfordshire, which encompassed Markyate, Harpenden, Wheathampstead and

Kimpton. It was that when the west wind blows up these valleys in December (season of storms and ghosts) hard enough to rattle the window panes, that it's the Wicked Lady galloping by.

The manor of Markyate is called Markyate Cell and it was built on the former 12th century nunnery, the Priory of St-Trinity-in-the-Wood. By the mid 17th century Markyate Cell had been the seat of the ancient Ferrers family for several generations and there was only one son, Sir Knighton Ferrers, left to continue the line. He married a beautiful heiress, the lady Katherine Walters of Hertingford, but within a year he was dead. He had produced no male heir, so the line had died out, but the couple did have a daughter, and she was also named Katherine. Her mother was now a rich widow and prey to fortune hunters during the perilous times of the Civil War. She was persuaded to marry Sir Simon Fanshawe of Ware Park, but he was an ardent Royalist and his estate was eventually overrun by Parliamentary forces and his wife and step-daughter were forced to flee to Huntingdonshire for their own safety. As soon as their daughter Katherine had reached the legal age to marry (which was 12), and in order to gain control of her large estates, Sir Simon had his step-daughter married off to his own son, Thomas, who was aged 16. Some years later her mother Katherine died and the new Katherine Walters (now that the Walters family had the estates that they had coveted) found herself neglected by her husband Thomas and the rest of his family. The lonely 18-year-old took herself off to a place where she had once known happiness – her father's rambling, brick-faced Tudor mansion, Markyate Cell.

Another chapter in Katherine's life began when she met farmer Ralph Chaplin. His land overlooked Watling Street, south of Markyate, but the farmer had a dark secret – by night he was a 'moonraker' and it is believed that he introduced the impressionable young girl to the thrilling adventures of being a highwayman. On one of his ventures further afield he was caught and shot while in the process of robbing a baggage wagon on Finchley Common. His heartbroken partner began a dreadful campaign of revenge, for she certainly didn't need the money, and no traveller in the vicinity of Markyate was safe. Not only were stagecoaches travelling along Watling Street under constant threat but houses were set ablaze, cattle were slaughtered and the Caddington parish constable was murdered on his own doorstep.

The trail of wanton destruction could not last for ever and during her final attempted robbery Lady Katherine received mortal wounds after an exchange of gunfire, with a traveller who was prepared to shoot back. She was still young and would only have been in her mid-twenties at that time. It happened at Nomansland Common, and began when a waggoner was travelling from St Albans with supplies for an inn at Gustard Wood village, near Wheathampstead. He gave a lift to two men, who settled themselves into the well of the wagon amongst the baggage. At dusk the wagon was rolling across the Nomansland Common when out of the gathering gloom a masked rider galloped up and rapidly closed with the lumbering wagon. Without warning the unfortunate wagon-driver was shot from his seat, dead before he hit the ground, but one of the men travelling under cover in the back had armed himself, he suddenly rose up and blasted the masked rider, who sheared away and raced for home. Somehow the mortally-wounded Katherine Ferrers managed the ride back to Markyate Cell and, pouring with blood, she staggered over the threshold to collapse and die in her own home.

Unsurprisingly Lady Ferrers has no grave in Markyate, she is thought to have been buried in secret at St Mary's Church at Ware, but certainly not in her husband's family, the Fanshawe's, vault.

Not long after her interment the hauntings began and it seemed that the Wicked Lady's thirst for revenge was reaching out beyond the grave. The phantom of a galloping highwayman was reported to travel the lanes as far north as Kimpton and along Watling Street. Markyate Cell was plagued by her ghost, which was seen by succeeding owners of the property.

Over three hundred years after her death Lady Ferrers continued to make her presence felt, as recently as December 1970 there was a 'visitation' attributed to her, when the landlord of The Wicked Lady pub, Douglas Payne, was walking his dog late at night on Nomansland Common. He heard the thunder of horse's hooves rapidly approaching him, they soon got nearer until they passed him, but there was no sign of any horse or rider and the dog was plainly terrified. The Wicked Lady is one of only two pubs in the county to be named after a ghost and it is believed that Katherine Ferrers met her partners in crime at this establishment, but the pub is not noted for being haunted by her. There is a ghost, however, it is that of a crying woman, and her sobbing has been heard from an upper room by several customers, only when this room is empty.

Another pub, the Tin Pot, has associations with the Wicked Lady, it is where she is alleged to have changed into her highwayman's garb before her forays and two people felt a strange 'presence' in the room that she is supposed to have used. One of them was moved to write some poetry about the experience and the lines were hung up in the bar.

The legend of the female highwayman is one that has captured many an imagination and such was its fame that a romanticised film was made about her life, *The Wicked Lady*, which starred Margaret Lockwood and James Mason. There is a rhyme which reminds us that local people considered it most likely that somewhere there is a hidden hoard of this outlaw's ill-gotten gains:

> Near the Cell there is a well,
> Near the well there is a tree,
> And 'neath the tree the treasure be.

If so it remains to be discovered...

So much for legend, but what about the facts? There is not a shred of evidence to back up the claims that Lady Katherine Ferrers was ever a highwayman! Fact: Lady Ferrers was born into wealth and married into another wealthy family. Fact: Katherine was probably living with her in-laws at Ware at the time she was supposedly holding up coaches, as Markyate Cell was sold to Thomas Coppin, who originated in Kent, in 1657. Fact: Katherine was buried on the 13th June 1660. The cause of death is unknown, but at age 26 and childless it is more than likely that she died of natural causes, in childbirth, after a miscarriage possibly. Unfortunately, in Oliver Cromwell's time, archive material was patchily maintained, particularly around 1643–1660, during and after the Civil War. With Katherine's death the Ferrers line died out too. Fact: Ralph Chaplin, her so-called 'partner-in-crime' exists nowhere but in legend. Hertfordshire Archive Library has no mention of Ralph Chaplin of Markyate. The Parish Register Indices have no mention of such a person; ergo he is a product of fiction.

How do such legends become so deeply entrenched in the public consciousness? In the mid 17th century highway robbery was practised by a number of 'gentlemen' of the road, men of property and influence who had been Royalists but had been left without property or income after supporting the losing side. Such men became desperate and desperation bred crime. The idea that the same 'romantic' occupation might be practised by a lady held a popular appeal, it still does. In a 19th century ballad, a lady, Maude of Allingham, was courted by numerous eligible bachelors but rejected them in favour of highway robbery until holding up one young lord, later Mayor of Redbourne, who had her hunted down. She was chased and shot but reached home where she died. Sound familiar?

Savay is an English folk song which tells how a young girl disguises herself as a highwayman in order to test her lover. The two themes of highwaymen and ladies who disguise themselves occur again and again in the folklore of England.

It is a matter of historical fact that in 1760 Laurence Shirley, 4th Earl of Ferrers, was hanged at Tyburn, after murdering an old and faithful servant. Ever after he was known as 'Wicked Lord Ferrers' –

it is easy to see how Lord Ferrers, in the course of the retelling of tales, might have ended up as the 'Wicked Lady Ferrers'...

Having exploded a myth we are still left with an intriguing mystery. If Lady Ferrers wasn't at all wicked, much less a highwayman who or what was sighted on a black steed with white blazes, haunting the lanes of Markyate? Who or what was seen swinging from the old sycamore tree in the grounds of Markyate Cell and whose entity was encountered on the secret staircase in the old house?

Chapter Twenty-Six

HEMEL HEMPSTEAD

Originally a forested area and mentioned in the Domesday Book as Hamelamesede, the town we know today as Hemel Hempstead has been occupied since the stone age. Haemele, its earliest title, is thought to be taken from the name of the man who owned these lands. It grew rapidly after the New Towns Act of 1947, first Stevenage and then Hemel were planned to combine residential, shopping, industrial and leisure areas together in discreet, self-contained 'neighbourhood communities', attracting many people from London as pressure for space continued to build up.

The Olde King's Arms is the best known of a trio of ancient haunted hostelries in Hemel, thanks to ace ghosthunter Peter Underwood, who interviewed the landlady during the 1960s. He was told about 'many unexplained noises', 'some manifestations' and that guests spent 'restless nights' in one particular, unspecified, bedroom. The apparition of a lady in white has also been recorded at the heavily timbered pub, which is believed to date back to Tudor times. Later sightings, by various members of staff, have described the laughing ghost of a big fat man in the haunted bedroom.

Another old pub is The Crown Inn, it dates back to 1523, and paranormal investigators, in 2000, reportedly felt 'suddenly chilled' and that 'we were no longer alone', a number of mysterious orbs, which are believed by mediums to be the essence of the deceased's souls, were captured on infra-red film that night.

The White Hart is also a 16th century inn with an eerie reputation, the stairs are associated with a feeling of terror for some visitors and one staff member felt unable to venture near them. Close by the stairs a frightened man's face has been seen. What terrible trauma could this ghost have experienced that still has the power to affect people today? Legend has it that a young man was killed on the stairs while trying to escape a Press Gang in the long-gone days of sailing ships.

There was also a haunted Georgian house at Piccott's End, where the apparition of a monk was reportedly seen during the 1940s and 1950s. Next to the house is a 500-year-old cottage where some unique monastic paintings were discovered some years after the ghost was first seen. It is known that there was an order of Bonhommes monks at nearby Ashridge monastery in the thirteenth century and the paintings are believed to be attributed to them. This house was later subjected to poltergeist activity during the 1960s. This included the familiar pattern of doors being slammed, knocking sounds, footsteps in an empty upstairs room, pictures thrown from walls, objects dematerialising and later materialising somewhere else and even crockery being smashed while it remained on the shelf.

BOVINGDON

Situated on the edge of the Chilterns just south of Hemel Hempstead this pleasant small town has evolved from a small village that was once home to a thriving cottage industry. People would carry out straw-plaiting in their own homes and the plait would then be collected and taken to Luton for the hat trade.

St Lawrence's churchyard is noted for being one of Hertfordshire's largest churchyards, with its fine avenues of yew trees, but it also has a sinister reputation for having been 'desecrated by bloodshed', when a murder was committed here long ago.

Box Lane for long held a haunted reputation with pedestrians (and their pets) in the past and Murvagh House (since renamed) in Box Lane gained a brief notoriety in the 1980s after some intense poltergeist activity. The phenomena culminated, at a winter's dinner party, in the hurling of a large candlestick, by unseen forces, in the dining room. This was witnessed by a number of people who were all seated at the dinner table that evening.

Chapter Twenty-Seven

ST ALBANS

ABBEY APPARITIONS

I am sometimes asked the question, 'What is the most haunted place in Hertfordshire?' I don't have to stop and think about it, the unequivocal answer has to be the City of St Albans. This is evidenced by the great success of the ghost walks, initiated in 1988, which rival anything that much larger competitors, like London, York or Chester, have to offer. I could almost write a separate book about the spectres of St Albans because they are so numerous, varied and well-documented.

In this most haunted city the most haunted building is undoubtedly St Albans Cathedral, which was built by the Normans as their Abbey Church, from recycled Roman brick, between the years 1077–1115. The Abbey's and the city's roots, however, are much older, dating back to AD 303 when the first English martyr, Alban, a soldier in Diocletian's army, was beheaded by the Romans. In AD 793 a grand monastery was built in his honour on the site where he was executed. Alban's Shrine became a centre of pilgrimage and many were the visitors who claimed that they had been miraculously cured of their disabilities after coming to the monastery, which was richly adorned with gold, silver and jewels donated by these grateful pilgrims. This sacred site has been a place of Christian worship for over seventeen centuries.

Like so many other visitors before me, I have been impressed by St Albans Cathedral's commanding presence, and I've felt a sense of its long, unbroken history. Its series of 12th–13th century wall paintings remain unequalled in England. Extensive renovations, paid for by Lord Grimthorpe of Batchwood Hall, were carried out in the 1870s and shortly afterwards the Abbey was granted cathedral status. One long-term resident of the city, who wished to remain anonymous, was a lady born and raised in the town, and she provided a modern, first-hand eyewitness account of ghostly encounters at the Abbey.

'For many years I lived near the Abbey and one evening I was walking home along by the railings on the south side path and enjoying the last fingers of the summer sunlight, when from within the Abbey I heard the sounds of the most beautiful music and choral accompaniment that I have ever experienced. When I decided to slip in through the main west door to hear more, I found the heavy oak door locked and as I pressed the knob the music ceased and the Abbey stood in eerie silence.' This 'heavenly music', as it has often been described, has been heard by numerous witnesses who have been passing by the Abbey, usually at night.

'Again near the Abbey one September evening, I saw approaching me four very tall monks, who swayed slowly from side to side, as they moved along the pathway from the Great Gateway to the west front of the Abbey and again the atmosphere was very eerie. I stood awhile but nothing seemed amiss with the scene, those monks were definitely swaying like thin trees as they walked forward and between them was something which looked like a coffin – I turned and fled!'

Humphrey, Duke of Gloucester, died in 1453, in most mysterious circumstances at Bury St Edmunds. His body was rushed back to St Albans where a tomb had been prepared for him in Saints Chapel and he was buried at night. Could this scene have been re-enacted for the lady from St Albans? The same lady also saw, on several occasions, a gloomy figure in a grey habit, 'with head cowled and hidden', where the new Chapter House is built. This figure has been reported as haunting the inside of the building as well, in the Hudson Library.

One of St Albans Abbey's canons during the 1920s was Canon George Glossop, who lived at Romeland House in the town. On a spring morning, soon after the First World War, he heard the organ being played as he walked to the Abbey. Curious as to the identity of the organ-player, the canon let himself in through the slype door, he made his way to the organ loft, but on reaching it the music stopped and there was no trace of any organist.

In 1921 Mr Willie Luttmann, organist at St Albans Abbey, staged a performance of the Fayrfax Mass, in commemoration of the 400th anniversary of the composer's death. Dr Robert Fayrfax was born around 1470 and he rose to become a pre-eminent musician, he had been Doctor of Music at Oxford and Cambridge Universities as well as head of the Royal Chapels' Music. He was appointed Master of the King's Musick at King Henry VIII's court. He not only composed many songs and the Missa Albanus (Mass for St Albans) but was also appointed organist and director of the Abbey choir at St Albans in his later years. He died here in October 1521, and was buried in the presbytery of the church. Luttman received permission to transcribe Fayrfax's original manuscript, kept at Oxford's Bodleian Library, into modern notation. After hearing the performance Canon Glossop told John Watkins, the head verger at the Abbey, 'This is the music I heard that morning.'

After the canon's death his widow revealed that her husband had heard the Fayrfax music on other occasions, one incident she mentioned happened late one night, as he was working on his sermon he heard the music, which grew louder and louder until it faded away. Other witnesses heard male voices singing in the night as they passed the west front from the Abbey Gateway and music was even heard in the Brown Owl café in George Street.

Canon Glossop was consulted about an ancient cottage near the Abbey which was purchased by a London man, who entrusted the place to his children's nanny to await the arrival of the family. Two nights in a row the unfortunate woman was shaken awake by a man in a black robe, who spoke to her in a strange language. She described the medal that the apparition wore about its neck and the canon was able to identify it as the medal of Saint Alban. An exorcism service put a stop to the unwelcome visits and Dr Elsie Toms, St Albans historian, pointed out that the house stood on the site of what had been the Abbey's charnel house. An interdict from the Pope in the past had prevented burial services from being held at the Abbey. If this monk died during that period he may not have 'gone to rest' without the last rites, until the later exorcism service gave him the peace he desired. Another point of view was that the 'strange language' spoken by the monk was Latin, and he may have been trying to impart knowledge about the lost Abbey treasure…

Strange happenings concerning the Abbey continued down the years and Dr Elsie Toms was told by Canon Glossop's daughter about an incident when she had heard singing outside the family home. She summoned her father and together they listened to an invisible choir pass by, towards the locked Abbey just across the road, and it seemed as if the phantom singers carried on into the main entrance.

In the early 1930s a man saw candle-light and heard singing coming from the Lady Chapel one night, 'It occurred to me that no ordinary choir sang so sweetly at 2am.' He was to hear it again, on several occasions. Two other witnesses in the 1930s heard organ music on the day after Boxing Day, at 1.30am, but were told it was impossible as the Abbey and organ were locked up, as was the engine house which provided wind for the instrument.

A lady and her five friends reported hearing 'simply heavenly strains' coming from the Abbey at 1.45am one morning.

The assistant verger's sighting on All Souls Day, 1931 was most spectacular. It was early in the morning when he saw a procession of monks moving towards him along the south side of the nave. They appeared to be real, wearing Benedictine dress, so he moved aside into the chairs, in order to let them pass, but as he did so they all vanished. Customarily the monks used to walk in procession around the Abbey lands' boundaries on All Souls Day and they were seen again by the curate a few years after the assistant verger's encounter.

Possibly the most famous ghostly experience reported at St Albans Abbey is the 'Firewatcher's Tale'. Basil Saville was a sixteen-year-old ex-chorister and team member of the firewatchers, whose job it was to check the whole building and its fire-fighting equipment, and to particularly watch out for incendiary bombs during air raids. He was alone, waiting for another firewatcher to join him, on the frosty night of Christmas Eve 1944. He began his solo patrol, by the light of a hooded torch, and soon began to feel some unseen presence; he made his way to the loft and was surprised to discover two monks' habits lying on the floor. It is easy to imagine what it must have been like for a young lad, with a duty to perform, to be alone at night in the vast emptiness of that venerable old building during the black-out.

The next anomaly was the peal of a single bell, which started tolling in the belfry. Basil knew that this was impossible because he had earlier seen the Abbey's twelve bells, all safely stored on the ground floor, due to the risk of bombing. The steady tolling continued as he approached the belfry, but as he got to the door it stopped, and when he checked inside there were no bells and no bell ringer.

He reached the roof and after taking a look around in the chilly evening air he made his way back downstairs, when suddenly he heard the organ being played and the light of a nearby candle illuminated the pages of a book of music, whose pages were being turned by invisible hands! Then he heard singing from the High Altar, so he hurried off in that direction. Here he saw some monks carrying candles, being led in a service by their Abbot. As he watched, the procession passed through the screen doors into the Saint's Chapel, where the doors closed behind them. Basil felt compelled to follow them yet when he reached the Chapel it was empty and in darkness. He ran back upstairs to the organ loft where he found a spent candle and a large book with plain black covers and yellowing pages; it was entitled *Albanus Mass* by Robert Fayrfax.

Eventually his fellow firewatcher arrived and Basil told him all about the mysterious events, so together they retraced the young man's steps, but this time there was no trace of the spent candle, the monks' robes or the book of music… Author Betty Puttick interviewed Basil Saville for her 1994 book *Ghosts of Hertfordshire* and he stuck to his story. 'I was stunned by it – overwhelmed,' he told the well known St Albans writer, 'I'm not psychic or anything like that and I've never seen anything like it either before or since. People may not believe me, but I know it happened.'

In 1983 the phantom Abbey music was heard again and it continues to be heard from time to time. There is even a reputedly Quasimodo-like figure that confines his hauntings to the shadowy heights of the Abbey; he is affectionately known as 'Henry'. Maybe he is reprising his former role as guardian of the Abbey treasures, as monks used to stand sentinel in the Watching Gallery, in order to keep an eye on pilgrims who visited the martyr's shrine.

An almost overpowering scent of incense smelt on the south side of the building is another phenomenon that has been experienced on occasion. These are many, but by no means all, of the paranormal phenomena reported over the years from the Abbey. Some people have said that when unusual occurrences are due to take place the whole building seems 'switched on', somehow transformed, so that those on the right wavelength sense it becoming a different place. Do witnesses encounter some kind of 'time slip', as, for brief seconds, the building reverts to times past, when it was the country's premiere Benedictine ecclesiastical establishment, and a centre of excellence as a seat of learning?

TAVERNS OF TERROR

St Albans is also famous for its haunted pubs (and ex-pubs) most of them are extremely old, with plenty of character and interesting histories. Ye Olde Fighting Cocks lays claim to be the oldest inhabited public house in England. It has a strange, octagonal shape, with a cellar built where the eighth century gatehouse to the Abbey used to be. There have been a series of odd happenings at this pub, like the keys which disappeared from the bar counter when a manager returned from a visit to the cellar. He was puzzled to rediscover the keys swinging violently from a key hook as he was alone in the building at the time. One of the bar staff was found in a state of fear after seeing a ghost, but he would not discuss any details of the haunting. Not so the staff member in 2001, who clearly saw a number of men dressed in the brown habits of monks. They were only visible as far down as their knees, when they emerged from the cellar, crossed the bar and briefly sat down at the fireside table before dematerialising.

Renamed The Tudor Tavern in 1963, the building on the corner of George Street has existed here for over six hundred years. Originally known as The Swan, it was later purchased by a rich merchant and transformed into the Abbey Guest House. There was a further change of use, when it became a hardware store and antiques centre, owned by Mr and Mrs Fred Mayle, during whose time the place was known as Mayle's Corner, which had the reputation of being haunted. Eventually this old building reverted to its original use, as licensed premises, this time becoming The Tudor Tavern. After customers have gone in the evening the bar staff reported a shadow which followed them around and it is said that somebody was actually chased out of the place by the ghost. Theories varied as to the identity of the wandering spirit; some said it was a former landlord, others that it was a former guest and a third opinion stated that the ghost was that of a soldier, brought here to die during the first battle of St Albans in the War of the Roses.

As well as 'the shadow' there is another apparition, affectionately known as 'Harry' who has been seen by a manageress. She described him as having 'dark, curly hair and a beard, wearing a black tunic with a neck ruff and buttons on his sleeves'. He was sighted at a table, quite at home, with glass in hand and leaning on his other elbow.

The Goat Inn at Sopwell Lane occupies a building which dates back to about 1500, originally built as a house with wings connected by a hall, producing an H-shaped structure. It became an inn in 1578, to provide accommodation and refreshment for the stage coaches which travelled up from London. It stood within sight of the city's gallows, where many prisoners were brought for execution. Strange, unaccountable noises and an unpleasant atmosphere pervaded a room at the back of the pub.

From 1979 to 1986 the inn was managed by Peter Ransom, who admitted to a weird night-time experience at The Goat when he awoke from a deep sleep to find, at the bottom of his bed, 'a ghastly face, scowling and staring at him', the room was icy cold and it is always cold, with a feeling of a 'presence', even in the present day. Ransom also used to find that his guitar was moved from where he left it on numerous occasions.

There is a door at the pub which opens and closes on its own and has even been known to lock itself. When The Goat was renovated, quite some time ago, an ancient, odd cellar was found, where old pewter pots were dug up. A director of the company that ran the pub found it difficult to open and close a particular door on his way to the yard, but when he returned he discovered that this door had swung open by itself.

On the edge of St Albans is the King William pub, which was built in 1937 and which soon gained a reputation for being haunted. A ghost was seen during 1939 in the bar and glasses were hurled around by invisible forces. Later reports point to a military ghost – he is 'a tall soldier with a moustache wearing a greenish uniform with buttons on the tunic' and there was a clear sighting reported as late as August 1987, by the chef, who looked up to see the soldier standing nearby. She yelled for the manager and he rushed downstairs just in time to see the apparition before it faded away (as old soldiers do). During the Second World War this hostelry was popular with the local Home Guard and it is thought that the haunting could have been connected with them.

An optician's shop at Market Place continues to be haunted by a famous St Albans ghostly manifestation which goes back to the seventeenth century. This site was occupied then by The Blue Boar, a popular coaching inn. A small boy is alleged to have been killed here when he ran out of the inn and was crushed under the wheels of a coach. His ghost, known as 'Charlie the crying boy', is believed to have returned in search of his long-dead mother. The ancient Blue Boar changed its name to The Wellington and the haunting continued. A barmaid claimed that an invisible presence had stroked her hair and kissed her forehead. A room over the saloon bar reverberated with the sounds of moving furniture, although it was empty, and footsteps were similarly heard on the landing. At one time the pumping gas for the beer was unaccountably turned off, a favourite trick of pub ghosts. Lights would turn themselves on and off and sleeping was made difficult by 'something' which jumped up and down on the beds. One disbelieving customer changed his opinion when a soda siphon rose into the air in front of his eyes. 'Charlie' was not the only ghost. One landlord's children asked their dad about a man seen in the upper rooms, saying 'Please ask that man in our bedroom to go away.'

Sylvia, one of the barmaids, seems to have been singled out for special attention by the ghost – maybe she reminded him of his long-lost mother? She was tidying up one day and had placed a clean ashtray on each table before cleaning the bar, when she turned around a packet of crisps had been placed in every ashtray. 'Charlie' was also known to clutch at women's skirts as well as breaking glassware. In 1971 new licensees were mentioned in the local press as being greeted by 'Bottles, jugs and glasses flying from shelves and smashing on the floor!'

September 1975 saw the extensive alteration of the old Wellington pub premises which were to be transformed into Matthews, a butchers' shop. Still the manifestations continued, with female staff claiming that something kept touching their faces. Tills would be interfered with, doors would slam shut and the manager blamed the spirit for mysterious punctures which happened when his car was parked. One butcher claimed that he saw a small misty figure in the cellar, which was behind the shop, and another worker reported seeing a shadowy figure of a man. Female shoppers complained of a classic haunted house impression – they felt as if they had cobwebs brushing across their faces and were even touched by the occasional chilly kiss!

One winter's morning a butcher called Kevin turned up for work at 5.30am. He saw a man standing with arms folded, in the yard, which was once the stabling for the old pub, where 'Charlie' had played centuries ago. As the butcher got out of his car the man's figure disappeared. Another day a young assistant went out to this same yard, to the dustbins, in the late afternoon. When he passed a pile of boxes he saw a hand appear above them, and then they were pushed down on top of him. He was startled to find no one about to account for the event, and he was certain that all the other members of staff were still in the shop at the time.

With the Christopher Place development both cellar and yard were swallowed up under new shops, yet still the paranormal happenings continued, in what was now an opticians' shop. Women still felt their hair or faces being stroked by invisible hands and one woman reportedly had her shirt pulled. In recent times CCTV cameras have recorded cleaning staff turning off lights, only for them to come back on again at 4am, in an empty building, yet subsequent electrical checks revealed no faults with any of the wiring…

The offices of estate agents Strutt and Parker are in the Tudor building which was originally used as an inn called The Crown and Anchor. It had a 14th century gallery, and the pub continued to serve the public until the 1950s, then it was later occupied by the estate agents. Leo Hickish of Strutt and Parker recounted the story of his arrival at the offices early one morning to be confronted with an 'agitated colleague', who showed Hickish a set of fresh wet footprints on the flagstone flooring at the foot of the stairs. The building was empty apart from the two colleagues and neither of them was either bare-footed or in possession of wet feet! It was later surmised that these may have been the phantom footprints of a long dead pilgrim, a visitor to the nearby Cathedral…

Some time in the late 1990s it was reported that a member of staff working upstairs was packing up to leave when he saw the gaunt face of a woman between two filing cabinets and the badly frightened man ran downstairs to tell his colleagues. It transpired that the face had appeared where there was once a window to the gallery in the original building. Weekend staff at the estate agents felt as if they were being watched in this upper office. During some filming at the building the camera battery pack mysteriously drained down and lights which had been turned off suddenly turned themselves back on again. Staff members have also reported the smell of tobacco smoke and downstairs a Cavalier's ghost has been seen, smoking a clay pipe. Next door was also part of The Crown and Anchor once, until it became a private residence, and the family living there got used to seeing the ghost of a monk standing by the fireplace, so much so that he was regarded as one of the family!

The Hare and Hounds proved to be a terrifying place for one unfortunate barmaid in recent years. One summer's early morning Marion Powell arrived at the pub to help with the cleaning and went down to the cellar, where the cleaning cupboard was located. She was about half way down when she experienced an intense cold and became aware of a strong presence near her, then she saw an 'overwhelming blackness' which rushed up the stairs towards her, enveloping her in what she felt was pure evil. She later described it as being like something was opening up to swallow her completely. Next she heard a voice screaming, telling her to get out, at which point she fled upstairs to the bar.

On occasion the sewage system would get blocked up and the landlord found a foul substance oozing through a cellar wall. Long ago the building next door was the site of the city gallows and the bodies of the executed criminals were pushed into a trough that now forms part of the pub's cellar. The 'oozing wall' now lies between the pub and the building where the gallows once stood.

A Medley Of Manifestations

As well as the multitude of haunted pubs and ex-pubs in the city there are many other buildings in charming, history-steeped St Albans that harbour 'uninvited guests'. The new City Hall, the Alban Arena, is built on land that once formed the garden of the Grange, and back in the 1980s at the City Hall, after a Mayoral banquet, a manager was working alone there when he heard someone pass his office door. He wondered if a guest had been left behind after everyone else had gone, so he got up to check and encountered a woman in a long grey dress who disappeared right in front of him, but more of her later…

At least one flat above the St Albans Antique Centre has ghostly connotations. Paul Rolfe lived in an apartment here in the late 1970s and he complained of being woken up at night by the sound of running water, when he investigated he found that his kitchen taps had turned themselves on.

At one in the morning, after a night out with friends, Paul saw the 'lime-coloured, translucent apparition of a woman in a lace dress.' She seemed to float a couple of feet off the floor down the corridor away from him before disappearing through the end wall.

The Gables, now Laura Ashley's, is another of the city's oldest buildings, which was once occupied by Boots the Chemists. It had long held the reputation for being haunted, even during the Second World War the top floor was known to be a spooky place. Stock in the shop was sometimes found jumbled up and in one store room an elderly lady was seen; on the top floor stock room a Saturday girl was frightened by an 'evil looking man' who stood by the fireplace.

A notorious ghost, known as 'the corset maker', haunts the premises that were to become the 'retro' shop, at 17 High Street. This three-storey building dates back to1665 and it stands on part of the site of what was once Fisk's, an enormous department store which occupied a large part of the High Street. The Fisk's store was demolished during the construction of Heritage Close, some 30 years ago. The tragic figure of the 'corset maker' (how she came by that name is not known for sure, but presumably that was once her trade) is said to be a former manager's daughter, who was kept locked in her room by her father after she fell in love with one of the young storemen, and she ended up committing suicide. She appeared to some of the shopgirls and was seen in the Abbey churchyard. She also haunted the basement of the store, to the consternation of the caretaker. Goods are still thrown about during the night in the present shops which occupy the site.

Stories of hauntings continue to emerge from all over St Albans, as in the case which made an appearance in the October 2003 issue of the excellent monthly magazine *Hertfordshire Countryside*. David Flatau was an ex-Londoner who had moved to the city in 1965, where he settled happily at Pilgrim Close, Park Street Lane, St Albans. One of his hobbies was photography, another was old houses, so it was that on a stroll around his neighbourhood he took some photographs of a 200-year-old residence, Park Cottage in Park Street Lane. An attractive building of half-timbered construction, it had a leaning chimney stack and it possessed an acre of gardens at the back. Mr Flatau was staggered to discover, on receiving his developed prints, a mysterious figure standing in an upper window of Park Cottage when he knew that the owners of the property were away on an extended holiday! No one else was residing at the cottage at the time the photograph was taken. Mr Flatau checked the negative and the figure could be clearly seen on that as well. The person at the window seems to have a bandage around their head and to be standing sideways on; to the right of the figure some ties hanging up are clearly visible. The photographer remembered that he had noticed the ties but there was certainly no figure in the window at the time of taking the picture.

David Flatau mentioned the incident to a man who was walking his dog and was told by this passer-by that, late at night, he had occasionally heard laughter coming from the back gardens of Park Cottage when he knew the place to be empty. He further related that his dog refused to walk on that side of the road and rumour had it that a murder had been committed there at some time in the past. Another strange St Albans story...

St Albans School

The Abbey Gateway in Romeland is part of St Albans School. The Gateway was the site of a prison for some 500 years and at least one schoolboy has heard strange sounds there, including screams. More recent ghostly sounds have been attributed to a long-dead caretaker who had served the school for many years. When the old biology department was closed down, before its demolition, the distinctive noise of hobnailed boots on the stairs was heard by the master who locked the place up for the final time, yet he knew he was alone. It was as if the caretaker's ghost was coming to say goodbye…

St Peter's Street's Phantoms

Once described as 'the most beautiful main street in Europe', St Peter's Street is on a main city thoroughfare. It is also a definite contender for the title of 'most haunted street' in this city of ghosts. One of the best known haunted houses in this location is the Ivy House, built by Edward Strong as his own residence (he was chief mason to Sir Christopher Wren for the construction of St Paul's Cathedral). The ghost that haunts Ivy House is believed to be that of a tragic young chambermaid called Meades, who was walled up in the chimney of a previous house on the site after becoming pregnant by a member of the household. She is the well known 'cleaning ghost' and is responsible for cleaning the handrail on the elegant staircase (thought to have been made by Grinling Gibbons), as well as the cellars. In modern times, when major renovations were carried out, despite there being dust everywhere else, the handrail remained remarkably dust-free! Ivy House became occupied by a firm of solicitors, Turner and Debenhams and staff members refused to enter the building after dark or to be the last one to leave on winter evenings. In 1975 a manager returned alone one dark and windy Friday night to collect some papers and as he entered the building he saw a young blonde-haired woman dressed in white standing at the top of the stairs. She glanced at the man then continued on up the stairs, the manager turned and hurriedly left, without his papers. The ghost of the sad serving girl was also seen at Christmas, by staff who had come in to decorate the tree. They saw her pale form staring down at them from the top of the stairs. Not only members of staff but also cleaners and visitors have all heard footsteps on the back stairs and other odd noises when there has been nobody else around to cause them. Taps sometimes turned themselves on too and doors were seen opening and closing without any human agency, as though someone had just walked through. The staircase handrail, apparently, continues to remain highly polished...

On the other side of the road St Peter's Church 'feels uncomfortable' for solitary workers, who say they sense a presence in this ancient place of worship, which is over 700 years old.

The Grange, previously mentioned, is also in St Peter's Street and was built by Mayor John Osborne in 1763. It was acquired by the Council in the 1940s and used as offices where typists and caretakers were frightened by ghostly appearances. In 1975 a new caretaker was alone in the cellars at one time said, 'I got this awful feeling there was someone else there and there was an eerie, icy atmosphere, so I turned on all the lights and the presence disappeared.' The identity of the spirit was allegedly Dorothy Osborne, daughter-in-law of John Osborne. Legend has it that 'sad Dorothy' killed herself after discovering that her husband had a mistress. This was claimed by a former Town Clerk; Miss Betty Entwhistle, but although her family are mentioned in the register at St Peter's Church there is no mention of Dorothy herself. She is supposed to be the lady in the long grey dress, mentioned earlier in this chapter, who also haunts the Alban Arena, as seen by the manager in the 1980s, in the area where her gardens used to be. It seems that the gardens, during Dorothy's lifetime, were much admired, they had their own courtyard entrance and they surrounded the Grange.

Another haunted building situated in St Peter's Street is Mallinson House, head office of the National Pharmaceutical Association, and in 1977 a builder was working late one evening when he encountered the apparition of a man which passed him on the stairs. It was not a full body manifestation however; the builder reported that the legs were missing. Staff discovered rulers and files had disappeared after the sighting. Research led to the conclusion that this ghost was the same one that was first reported back in 1872. It was supposedly the restless spirit of Dr William Russell's butler, whose ghost was made famous one Sunday evening at 7pm in 1872, when a crowd of two hundred people gathered in front of Donnington House, as Mallinson House was called in those times. A passer-by had seen a ghostly figure, which tapped at an upstairs window; it was wearing silver-buttoned butler's livery and a white wig. The passer-by attracted the attention of others until the sizeable gathering amassed. The story was reported in the *Herts Advertiser* in 1872, which summed up by concluding that the policemen who entered and examined the house believed someone had got in via the back of the late surgeon's house 'for a lark'. What is known is that Dr Russell's butler had committed suicide in this upstairs room.

He had been sacked after being caught red-handed drinking his master's brandy and had been unable to live with his shame.

There are many ghosts in the immediate vicinity of St Peter's Street, in one small house a staircase was moved, but a soldier has been seen coming down the original stairs. In one of the Pemberton Almshouses (founded in 1620 by the High Sheriff of Hertfordshire, Roger Pemberton) a non-smoking lady tenant remarked on her unseen 'guest' who left behind a smell of rough tobacco as well as a heavy indentation on the bedcovers.

HOLYWELL HILL HAUNTS

Holywell Hill (formerly known as Halliwelle Street) is one of the oldest streets in St Albans, and one of the most interesting if your hobby is ghost-hunting! A Georgian house on the Hill has been the subject of poltergeist phenomena in recent times. The couple involved wish to remain anonymous, but their story is intriguing. The wife was in bed alone one night when the heavy bedroom door slowly opened of its own accord, later on the neighbours, accompanied by the police, called round to tell the family that all their lights were on and electric bells were ringing – bells had been fitted to every room. The police investigated but could find no intruder, so they turned off all the lights and locked up before leaving, yet in the morning all the lights were found on again.

The next occurrence was in the early hours when the couple (the husband was back at home this time) were woken up by their son, who couldn't sleep because he felt someone else in his room. The son went to sleep in his parents' bedroom while the father swapped bedrooms and went to sleep upstairs.

'I had only been in bed a little while when I suddenly had a premonition that all was not normal. I knew immediately that there was a presence in the room with me; I felt no alarm for it seemed to have a soothing effect on me and I spoke to it and shortly afterwards I fell asleep and awoke in the morning quite converted to 'there are more things in heaven and earth than are dreamed of in our philosophy,' he said later.

Although the house was early 18th century the cellars and foundations were found to date back to the 12th century. A passage here used to lead to the tomb of St Alban, but was filled in many years previously and it was thought that pilgrims held services in the cellars before visiting the tomb.

The daughter of the house never liked going upstairs on her own, and a sceptic family friend expressed his disbelief in poltergeists. As he made his comments a door slowly opened, but there was no one there, and the friend left rather hurriedly, and didn't return.

Things quietened down after an extra staircase was installed in the old house, for some months there was no paranormal activity. Strangely building work involving alterations to a structure can either set off poltergeist phenomena or quieten it down for a time.

The husband took up the story, 'After about a year I was working on some odd job in the cellar when suddenly I felt his or her presence, so vivid it was that I exclaimed "Good heavens, poltie, where have you been? We have missed you," – and a feeling of contentment filled me. Then frequently after that we felt the presence with us – in a room, on the stairs, or in the cellar.'

The wife had the final word, 'He or she was very naughty really but never spiteful, although he had me up in the night many times ringing bells, turning on lights, and leaving doors open, particularly in the cellars. I wonder where poltie is now and whether he missed me when we moved away.'

Another Holywell Hill residence is home to a ghost that wanders about and whose heavy footsteps are heard and whose presence is felt. She is known as Granny Sheldrake and young people seem more sensitive to her and similarly she seems interested in the children of the house.

The White Hart Hotel haunting has attracted the most interest of any location in Holywell Hill as the case has provided numerous witnesses to the plentiful ghostly activity to be found there. Paranormal investigators set up a vigil here in 2001, with all the latest electronic paraphernalia at their disposal and what they discovered added to the 15th century coaching inn's reputation as a prime St Albans paranormal 'hot spot'. One of the group's control room monitor screens went blank not long into the investigation – it was discovered that the wires had been wrenched out of the back of a camera, which was found still standing on its tripod in an empty cellar!

The medium and psychic artist Marion Goodfellow, while attending a séance held at The White Hart Hotel, encountered the spirit of a child who died in a fire in 1803. Her parents were called John and Elizabeth. Research later revealed that there had been a John Rudnan-Heywood (married to Elizabeth) who had been a landlord during the time of a fire, which occurred in 1803... Marion also captured the image of a young Georgian woman and associated the date 1820 with her. Many people have seen the ghost of a young lady who seems to fit in with this era and she is thought to be the spirit of Elizabeth Wilson who was decapitated when her stagecoach thundered under the low hotel archway... in 1820.

A guest staying at the hotel claimed to have seen a stranger, a man, sitting on the edge of his bed. Next thing a message formed on his bedroom mirror – 'Meet me in room 7 at 7.30'. The shaken guest told Evie Scully, the landlady, who went upstairs to investigate. She later said, 'The writing was big and bold, sort of childish and written in a chalky substance.' The landlady erased the message and went back downstairs to her guest, who returned to his room but came back minutes later to say that the writing was back again. Other guests using that room (room 8) have told of waking in the morning to find towels strewn around the floor.

Sue Pearce used to work in the hotel in the late 1990s, and she recalled feeling a cold breeze (as if someone had rushed by) and sensing a strong presence, while she was laying out the breakfast tables on her own.

Jon Woolard is another ex-employee who experienced paranormal activity – heavy barrels which were difficult, even for strong men to handle, would move about the cellar at night. They were left carefully stacked one night yet next day they would be found scattered all over the cellar. Lights went on and off by themselves and the cellar door would lock itself without its key.

Several guests have seen a little girl's ghost, which usually appears by the fireplace in the bar. The fireplace in room 7 has been seen engulfed in flames despite the fact that it has been bricked up for many years now.

FISHPOOL STREET ... ANOTHER CURIOUS PLACE

Once the main coaching route into St Albans, Fishpool Street suffered a decline in fortunes when Verulam Road was built in the late 19th century, and it became a notorious slum area. In its coaching heyday nearly every other building was an inn, but now they are all long gone – pubs like The Angel, the Blockers Arms, The Crow, The Cock and Flowerpot, The Queen, The Royal Oak, The Rule and Compasses and The Welclose Arms.

Nowadays Fishpool Street is a quietly prosperous old street in a middle class city. It also has numerous hauntings and a wide variety of ghosts. Well known local stories include the 'lady in blue', rumoured to have suffocated her daughter by accident when she lived in the 18th century, near the Red Lion pub. She turns up at 3am looking suitably anguished in her long blue dress as she wanders between house and street, wiping her face with a handkerchief.

There is another home in this street where a strangling is alleged to have happened, in a bedroom where people still awake in panic, with the feel of invisible hands around their throat. A former shop in the area boasts the spirit of 'Charlie', who shifts phantom biscuit tins around the stone-flagged floor. The grey figure of a man has been seen in yet another property, he appears at night by the bedside, and a window fitment vanished here only to reappear weeks later. The attentions of this particular ghost are reputedly the cause of some owners moving out after short periods living there. 'Old George' is another ghostly Fishpool Street inhabitant who appears, complete with top hat to 'welcome' new arrivals at his former home.

One of the most attractive private houses in the road betrays its ancient origins as a former coaching inn (The Crow) and it has been home to at least four restless spirits. A family with three daughters lived here between 1959 and 1969 and they were quite open about their 'phantom lodgers'. In a small room at the rear of the building doors would noisily have their latches lifted and be opened by unseen entities. Pets would follow these invisible presences with their eyes, indicating that they, at least, could detect them. Popular opinion was that the haunter was Tom Baker, a landlord of what was The Crow inn, before the First World War. Tom used to travel up to London in the early hours of the morning, to his forge at Sloane Square, as he was blacksmith to King Edward VII. This industrious man would then return to serve his customers at The Crow in the evening. Another ghost is thought to be responsible for tapping noises heard on a partition wall; she was a former inhabitant, an invalid who would constantly rap on the floor to attract the attention of her daughter, who was a nurse. The daughter died before her mother and her ghost, in nurse's uniform, has been seen in the house. Furniture has also been regularly moved around in the dining room by paranormal forces. Perhaps the oddest story about the former pub concerns a man who lived here and he was woken up one night by the apparition of a young Boer War soldier at the bedside. 'What do you want?' the man asked. 'I am Charlie Rowley and I have come to see my mother,' replied the soldier. 'Well she's not here,' responded the man. With that the soldier politely shook hands and left, the startled witness observed that the soldier's hand had been 'ice cold'.

VERULAMIUM VISITATIONS

The remnants of the Roman city of Verulamium can be seen in the parkland through which the river Ver runs. Verulamium was razed to the ground by Boudicca, Queen of the Iceni tribe and her armies, who slaughtered the Roman garrison here in AD 61.

In 1970, around Christmas time, two young lads cycling through the park encountered the ghost of a Cavalier. Their description was fairly detailed, the soldier seemed to be floating in a silver mist and he was wearing a silver-buttoned tunic with tassels. His loose-fitting trousers were tucked into high boots, his long hair was curly and he carried a sword.

Ginger Mills was a local character who lived for a while in a caravan parked beside the lakes at Verulamium and it was his custom, in the early hours of the morning, to stroll around these lakes. On one of his walks he heard the tramp of marching feet coming from behind and he instinctively moved aside to let the marchers through. He was shocked by the passage of a phantom army and said that he felt an icy breeze as they went by him.

It was the summer of 1985, and a young man was walking home through Verulamium when he was confronted by a Roman Centurion on horseback. The panic-stricken witness fled the spot only to trip up and injure himself so badly that he had to attend the local hospital.

BERNARDS HEATH MEMORIES

A lady attending one of St Albans' celebrated ghost walks had her own ghost story to recount. Her daughter and a friend were passing St Peters late one night when they both heard the sounds of hoof beats which passed them travelling in the direction of Bernards Heath.

One of my favourite true stories from St Albans' haunted history is the experience of writer Betty Puttick, well known resident of St Albans and author of *Ghosts of Hertfordshire*. In her book she describes her own ghostly confrontation;

'Bernards Heath is a stone's throw from my own home, and from time to time while exercising my dog there I have picked up small completely round stones and idly wondered if they could be stone shot from the battle (*The second battle of St Albans in 1461*).

One day I had a curious experience there. As I walked towards the wooded part of the Common I noticed something odd about the trees. They were completely still, with no movement in the leaves and branches, appearing to resemble a painted backdrop and everywhere seemed unnaturally quiet. I walked on into the trees and suddenly all hell broke loose. I could feel movement, violent movement, all around me. I felt that horses were rearing up almost on top of me and I could hear neighing, shouts and the clash of metal so close that I threw my arms over my head to protect myself from I knew not what, as there was absolutely nothing to see.

As I whirled round to get away, there in front of me with his back to a tree sat a man. He was wearing a leather cap and jerkin, boots and some sort of leggings and he had a bow and arrows. He was holding his head in his hands and I could tell he was wounded and in pain.

As I looked at him he began to fade and I realised I could see the trunk of the tree through him and seconds later he had vanished.

Somehow I found myself out of the trees with the feel of the breeze on my face and the sound of birds and the traffic on the Harpenden Road just as usual. My dog came running towards me and we walked home, as I tried to come to terms with what had happened and find some rational explanation for it. Nothing like that has ever happened again and I visit Bernards Heath often, but I have never forgotten the day when I really believe I may have walked into a re-enactment of part of that Shrove Tuesday battle so long ago.'

A remarkable encounter with another world, which I am convinced, was a rare 'time slip'. Betty was transported back to Bernards Heath as it was in 1461. It is reminiscent, in many respects, of time slips as described by other people, Jourdain and Moberly at Versailles, for instance, as discussed earlier in the chapter about Watford. The fact that she was in a relaxed (and therefore receptive) frame of mind, walking her dog and 'idly wondering' about the second battle of St Albans is most interesting. Betty's observations that the scene wasn't quite right somehow, the 'painted backdrop of the trees', the 'unnatural quiet', all have resonance. 'Retrocognition of the past' would seem to be an appropriate category for this particular experience.

BATCHWOOD HALL MYSTERIES

I have mentioned Lord Grimthorpe previously, and his philanthropy which made possible the restoration of St Albans Abbey with a £130,000 donation from his own money. This eccentric lawyer's country house, Batchwood Hall, was just on the other side of Watling Street from Gorhambury. He designed Batchwood Hall himself and when he died, in 1905, Grimthorpe was worth several million pounds, a colossal fortune in those days. Now his grand old house is a nightclub and sports centre, which suffered a fire in 1995. People escaping the fire told of a ghostly woman scattering burning coals over the floor from a shovel! There was another fire here a hundred years earlier, when a man named John Beckett ran into the Hall to save his wife. In recent years John was said to still search for his wife's body, which was never found. After the 1995 fire it was speculated that the ghostly woman may have been the spirit of John's wife, who just might have started the original inferno... In 1989 Batchwood Hall was being refurbished when various supernatural activities in the hall and cellar were reported. Objects mysteriously seemed to move themselves from their original positions, lights turned themselves on and off and padlocks, inexplicably, were found opened. Soon after a Victorian fireplace was removed these strange events began... the paranormal work of an irate former peer of the realm perhaps?

190

SALISBURY HALL SPECTRES

Sir William Beech Thomas, in 1950, called Salisbury Hall 'quaintly isolated' and so it was to remain until the arrival of 'the road to hell' (aka the M25). The Hall's very isolation ideally suited the purpose of King Charles II, who kept his lover Mistress Eleanor Gwynne here, away from the prying eyes of his courtiers. Like many others before me I was captivated by the place when I first saw it about twenty years ago, prior to the incursion of London's overcrowded orbital motorway. Then it was just off the road to Barnet and still had a rural feel to it. Not only is it an attractive brick-built house surrounded by a moat, but the fascinating history of the building is the history of England. Together with my sister Valerie, who was equally smitten by the romantic and precious old place, we joined the other visitors for a guided tour of one of the smallest and least-known of English stately homes. Now it is no longer open to the public as it is a business premises.

Situated near London Colney, some four miles to the south east of St Albans Cathedral this site was owned, in the year 800, by a Saxon dignitary, Asgar the Staller. William the Conqueror later gave it to his wealthy and powerful ally, Geoffrey de Mandeville. Later still, in 1380, Sir John Montague, Earl of Salisbury and Knight of the Garter, married into it and so the property acquired its present title. Eventually it came into the possession of the Nevill family's most famous son, Warwick the Kingmaker, who was to die close to the Hall, at the Battle of Barnet, along with his younger brother, the Earl of Northumberland. It fell into obscurity for a while before Henry VIII's treasurer, Sir John Cutte, discovered it and rebuilt it in 1507 and it remained in his family for two hundred and fifty years. During the Civil War, Charles I used Salisbury Hall for a headquarters and armoury; it had been modernised and now boasted tunnels, useful for concealing Royalists. After his execution his son, Charles II, spent many happy hours here with his mistress and legend has it that Nell Gwynne threatened to drop her son into the moat, as he had no royal title, and the King's reply was 'No, spare the first Duke of St Albans.' Not only was Nell a great beauty of her times she was also shrewd and acquisitive.

Moving into the twentieth century, in 1905 widowed Lady Jenny Churchill, mother of Winston, bought Salisbury Hall with her new husband George Cornwallis-West. Winston Churchill would sometimes stay with his mother and step-father. George Cornwallis-West reported seeing the ghost of Nell Gwynne in his autobiography *Edwardian Hey-Days*, published in 1930:

'One evening at Salisbury Hall just as it was getting dusk, I came down the staircase which leads into the old panelled room that we used as a dining-room, and there, standing in a corner, I saw the figure of a youngish and beautiful woman with a blue fichu (a small triangular shawl, worn around a woman's shoulders and neck) round her shoulders. She looked intently at me, and then turned and disappeared through the door into the passage. I followed and found nothing.'

A medium was later consulted and confirmed that Cornwallis-West had indeed seen the ghost of Nell Gwynne, who had come to warn him of an impending danger. Within six months of the sighting a solicitor absconded with over ten thousand pounds, money entrusted to him by Cornwallis-West, to pay off some mortgages...

A Mrs Rosamund Stutzel lived in the house as a child during 1919 and her childhood memories were expressed in a letter, sent in 1959 to the then owners, the Goldsmiths. Mrs Stutzel recalled a 'something' that stood by the bed in the bedroom over the entrance porch, and it was experienced by her brother and sister, who were often awakened by the entity as small children. A governess who spent the night in this same room refused to sleep another night in the house after saying 'something terrifying came out of the wall near the fireplace and stood by the bed'.

From 1934 to 1939 Salisbury Hall was owned by Sir Nigel Gresley, the designer of record-breaking Pacific steam locomotives. Guests who stayed in the large red bedroom were always troubled by strange footsteps in the night.

During the Second World War Salisbury Hall was taken over by Sir Geoffrey de Havilland as a top secret establishment and in late 1940 the reason for the security was revealed, in the shape of the 'Wooden Wonder', the revolutionary, ultra fast and manoeuvrable fighter-bomber called the Mosquito. This most versatile of aeroplanes was one of the aircraft that helped the Allies win the war. When fitted with cameras it was used in photo-reconnaissance work, it served as a night fighter, intercepting German bombers, and as a light bomber for small, precision bombing raids. Although Salisbury Hall is no longer open to the public the Mosquito Aircraft Museum in the grounds is accessible.

One of the 1960's most notable British clairvoyants was Tom Corbett and in company with the writer Diana Norman he visited Salisbury Hall to investigate the ghosts for himself. In her book *The Stately Ghosts of England* Diana Norman gives details of their researches. After De Havilland moved out, the Hall suffered many years of neglect until it was rescued by Walter Goldsmith, a painter and art dealer, in 1956. Goldsmith was to transform the property from its near derelict state, with a garden overgrown with brambles, but it required many years of renovation work. During this project Goldsmith discovered secret rooms, passageways and cellars. Without any prior knowledge of the house, or its history, Tom

Corbett quickly identified the ghost of 'a very beautiful woman' in the Green Bedroom and correctly added, 'Somewhere in the house you have a portrait of her', and this turned out to be Nell Gwynne.

The Goldsmiths admitted to a number of ghostly encounters, Walter Goldsmith felt a 'warm and friendly, supernatural presence' in his top floor studio where a bloodstain was reputed to appear and re-appear on the wall in times past. His wife, Audrey Goldsmith, heard ghostly footsteps in the passage outside her bedroom and their children heard something pass their bedroom door in the night. Tom Corbett thought that there was a second ghost, a man, who was responsible for the footsteps that walked a passage, most of which didn't exist any more, in the old Tudor Wing which was destroyed in 1818. The clairvoyant finally sensed another female spirit, quite harmless, on the little medieval causeway bridge leading to the house.

In more recent times author Betty Puttick visited the Goldsmith family when Walter and Audrey's son Robin and his wife Maria, lived here in the Tudor cottage long known as 'Nell Gwynne's cottage', in the grounds of Salisbury Hall, which continued to be haunted. Betty Puttick interviewed the Goldsmiths for her book, *Ghosts of Hertfordshire*. Maria gave a good description of her encounter, one summer's night by the coach house, with a Cavalier who haunted the site; he was dressed in frilly white shirt and knee breeches and his shoes were adorned with large, shiny buckles. He was tall with long fair hair tied back in a pony tail and he had a young, serious face although he seemed to be smiling as he looked directly at her until his image slowly dissolved in front of her eyes. Persistent stories of a ghostly Cavalier have been linked with Salisbury Hall over the years. It is believed that he was a messenger, carrying secret despatches during the Civil War, who was cornered by a force of Roundheads and rather than be captured he committed suicide.

On another occasion Maria slept in the room over the porch at the Hall as there was no other bedroom available at the time. There was a chiming clock in here which Robin stopped in case it woke her up. Maria had a bad feeling about the room, although she didn't know about its haunted reputation, she just wanted to get away and retired to bed feeling rather depressed. At 2am she awoke to the sound of the ticking clock, which seemed to have restarted itself. Then the bed violently rocked back and forth for some three minutes. Maria huddled under the bedclothes in terror and left her bed early in the morning. Eventually she shared her experience with Robin's mother, who recalled the governess's ghostly encounter in the same room, circa 1919, which had caused her to refuse to sleep in the house ever again. Maria also talked about the haunted gardens where people have heard ghostly laughter... memories from a 'Merry Monarch' and his beautiful Mistress Nell?

Chapter Twenty-Eight
TRING

Situated on the far western tip of Hertfordshire the Tring Salient juts out deep into surrounding Buckinghamshire like the Cornish Peninsula into the English Channel. It certainly has a different feel to anywhere else in Hertfordshire and has recently been listed by a newspaper as one of the most desirable places to live in the UK. Tring stands at the highest point of the Grand Union Canal in the Chilterns Area of Outstanding Beauty, with the surrounding woodlands of the National Trust's Ashridge Estate and the Forestry Commission's Wendover Woods close by. It has certainly proved equally attractive to the local wildlife and to people, be they walkers, horse riders, canal boat owners or film crews.

Fabulously wealthy, the Rothschild family, who owned 1,000 acres of land in Buckinghamshire, held lavish parties in the nineteenth century at their Tring Park Mansion, where zebras pulled traps around the grounds. Lionel Rothschild acquired the Mansion in 1873 and it was his family's bank that loaned Prime Minister Benjamin Disraeli four million pounds to purchase a half share in the Suez Canal in 1875. Around this time there was heavy canal trade through the Tring Gap and the town had a thriving silk industry as well as plenty of straw-plaiting work.

The most tragic story associated with Tring concerns witchcraft and the notorious case of the last trial by ordeal in England, which happened in 1751 (thought to be one April morning) at Wilstone, near Tring. A farmer called John Butterfield of Gubblecote in the same parish, refused to give some buttermilk to an old woman, Ruth Osborne. She cursed him for his meanness. Shortly afterwards his calves fell ill and he himself suffered fits. Butterfield had been subject to fits all his life, and the calves' illness was most likely an unfortunate coincidence, but in those superstitious times it was proof enough of Ruth's being a witch, so the farmer ordered a witch-hunt.

The unfortunate Ruth, with her husband John, sought sanctuary in the workhouse at Tring, but the angry crowd gathering outside convinced the workhouse-master that it would be best to usher them into the vestry of the church. The old, (probably in their 70s) confused couple were dragged out by a crowd of some 4,000 people (most likely somewhat inebriated), who tied the Osbornes' thumbs to their toes, allegedly stripped them, wrapped them in sheets and threw them into a muddy Wilstone pond (since filled in) before dragging them up and down in the water. Trial by ordeal could only ever result in one outcome – if you sank you were presumed innocent and if you swam you were adjudged guilty of witchcraft. Mrs Osborne died quite quickly and her husband died soon after being pulled out, both as the result of suffocation and exposure. Local chimney sweep Luke Colley amused himself and his friends by prodding Mrs Osborne's body with a stick and turning it over and over in the water before passing his hat round. As perpetrator of the crime Colley was arrested for his part in the affair, but though he wrote a letter before he died, which was full of remorse, he was sentenced at Hertford assizes and 108 troopers of the Horse Guards escorted him away. He was later hanged and gibbeted in chains in Luke's Lane at Gubblecote Cross, near Long Marston. His body was left to swing there for many years, as a grim warning to all who passed by. The area of execution was shunned by locals thereafter as being haunted by a hell-hound, supposedly the spirit of the hanged chimney sweep. Until the widening of the lane during the Second World War (made necessary by the construction of the Marsworth airfield) strange stories were told by passers-by in Lukes Lane, of odd happenings there including the sounds of phantom chains which were heard rattling…

The trouble with Tring's true ghost stories is that they are mainly anecdotal and the most interesting ones are about events that happened in the distant past, so they may be of less interest to the modern reader. An attempt was made to collect them into a single source, and a slim volume, of just a dozen pages, called *Ghosts of Tring* was written by Sheila Richards in 1976. For keen students of the paranormal this has been the definitive source for hauntings in this far-flung outpost of Hertfordshire. With such a small reference work there is inevitably a frustrating shortage of detail about names, dates and places and there are no corroborative witnesses to these accounts, many of which are of incidents from the long ago past, not currently active sites, and therefore of much less interest than contemporary manifestations. They are many and varied and one of my favourites is not really a ghost story but an amusing tale of Tring;

At Startops End lived a man who drank and his wife who wanted to cure him. She put on a nightshirt and waited in the hedge in the dark until she heard him, when she popped out crying 'I'm the Devil!' 'Married yer sister' was the reply.

Sightings of Roman soldiers have featured in Tring territory on a number of occasions; they have mainly been confined to the areas of Miswell and Wigginton Common. The latter area featured in the *Bucks Advertiser* of July 1835, as haunted by a ghostly Roman army.

Oliver Cromwell's troops were once billeted on Wigginton Common and ghostly Roundheads have been reported there.

Other legendary Tring apparitions include a 'farmer' in smock and gaiters. This figure has been seen several times, leaning over a gate looking into a field at Buckland, on the road from the Wharf to the Rothschild Arms.

Pendley Beeches is one more supposedly haunted spot. In the early 1950s a 'tall figure, wearing a top hat and cloak with head bowed' was spotted by a motorist crossing the road. As if the old-fashioned garb wasn't enough of a clue the fact that the figure's lower legs were missing was further evidence of an apparition.

Another intriguing story concerns a disappearing postman, who was on the Wilstone to Puttenham round one day when he was seen coming up to the bridge in Little Tring, but he didn't manage to get across it. 'He was never seen again, nor his bike, nor yet his mail bag.' It seems that his bicycle lamp was seen again, however, on occasion, at the bridge approach.

On the road from Aldbury village to nearby Tring the sound of horses' hooves and the jingle of harness bells have been heard on occasion, and one motorist, during a late night journey, claimed to have actually seen a phantom coach 'in a blaze of light' beside the road at Two Waters. It is believed to be the (sometimes invisible) coach and horses of Simon Harcourt, the long dead Lord of Aldbury, who figures in several accounts where his conveyance has been merely heard but not seen by local people. Signalmen used to report the Harcourt coach, complete with running dog, crossing the railway line between Tring station and the signal box. A traveller returning late one night from Tring station attempted to pat a strange dog. He described an extremely large animal, although the man didn't recognise the breed, and as he tried to stroke the hound his hand went straight through the 'creature'. My guess would be that this was Lord Harcourt's ghostly dog and it would have been a Talbot, a type of hound that is now extinct, it was a big, strong beast, used for hunting and tracking. These dogs were popular in coaching times, when their function was to deter highwaymen. Talbots would happily trot alongside coaches, which they would then loyally guard with their lives.

A man on a white horse has been seen by at least three different witnesses on separate occasions, an older woman, a young woman and a man all saw the figure on the road near Tring station. These are also believed to be manifestations of the well-travelled spirit of Simon Harcourt.

BIBLIOGRAPHY

Carrington, Beryl and Thresher, Muriel, *The Ghost Book – St Albans Favourite Haunts*, (Self published pamphlet)

Glendinning, Victoria, *Victoria Glendinning's Hertfordshire*, Weidenfield and Nicolson, 1989

Guiley, Rosemary Ellen, *Encyclopedia of Mystical & Paranormal Experience*, Grange Books, 1993

Herts Federation of Women's Institutes, *The Hertfordshire Village Book*, Countryside Books/HFWI, 1986

Jones-Baker, Doris, *Tales of Old Hertfordshire*, Countryside Books, 1987

Norman, Diana, *The Stately Ghosts of England*, Robin Clark Ltd., 1977

Puttick, Betty, *Ghosts of Hertfordshire*, Countryside Books, 1994

Richards, Sheila, *Ghosts of Tring*, Printed by Maund and Irvine Ltd, 1976

Spencer, John and Anne, *The Encyclopedia of Ghosts and Spirits*, Headline Book Publishing, 1992

Stratton, Ruth and Connell, Nicholas, *Haunted Hertfordshire*, The Book Castle, 2002

Underwood, Peter, *The A-Z of British Ghosts*, Chancellor Press, 1971